UNFORGOTTEN

FINDING HOPE
IN BANGKOK PRISONS

To Melodie:
Thank You so much

♡ HEATHER
Oct. 3, 2015

HEATHER LUNA-ROSE

ISBN: 978-0-9948252-0-9

Cover design by Natasha Kong
Cover photograph by Heather Luna-Rose
Author photo by Billie Woods
All interior photographs, copyright, Heather Luna-Rose
Typeset in *Swift* with *Trade Gothic* display at SpicaBookDesign

Printed in Canada by Printorium Bookworks / IslandBlue, Victoria BC

ACKNOWLEDGEMENTS

I AM GRATEFUL for friends and supporters of *Luna-Rose Prisoner Support* for your encouragement and contributions that have kept me doing this work even when I wanted to give up: especially, Yvonne, for your cheerleading in all ways, and, Kaz, for fantastic feedback and support with editing of this book. I am indebted to my recovery communities in Bangkok and Salt Spring Island for holding me in your healing embrace.

I am grateful to each of the men I walked this path with. To Pete, Adrian, Felix, and Jesse: thank you especially for your friendship and your love, for giving me unimaginable strength and hope. I carry you always with me.

Finally, this book is for my daughter, Morgan, who saved my life, who taught me to love unconditionally, who inspires me every day to be a better person and to never stop dreaming and learning, and for whom I continue to strive to create a better world.

PROLOGUE

STANDING ON sun-bleached concrete, bathed in thick unmoving air, sweat soaking through the shirt that covers my shoulders and tattoos, I push up long sleeves in an attempt to cool my arms, but the 36 degree Bangkok air is a heavy sopping blanket. In an open courtyard inside the prison, directly beneath the iconic concrete guard tower, I wait, skin burning in the sun. Twenty minutes from now the inmate I've come to see will arrive from his building for our visit. A smattering of other 'foreigners' mill around this area, waiting in the oppressive unmoving humidity.

An older Thai man in blue shorts, blue shirt and flip-flops slowly drags a garden hose towards a bright pink flowering shrub. He soaks the first potted plant for a few minutes then moves to the next, neither paying attention to, nor getting much notice from the various visitors who stand around this courtyard, sweating profusely. This inmate has probably completed almost all of a lengthy sentence and has paid for this very privileged duty. He may be considered a low escape risk and thus is allowed to spend parts of his days in this in-between space. Unlike the majority of the 7000 or so inmates on the other side of the thick concrete walls and guard tower, this older man gets to spend his remaining days in this liminal place that is neither inside nor outside. Here, in this place where I, too, spend much of each day, this man gets a glimpse of 'regular people': women, children, all manner of family members, coming for visits with their incarcerated loved ones.

I watch the old man water the plants that were added to this dusty courtyard a few years ago in an attempt to prettify the only part of this infamous prison that we visitors can access. Across the courtyard from the 'foreigner' side of the visiting area, dozens of Thai families wait for their visits with a loved one to start, while others trickle out slowly towards the large exit gates.

As I wait for an Australian inmate, I fan myself with a photocopy of my passport, the only item I am allowed to carry with me, using it to push the thick air slightly in an unsuccessful attempt to cool my skin. I hear the unmistakable clanking sound of chains: a shackled inmate is being taken into the prison. Turning towards the centre of this inner courtyard, I see six prison guards in brown uniforms surrounding a young white man shuffling awkwardly, the weight and slow clanging of the heavy iron thumping on his legs and hands. The young inmate wears thin shorts and a ratty t-shirt. In his hands he carries a small bundle of what I presume are his few allowed possessions. He stumbles, then regains his balance, clutching a thin string that lifts the heavy chains running between his legs to keep them from dragging or tripping him.

The guards and young man proceed slowly from the outer gates on my right towards the set of large inner doors located directly under the guard tower on my left. The few scattered foreigners and Thais ignore this all-too familiar scene. Normally, I ignore shackled inmates being brought through this prison courtyard, trying not to compound their humiliation as they are taken to and from court appearances. Today, however, something compels me to watch the slow procession. As the small group draws near me, I am struck by the terror and shock on the young man's face, this a stark contrast to the hard stony mask most inmates adopt. I don't recognize this foreigner, and judging by his wide-eyed look of fear, eyes darting around, I assume he is a new arrival. I cannot imagine what is going through his mind as he walks these last steps into Thailand's infamous Bangkwang prison, where he will serve a sentence of at least 25 years, perhaps as much as 100 years or a death penalty. The six bored-looking guards flanking him keep his reluctant legs moving forward.

As they pass me, his eyes find mine and our gaze locks. I am caught by his fear and bewilderment. I stare at him, breath caught in my throat. I hope my face does not convey pity. The enormity of the journey this man is about to embark on hits me. I don't know what country he's from or if he speaks English or whether his family even knows he's here. Images of all of the men I have visited over the past years in this prison flood me, the hundreds of foreigners struggling to maintain their humanity. I think of all those who succumb to mental illness, suicide or disease, crushed by this juggernaut. I think of the thousands of men struggling to maintain hope with years behind them, years in front of them, played out day by interminably long day. The horror, pain and agony I've witnessed of people barely surviving, isolated from their friends and loved ones grips me. This man's whole journey stretches before him. I want to reassure him that I see him, that I know he's there, and that he won't be forgotten. I want to offer a connection, an acknowledgement, anything, but I feel helpless. The guards fumble to unlock the great inner doors.

As he is led into a long prison sentence in a foreign country, I wonder what chain of events has brought him in this moment to this notorious prison, known by locals as *The Big Tiger* for its reputation of devouring men. I note this man's youth and I wonder if he will be one of the resilient ones, or one of the ones eaten alive. Is every cell in his body screaming? I wonder at the regret, remorse, worry, confusion, fear, he must feel. I cannot imagine the terror he is experiencing as he waits for these large prison doors to swing open. He turns at the last to find me frozen on the spot, still staring at him. Without thinking, my right hand moves over my heart. Staring back, he returns the gesture, hand over his heart, in response. The doors open and the guards shuffle him slowly inside.

One of the regular prison visitors approaches to greet me and I feel myself turning to answer his questions automatically. I can't hear what he is saying, but I smile and nod mechanically, lump in my throat. My hand is still on my heart, and I know that something has ripped open in my chest. My friend's mouth is moving, so I know he's talking to me, but I can't hear him. Although I have seen inmates being marched into the prison many times before, today, I can't bear it. Today, the years of watching men struggle and succumb to despair overrides all else. In this moment, I cannot recall all the joy and hope we carve out in this darkness. I am ripped apart by seeing this young man's terror. I hate knowing that he will soon disappear into the mass of thousands of men identified by their prison number who can only be accessed if someone knows they are behind these walls and seeks them out in person. I can't stand to see yet another person erased by this place: made invisible and forgotten. I can't do *nothing*. As the large doors slowly shut behind him, I turn back and desperately shriek across the courtyard: "What's your Name?" It is too late, the great doors have swallowed him up inside Bangkwang Prison.

INTRODUCTION

BANGKWANG PRISON is located in Nonthaburi Province, Thailand, just north of Bangkok. Built a century ago, this maximum security prison houses roughly 7000 inmates, including foreigners from all over the world, many of whom are serving 100 year sentences for drug charges. Strict regulations control the dissemination of information about the exact nature of the inmates' existence, as well as limit their access to outside information. Several highly sensationalistic and disturbing accounts have been published by former inmates highlighting the abuse, corruption, and brutal conditions. Newspapers, internet and cell phones are forbidden; only written correspondence is allowed between inmates and the outside world. Photographs of inmates are not allowed; it is also forbidden to take a picture of the outside of this prison, or to bring any type of recording device into the prison visiting area. These measures are designed to keep this population invisible, absent, at some level, from the mind and consciousness of the public. Thailand's prisons have historically not been designed for human dignity or rehabilitation; rather, only to support bare life and punishment.

With as many as 100 men sleeping on the floor in each cell, shoulder to shoulder in each cell and lack of minimum standards of sanitation or medical attention, diarrhea, skin rashes and other illnesses are so common as to be unremarkable, while tuberculosis, HIV, Hep C, mental illness and other serious diseases are dangerously common. Food and all necessities for survival must be purchased by the prisoners. There is a great disparity in the quality of life between prisoners who get financial (and moral) support from their families and friends, and those who don't.

In 2006, I started visiting foreigner male inmates at Bangkwang Prison, Bangkok, bringing food, emotional support, toiletries, books, conversation, and human connection. I first visited a fellow Canadian, then expanded this mission to include many incarcerated men who hailed from Australia, Europe, the US, and other countries. What was at first a gnawing and inexplicable need to visit these forgotten men grew into my soul's calling, and I have returned to Bangkwang prison every year, making this my full-time mission. Over the years, I added five other prisons near and around Bangkok, including Klong Prem, Khao Bin, Bang Khen, Pattaya Remand, and Bangkok Remand. I had no idea at the beginning how life-changing this would be, transforming me in ways I couldn't anticipate.

People often ask me how I started doing this work. I tell them about backpacking through Bangkok a decade ago with my young daughter and picking up a book called *The Damage Done,* by Australian Warren Fellows in a local used bookshop. Haunted by his account of the fourteen years spent in Bangkwang Prison for heroin trafficking, and, identifying deeply with people thrown away by the world and suffering in isolation, I felt called to go to the prison to offer my support. In 2006, I approached the Canadian Embassy of Bangkok and obtained a list of Canadian inmates wanting visitors. The first person on the list was Johann, a 47-year old man serving a 100-year sentence for drugs.*

Learning from Johann that prisoners must buy everything they need for survival, including food and drinking water, I returned to try to visit him and even more marginalized foreigners: those from Burma, Nepal or Laos, or those without family or Embassy support. I brought vitamins, cooked food and fresh fruit from street vendors, books and toiletries. When prison rules changed a few years later to no longer allow visitors to bring food or books, I filled my daily schedule with emotional support visits at several prisons daily. Over the years, I have also helped other volunteers to come to Bangkwang and set up pen-pal correspondences between inmates and people in my home community on the West Coast of Canada. In the months each year I spend working and fundraising in Canada, I keep in correspondence with some of the inmates, exchanging letters and mailing them care packages of vitamins and sundries (until November 2012, when all but letters were banned from entering the prison).

In 2009, I registered a BC non-profit society, enlisting a Board of Directors, a group of supportive compassionate people in my home community, who encouraged my crazy one-woman mission. In order to finance this work, I worked many jobs, sometimes up to 80 hours per week, while raising my daughter on my own and helping to care for my mom with dementia. I drove taxi, waitressed, landscaped, and spoke and wrote at length to anyone who would listen about my mission, to

---

* Names have been changed.

try to raise awareness and funds for this work. Living very frugally and often sleeping on people's couches in order to raise the funds, I have never drawn a salary, devoting most my time, energy and money to continue this work.

In 2010, I curated the first of several prisoner art exhibits on Salt Spring Island, BC. Showcasing the artwork of one Russian inmate, Ivan, who has become an incredible self-taught artist inside the prison, I shared his story of determination and perseverance and sold many of his works. When I returned to Bangkwang that Fall, I deposited all the proceeds from his art sales into his prison account, which then allowed him, for the first time in his seven years of incarceration to be able to support himself inside. At that exhibit, I created and sold a sculpture made from found scavenged material, which helped to finance six months of prison work that year. Other years, I helped cover the costs by fundraising through social media and friends. Although my ongoing efforts and devotion to continue this calling have been tremendous, I could never have continued this journey without the support of friends who rented me cheap rooms or gave me cash jobs and offered emotional support and encouragement, as well as the supporters who donated funds.

Many have asked me repeatedly over the years why I continue to put all my financial and emotional resources to bring visits, connection and conversation to criminals. My answers vary, depending on my mood, the context, and the audience and are all true, but like all truths, partial, and incomplete. I believe passionately in the need to bear witness to all those who suffer, no matter who we are and what mistakes we've made. I will speak about how depriving someone of their liberty for a crime may be a legitimate form of consequence, however, degrading, humiliating and imposing suffering and punishment at the levels displayed in those prisons and with 100-year sentences that destroy entire lives, is unacceptable. That the abuse of and degradation of any human is never an acceptable way for us to deal with the transgressions against society that we want to stop. That while I understand the human impulse for revenge, a just and humane society that aims to reduce the suffering of all and to increase the well-being of all must rely on principles of deterrence, of rehabilitation and humanity when imposing criminal sanctions. And that no one deserves to be forgotten.

My journey into these prisons started long before I backpacked with my daughter through South-East Asia and picked up a book about Bangkwang prison. I grew up too quickly, adopting a hard outer shell as I learned to survive counting on no-one, experiencing neglect and psychological, sexual and physical violence in my youth. As a hardened teen working full-time and putting myself through college, I gravitated towards women's groups and feminism for healing, strength and support. Deeply sensitive to suffering, I became an activist, a gender radical, speaking out about violence against women and radicalizing my growing social justice conscience. Pregnant at 20, I continued on to complete a degree in psychology and women's studies while working and raising my daughter alone. On the outside I was a tough, angry warrior, a sex/gender radical who railed against injustice, spoke my mind, and fought to make the world a safe place emotionally for my daughter, while on the inside, I struggled with debilitating depression and anxiety, feeling always like an outsider, an alien on a planet with values that I couldn't reconcile with my own.

Working hard to raise my child, living under the poverty line, debt collectors at our door for student loans, I moved out of Vancouver and found work researching gender-based violence prevention in the small rural community of Salt Spring Island. Gradually, my depression and anxiety lessened and although I was exhausted and overwhelmed as a single low-income parent juggling so many balls, I found much joy in raising my daughter, who was the centre of my world. After an acute trauma at the age of thirty, I entered several of my darkest years, using alcohol to medicate overwhelming stress and pain. I drank, cried, worked and raged through a graduate degree, while continuing to try to create a playful, hopeful existence for my daughter and I. An adrenaline junkie, passionate about challenging myself in all areas of my life, I have always gravitated towards new challenges. Wanting to fuel the part of my soul that was yearning to find an emotionally and spiritually more meaningful life, in 2004, I sold our few items of furniture and possessions and took my then ten year old daughter backpacking to Asia with the hope of finding adventure, purpose and work in social justice.

Finding my way into that prison and bringing a human connection to those men suffering alone in their hell allowed me to escape my own demons and self-pity and sense of dis-connection from others: I finally felt of real use to someone whose situation was incomparably worse than my own. I brought my fighting spirit, feminist ethics, intolerance of suffering, belief and practice of non-violence to this place and set it loose, fumbling and bumbling along the way to make sense of what was at first an inexplicable drive to feed and visit these men who had no one else to fend for them.

This book is a small selection of letters written to friends, to inmates, and journal entries from over the nine years of supporting foreigner inmates in Bangkok prisons. I worry that these written reflections reveal only one dimension of my experience: my rants and struggles to unload the horror and the stress of each day in the visiting area of a horrific prison. This offering is by no means a comprehensive or full picture of my journey. These dispatches offer instead an unique perspective into the tireless undertaking of one profoundly hopeful woman, deeply mistrustful of people, who found her soul's calling bringing support and connection to isolated and wounded men.

Many inmates I visited only once or twice, others a few times, and still others I built a long-standing relationship with over many years. Most of those I visited were nominated by other inmates I was already visiting. Although I initially tried to visit people from the poorest countries, because the Westerners got the bulk of the 'backpacker' and tourist 'banana visitors,' I found myself in more recent years visiting also European, North American and Iranian inmates, as they seemed more able to accept me at face value when I said I was there to support, and that I did not want anything from them, nor would I be providing them with cash funds. I grew weary of the men from certain countries with ready-made scripts, detailing their poor health, lack of family and great need for immediate financial support. Too many of my interactions with these men were only manipulative, with no agenda other than financial gain and they seemed to have no interest in what I could offer in emotional support. It's understandable that any person in a very difficult circumstance try to get as much as possible from whatever 'charity' they can, but the repeated manipulations turned me off. As my workload increased, with so many more hundreds in need of support than could ever be reached, I could pick and choose and thus found myself gravitating towards supporting people who could most benefit from what I offered, and sometimes choosing, albeit with some guilt, those whose culture of origin was closer to my own, for ease and convenience sake.

Over the years, I grappled with a great unease that arose from operating within cultural and institutional contexts which greatly limited my ability to reach a larger number of people in need and that stifled my voice as an activist. In order to be able to operate within Thailand's political and cultural context, I chose not to denounce or try to reform a system, but to engage respectfully within it. This never sat easily with me. My humanitarian mandate 'to ease suffering,' rather than to denounce or try to reform the conditions of their incarceration was both realistic and pragmatic, but also a great source of dis-ease for this formerly shit-disturbing activist.

Acquaintances repeatedly questioned me about working with this population, as I had oriented my activism, education and work in my first thirty years towards ending oppression of women, and of all those on the margins of sexual or gender categories, including sex trade workers, single moms, queer and trans folk. Why was I working with criminal men? A survivor of much male violence, I was aware of the irony and re-traumatizing potential of spending much of my time in misogynist, racist, violent institutions, supporting men experiencing unimaginable suffering. In choosing to spend my time with these men, though, I discovered that my views had shifted: after years of feminist activism, theorizing about identity politics and analyzing systemic and institutional levels of gender and race oppression, I was experiencing the quiet change in being present with another human in loving compassion. For me, it was never that criminal men were somehow 'more deserving' of care than battered women, lgbt youth, sex trafficked or neglected children, as I was often challenged, but that in sitting in dark spaces with these men and seeing the effects on me and on them of bearing witness and giving and receiving loving kindness, I realized I no longer supported the notion that *anyone* was more or less deserving of simple human kindness than another.

My commitment to non-violent practice evolves and continues to grow. Still prone to judging others unfairly, I nonetheless believe that we can only heal ourselves and our broken communities when we actively work to lift each other up and not put each other down, in word, spirit or act. I hope these stories will help to illuminate some of the human sides of a wounded healer making imperfect choices trying to heal herself and to make a difference in a broken world. Many pieces of my journey with these men are left unwritten: the triumphs, the small of moments of grace carved out in a smile, a look, laughter, hope renewed, a song shared. Like so many drawn to helping professions, the friendships, love, and healing I received from my criminal 'clients' renewed my hope and faith in people, paradoxically rekindling a hope in me that I was not, as I secretly feared, too broken to be fixed. There were many days I would float out of the prisons after a visit, higher than a kite after spending hours with an inmate, sharing joy and laughter. Our light-hearted musings or profound talks about spirituality and the complexities and struggles being human fueled and nurtured much hope amidst such darkness.

Far too many other days, the heavy weight of the horror I saw would threaten to sink me, and I would drink at a local bar at night, trying to numb what I could share with no one. I had many drunken conversations with backpackers travelling through Bangkok on their way to resort islands for drug-fuelled raves, warning them of the draconian penalties meted out for being caught with even tiny amounts of drugs in South-East Asia. Invariably, the people I spoke with would grill me for the sordid details of the slave labour and sex trade in the prisons, the suicides, and torture or for details of the crimes I had learned from the men. I would shut down, unwilling to fuel a voyeuristic obsession with sordid details of "life in a Thai prison." I used instead my journal and letters to help unravel the questions raised for me of daily engaging with the unspeakable. When people heard I drew no salary, had no possessions to speak of, nor stable housing, and landed back in Canada each spring with $20 in my pocket, exhausted, emotionally and physically burned out, yet taking any and all jobs immediately to sustain me, my child and the prison work, I was either characterized as a saint, or dismissed as a lunatic. I couldn't find words to describe what my soul felt called to do, from the first time I entered Bangkwang.

People frequently asked me: "Do you ever want to quit?" Not a week of daily prison visits passed that I didn't have a meltdown and wonder if I could sustain this emotionally and financially, the toll on my heart and spirits the hardest. Clearly experiencing burnout and pstd, I couldn't explain that the incredible joy we managed to carve out in such a dark place also gave me unimaginable strength to face my own demons; and that the moments I unraveled were often triggered not by the most violent or obscene of human violations I witnessed; rather, it was the quiet moments of grace that threatened to undo me.

I do not write this book to tell the inmates' stories, as theirs are not mine to tell, even as I carry these men with me, always, every day. Neither is my purpose to add to the collection of sensationalist exposés of life in a Thai prison nor to critique Thailand's criminal justice system. This country is the context in which I found myself grappling with questions of what we do to each other as humans and how we come to terms with that. Although I disagree with the penalties and prison conditions imposed, I want to make clear my deepest respect for the people of Thailand, the Kingdom and Monarchy of Thailand and my deepest appreciation to the prison authorities for allowing me to support incarcerated foreigners. As a social justice activist from a multi-cultural country, I grew this mission through a large amount of trial and error as a White Western woman negotiating and learning a cultural context vastly different than my own. Although I was deeply uncomfortable by the manner in which people are referred to only by their ethnicity at the prison, and indeed in Thailand in general, I have nonetheless adopted this custom that reflects the context in which I work. So too did I adopt the Buddhist Calendar, as reflected in my journal entries, starting in 2555 (2012).

Sometimes I condense conversations that occurred over many visits for narrative simplicity or refer only to Bangkwang, the prison I spend most of my time in, although some of the conversations with inmates occurred at other prisons around Bangkok. Where I quote someone, I am recalling to the best of my ability their exact words. Where I repeat a 'fact' about a prisoner's life, I am aware that it may not be true, my only source being the inmate himself. I reported my experience as accurately as I could and have resisted changing or editing the journals to reflect more recent changes in understanding. Any mistakes or inaccuracies are unintentional and are mine alone.

While my solitary mission is my own, I never want to imply that I am the only person doing this. I have met and forged friendships with a small group of women and men from various countries who have also devoted much of their time over the years to bring support to inmates in Bangkok's prisons, for varying religious or secular reasons. I am grateful for their presence at the prisons, in my life and in the lives of so many inmates, who have derived much hope and comfort from their tireless efforts.

In order to guard the privacy and dignity of the men, and for my own safety, I do not plumb the depths of all thousands of intimate moments we shared, nor some of the unspeakable moments that may be impossible for a reader to believe. There are many books that offer those types of details. Instead, the following pages contain some of my experiences from an unique vantage point in a decade long journey that changed me in ways I could never have anticipated. Here, the strands and fibres of these men's daily struggles to stay sane, to keep body and soul together and to maintain hope and derive meaning from their lives are only hinted at, woven through my own attempts to do the same.

Each day over years, I bore witness to events that were the worst days of many people's lives – experiences that I carried in my bones, in my heart and could not release: desperate families from the world's poorest countries begging impassive guards to let them visit when they have saved money for years to make one trip to Thailand for a few days to see their son or brother, only to learn that the three days they are here are not the days allotted to this inmate's visiting days. Listening to a man share in a deadened monotone about his father who died waiting for years for a chance to see his son once in a faraway prison, or hearing of a cell-mate who sharpened a toothbrush and placed it in his ear, banging his head against the wall until it pierced his brain. Or a person I have visited for years sharing with me his new HIV positive status. The days that an arbitrary rule change means inmates are no longer allowed water when they are locked up in the afternoon, 20 to 80 men in a room from 3 pm to 7 am the following day: in the oppressive heat, one ceiling fan slowly turning while they sweat out the night, sleeping on the floor in rows, no space between bodies. An inmate's account of torture and beatings by the police and his fear that he will be killed inside for reporting. Watching a man I have visited for years visibly struggle to keep his composure as he confesses his terror at seeing his mind slip away from him. Crying with another as he tells me that he no longer wants me to visit, because after fifteen years inside, and countless more to go, he no longer wants to be reminded that a world he will never again see exists outside the walls. Laughing hysterically with another as we trade impersonations of famous actors or tell dirty jokes to try to gross each other out, then seeing the veil of the dead settle over his eyes and face when it is time to leave our visit and return to his building.

Thousands of instances of horror have mercifully faded from my mind, and yet the memory of that brief shared moment with the young inmate entering Bangkwang remains with me. I have not seen him since and have no idea whether he is still there. I didn't learn his nationality or name, so it is impossible for me to make enquiries to locate him. At times, my chest hurts as I recall the moment he entered the great inner prison doors, our eyes locked. In his eyes I saw my own fear – the terror of being taken into a dark horrific nightmare with no escape and being left alone, with no one knowing I was there and no one to help me. This gets at the core of why I come year after year to this prison – I cannot abandon people to suffer nightmares alone. Years have passed, but I revisit the look in his eyes, and the small gesture we shared, hands on our hearts. I have taken to singing out loud as I wait in the registration area outside the prison, and as I wait inside the courtyard: singing soothes me and helps me to enter this dark place with a protective layer of light.

TABLE OF CONTENTS

Prologue v

Introduction ix

I: THAILAND

First Visits. 3

Incarceration & Choice 9

Early Days. 19

The Shitshow 28

The Corpse Gatherers: What is Taken .38

The Corpse Gatherers: What Remains. 41

Holistic Healing: Bangkwang-Style 47

Safety & Security 51

Journal 2011. 62

Dignity 81

No One Makes It Out 85

Paedophiles & Bananas 91

PART II: CANADA

Fishing I: Letter To James 99

Fishing II. 143

Fishing III 202

PART III: THAILAND

Bangkok Journal. 243

White Fungus Bird's Nest:

Greasing the Wheels, Thailand-style 249

Letters 254

Going Inside. 261

Your Job is Not To Judge. 273

Epilogue 281

Author's Note. 299

When will our consciences grow so tender that we will act to prevent human misery rather than avenge it?

~ ELEANOR ROOSEVELT

I:
THAILAND

FIRST VISITS

Dear friends:

I am in Kanchanaburi, Thailand having just had my passport, bank cards, and all my cash ripped off my shoulder by two guys on a motorcycle. I am spending the day waiting for my evening bus back to Bangkok, writing this year-end greeting, periodically taking a break to walk around the town, checking garbage bins for my passport, hoping it was tossed out.

Most of you know I spent eight months in Thailand last year with Morgan and a friend's son, travelling, teaching, then volunteering with a Burmese Migrant Workers' organization in Mae Sot, on the Thai/ Burma border. I fell in love with Mae Sot, and felt called to continue to support grassroots' humanitarian and social justice projects with Burmese people, but I need to return to Canada to try to finance longer term work and projects in Thailand.

The high cost of living in Vancouver made it very hard to stay afloat there, though, and even though I was working seven days a week in the summer and fall, I could only barely support Morgan, myself and Sally (A friend's teenage daughter, whom we had taken in, as her mom was unable to care for her properly). I felt increasingly trapped in Vancouver by an expensive, rat-race system where I always was running as fast as possible to still be behind, and as Fall turned to Winter I started to get more depressed. I knew I needed to leave Canada in order to try to make a life for me and the two girls that would be more meaningful than existing paycheck to paycheck working soul-less jobs. I applied for and was accepted to run a school in Chandigarh, India, but was told the company could not accommodate the two girls, initially.

At the beginning of December, I borrowed money for a plane ticket to India, with a month stopover in Thailand, with the highly developed plan of "finding work then sending for the girls." My sister and mother generously agreed to take care of the two girls in Vancouver, until they could join me.

Of course I have had many moments of doubt, wondering if I made a mistake, wondering if I can really create a life of humanitarian work, and of course feeling worried about leaving the girls but I was certain that they understood that I had to try to open possibilities for us outside Canada. It has been challenging and lonely this past month, but also an amazing experience. I have had many moments of doubt, fear, wondering about the wisdom of my plan – wondering if I was just foolishly running away from pressures and responsibilities of my life. The images that have sustained me this past month during loneliness and fear are images of flying: of jumping into the unknown, into uncertainty and trusting that I will fly.

I have missed Morgan very much. It's been incredibly hard being away from her, but also wonderful to appreciate from a greater distance the beautiful person she is, making her way in the world with so much wisdom and grace. So guilty for the hurt it causes her to be away from me for these months, I am convinced that there lies a better life for us, one in which she doesn't have to see her mom struggle so. I feel even more guilty for not being joyous, only wanting escape from the shitty existence we spin in.

I am also missing my French boyfriend I met last year in Thailand, who remains in Vancouver, caught in a self-destructive cycle of alcohol abuse. Simple sentences like the previous one just don't capture the complexity and the heartbreak of watching someone you love spiral deeper into inner hell of addiction and feeling totally powerless to help them. Trying to support, encourage and love this man has taken a huge emotional toll on me this year, and I am still reeling from the intense combination of pain and love, and the see-saw of hope versus hopelessness, promise and betrayal that get played out over and over as I support him in his struggles.

Feeling quite lonely during the December holiday season, missing my daughter most acutely, I decided to spend time visiting Canadian prisoners in Bangkok prisons. Having read about the need of foreigners incarcerated in Bangkok to get visitors, I thought I might offer some comfort to a Canadian far from friends and family and so I went to the prison and brought some books and food. I spent several hours talking to an inmate who is five years into a life sentence for possession of drugs. My time spent with this man was very humbling, as I found him to be one of the most optimistic and joyful people I have ever met. Despite the horrific and inhumane conditions he was existing in, he was cheer-ful – determined, he said, to choose gratitude and joy in each moment, rather than to live in despair. In this infamously overcrowded prison, this man was sleeping during the day and meditating at night to find some peace. His ability to transcend his physical situation, and to use his time of reflection and meditation to show gratitude overwhelmed me, and put my fairly insignificant worries into perspective. I find myself thinking a lot these days about freedom and gratitude, and the barriers in my mind that often prevent me from choosing joy.

After Bangkok, I spent two weeks in Mae Sot, visiting Burmese friends I made last year who are living in Umpiem refugee camp. The border situation is so difficult for Burmese, as the lucky ones who flee persecution in their country are used as slave labour in Thailand, working for as little as $1 a month in exchange for not being shot or tortured by their own military government. The hundreds of thousands of undocumented Burmese migrant workers in Thailand are in political limbo, with no rights, used for their cheap labour, fueling this coun-try's booming economy. They endure harassment and extortion from the Thais but some register as refugees and live in the camps for years, hopeful that one day they will be 'chosen' by a Western country and given a chance at jobs, a home and a future to build anew.

When I was in Mae Sot, I confirmed my contract to teach in India starting January 6. I left Mae Sot, hoping to return in the future to live and work there. Saying good bye to my friends, I was aware of my privilege at being able to leave the camp easily, while they are stuck indefinitely, hoping I can find them sponsorship to Canada.

These words seem trite and I hope people will forgive my awk-wardness, but I have had such overwhelming experiences and I wonder how hope is created, sustained, and what it takes to leave the barriers in my mind that have prevented me so many times in my life from seeing that I have freedom.

How do I sustain hope? I don't know, it's a mystery to me. I have felt at many times in my life at the complete mercy of my inner hell, a prisoner of debilitating depression and anxiety. For years I was incapac-itated by the inner demons that raged in my head and lead to chronic anxiety, despair and hopelessness. Although I feel released from the grip of those demons, I don't know what to make of all of this. I now deeply appreciate my health and that of my family's, and I try to express gratitude in the midst of this crazy and unjust world for the presence of compassion and love and friendship in the midst of suffering. I hope that this letter reads as one of appreciation: for my family, for love, for learning and for kindness in unexpected places.

I hate clichés about not being able to save people. I have learned so much loving a man for whom I only wish happiness, but who is destroying himself with alcohol. I do believe that humans try the best we can all the time and that this deeply unjust world is not really understandable. I do believe in trying to love people who are lost. I don't know if I would have survived my hell if I hadn't known that someone believed in me, and was willing to stay through hell and give me love. So I have gratitude for all the learning I am doing... even if I am a slow learner.

So, shortly I will return to Bangkok, to wait out the holidays until the Consulate opens Jan. 3. We shall see if I can get a replacement passport in time for my flight to India – I doubt it, but my challenges feel fairly insignificant and definitely surmountable.

I wish all of you much love and joy and good health for this coming year.

Love, Heather.

Hello folks:

Just to let you know I am safe and well, in case you heard about the bombings in Bangkok.

I caught the bus back from Kanchanaburi to Bangkok last night at 6:30, just after sending my Year End email greeting. I was nervous in the two-hour ride as we weaved in and out of traffic at lightening speed, gripping our seats that have no seat belts, having just learned that New Year's is the most accident-prone day on the roads of Thailand. We made it safely to Bangkok, totally unaware that six bombs had just gone off in the city centre and touristy areas, injuring dozens and killing three. New Year's celebrations were supposedly cancelled by Bangkok's mayor, but not a single one of the thousands of people I saw on the streets, in cafes, in clubs and wandering around, were apparently aware of this.

UNFORGOTTEN

I met a couple on the mini-bus to Bangkok, a Canadian man and German woman. They were staying in the same guesthouse as I, and as we were all tired, feeling mellow and not into partying (and I have no money), we showered then met up to go wander around together and watch all the drunks celebrate.

We passed a lot of subdued looking people around 11 o'clock, but the crowds got progressively intoxicated the closer we got to Khao San Road. Thousands of drunken, barely coherent, shouting, stumbling, drugged up mostly foreign revelers packed the streets, dancing, fighting, eating, while dozens of street vendors sold Pad Thai, cheap whiskey and beer.

Stone cold sober, we laughed our asses off watching the ludicrous antics of the barely-functioning partiers. We stopped to hear a live Thai band and suddenly the whole street shouted: 'Happy New Year!' which took us by surprise, because we had heard no countdown. Fairly typically of Thailand, the band eventually did a countdown in English a few minutes later, even though it was now past midnight. Drunk European men drenched in sweat from dancing embraced me and wished me Happy New Year, and we moved on.

We continued to Khao San Road, the 'backpacker ghetto' of Bangkok, a short street packed with stalls selling cheap goods, bars, dirt cheap hostels, tattoos parlours and drunken parties. We saw what seemed like hundreds of military police and tanks surrounding the entire area. Still ignorant of the bombings, I assumed the military were there to deal with partiers. We wandered down the road, where people-watching was really good, but the energy started to get a little crazy: people throwing beer bottles, starting fights, and we decided to move on.

I heard a loud bang like a firecracker. In front of us, people were running directly towards us, panicked looks on their faces and we saw a guy with a handgun shooting directly at the fleeing crowd, just 50 feet from us. We turned and started running, heard two more shots, and continued into the drunken crowd which was oblivious to the shooter. We turned down a side street. A little numb from the surreal experience, I was ready to head back to unwind at our guesthouse. On the way we tried to get a drink on Soi Rambuttri, but the normally 24-hour bars were closing, staff members shooing people away because a bomb had gone off in the adjacent street.

I didn't realize the extent of the bombings until this morning, reading the *Bangkok Post*. No one has claimed responsibility, but most newspapers are speculating it may be the actions of opponents of the military coup. There are travel warnings to foreigners that more bombs are expected in the coming days in the Bang Lampu area (where I am) as well as other tourist areas. It's mildly nerve-wracking at times, as I carry on, but there's nothing to do but wait it out.

I hope you have a safe and peaceful New Year's.

xoxo Heather.

INCARCERATION & CHOICE

I am hanging around Bangkok in a bit of a limbo, waiting until the Canadian Embassy opens tomorrow and wondering whether they'll issue me documents to continue on to India in two days, or whether I will have to forget my flights, my job and stay in Bangkok for 15 days waiting for a new passport to start my teaching job.

I met and hung out with few travellers, an Indo-Canadian, a Chinese-Austrian, and an ethnic German. They were interested in hearing about my time spent at the men's prison, and they decided they wanted to accompany me today to Bangkwang. Last night, they peppered me with thousands of questions about my first experience in the prison a few weeks ago and subsequent visits. They asked about every detail: the visiting room they would be in; the time allotted to spend with the prisoners; the types of conversations they might have with an inmate; and, whether they were free to leave before the time was up. They were getting increasingly nervous at the prospect of visiting an inmate. I told them they needed to look up the list of foreign prisoners on the internet to choose which one to visit, and we all traipsed over to an internet café. After twenty minutes of browsing a long list of foreigner inmates, reading their names, crimes, and sentences, sometimes accompanied by a brief blurb about the prisoner, stating that he speaks English and really wants visitors, or that he has no money and hopes for a donation, or, that he hasn't had a visitor in over 6 years, one guy picked out the names of several men: a Malaysian, a Nigerian and a Nepali, all people he thought might not get many visitors, and he would decide later on which one of them to visit. The other two found the process of picking inmates' names off a list on the internet too bizarre, and decided they would not go to the prison after all. I was frustrated at them, angry and tried not to show it, but they sensed it anyway. I'm not exactly a master at hiding my emotions.

I wanted to acknowledge their questions, doubts and fears, and support their decision not to go, understanding that this process of going to Bangkwang as a tourist, picking the name of a foreign inmate off a list and visiting him in prison really was 'just too weird.' I could relate to their fears and support the myriad of questions and emotions, but I still found myself impatient and annoyed at their cowardice.

I know that each visit of two hours creates an unimaginable difference in the life of a person who will spend every day until he dies in a concrete overcrowded hell with little or no contact with the outside world. I don't know how to convey that. I didn't want to let these two off the hook, just because they were experiencing discomfort at the idea of going to a prison. "I just don't know anything about these people," complained the German woman.

What does she want to know, I questioned her: their politics, their hair colour, their music preferences, a complete biography? What difference does it make? I know that these people are human, that they are incarcerated in inhumane conditions and that regardless of their crime, they deserve to be treated with dignity and they are not. A moment of contact with another human is precious and may give a lot of comfort. I told her she can always leave if she doesn't like the inmate, or if she doesn't know what to say.

We walked back to the guesthouse and I asked Shawn if I could speak with him a little more about it. I told him that I had been really nervous before I went the first time, and that the feelings and questions that came up in me had given me a lot to explore and challenge in myself, which had ultimately made the experience very powerful. I told him that I had to look at my fears: why am I so afraid of a prison? Is it fear of contamination? An us vs. them bias raging strong despite my knowledge of the arbitrariness of such a construct: was I afraid somehow I will be associated with people who are on THAT side of the wall, the moral wall, the criminal wall? Partly. I had worries in the days before the prison visit that I would be suspected of being in 'criminal cahoots' with the inmate and might be thrown into prison myself. I realized how much I had internalized the divide between 'me' and the 'other,' the inmate. Although I kept telling myself that he was human and deserved humane treatment and company, I was also afraid of his situation, of incarceration. Determined to overcome my fear of the prison itself, of the building and guards, very physical reminders of lack of freedom, I had put forward many internal arguments to convince myself that spending two hours with an inmate was the 'right' thing to do. Sure, there was the social approval, for doing a 'good deed' and there was the need each inmate had for company, conversation, a human visitor, and more reasons too. I thought about these reasons extensively in the days leading up to my decision to go. As the day approached, my fears and uncertainty grew, as did my worry of potentially disrespecting an inmate as a perceived 'voyeur' into his misery. I consoled myself by reasoning that I could simply leave if I was uncomfortable or if it was awkward. Ultimately though, what tipped the scales for me was a selfish argument I kept returning to: I imagined a scenario where someone threw drugs into my bag at BKK international airport as I was boarding a plane and I was thrown in a hellish Thai prison for life.

Having heard of many cases of false charges, an unjust legal system where an accused cannot defend himself and harsh sentences, I have a fear of that very scenario occurring to me. I imagine a situation where I am incarcerated in a foreign prison with no help and no legal recourse. If it were me in that hell-hole, trying to stay sane against horrible loneliness and desperate conditions, would I not hope that anybody, absolutely ANYBODY would come and visit me? My fear of visiting the prison I overrode with a karmic debt argument – maybe if I visit someone incarcerated in that hell, I will ensure that I will never have to sit on the other side of the barrier, or at least that if I am stuck in there, I will not be forgotten. That is what finally convinced me to go the first time, I tell Shawn. He says he will go back to the internet cafe and look over the list of names again and will probably join us the following morning.

The next morning, three of us leave for the river boat, me anxious that we not get to the prison too late to register for the 9 – 11 am visitor's slot. Shawn has not shown up at the guesthouse by 8:10, and I am disappointed, thinking I had convinced him the night before. After 40 minutes on the river express boat, we arrive in Nonthaburi and walk towards the prison in silence. I worry that the guards will not accept a photocopy of my passport – the original having been stolen. We buy bags of oranges for the inmates and look around for cooked chicken, but, curiously, there is an unusual lack of street vendors.

Walking down the wide boulevard towards the prison, we fall silent as the imposing structure comes into sight. We walk along the high concrete walls, barbed wire, a guard tower and pass a small, newer building called "The Learning Center: For the Welfare and Education of Guards and Employees." I shake my head: this recently built internet room is promoted on the prison website as if it is for prisoners' use. What a joke. We reach the main entrance and I notice that the gates are closed, padlocks on the iron gate leading to the visiting area. With a sinking feeling, I realize that on Thai national holidays the prison is closed to visitors. We talk to a man outside the guard station who confirms that the prison is 'closed'. We are not even allowed to leave the oranges for the prisoners.

We walk back to the riverboat and return to the guesthouse disappointed. All three of us are separately leaving to continue our respective travels within the next 48 hours and probably will not make it back to Bangkwang.

The rest of today I have spent thinking about the concept of choice. I go to an internet cafe and read ten messages left by my boyfriend, all of them equally bizarre and cryptic, as he drinks himself into oblivion, delusion, paranoia and god-knows-what-else, convincing himself that I am cheating on him or doing I don't know what. I used to be devastated, enraged and saddened by these accusations: how could he accuse me of this, how dare he question my integrity and my behaviour? Especially when I have spent so much time supporting and loving him, encouraging him to seek help when he fucks up, and enduring painful lies, deceit and hurtful behaviour. Nothing he says in this state is rational; unfortunately, I am used to the bizarre places his mind goes to when he is lost in one of his prolonged drunken spells. Spell is the right word, because there is an alternate reality and world that he inhabits when he is drinking that probably makes a lot of sense to him, but that is heartbreaking to me: it is a world where he trusts no one, nothing that is said makes any sense, where he verbally berates me in nonsensical ways as the threads of rational thought and sanity elude him. In this world, I am his enemy. He threatens to harm me, to kill me, to punish all who defile me, his emails get very heavy and incoherent and nasty, but they generally follow the same theme: "I can't live without you, you are the love of my life, you bitch, I will find out what you are doing and you will pay for it." He will drink non-stop day in, day out, until he is completely incapacitated. Then, when he can move again, he will pull enough strength together to maneuver to the closest bottle, and consume it.

Yes, it is disturbing. It is awful. And I also know that there exists under this alcohol-induced paranoia and delusion a man who is scared shitless about his total lack of control over his delusional thinking, doesn't know what to do, and whose brain is telling him that the only way to cope is to drink and to sink into that other world that offers him some kind of hellish comfort. In moments, between the rambling delusion, the incoherent mumblings, and the endless declarations of undying love and verbal harassment and death threats, I see glimpses of the pain he is trying to mask. Of his terror. In this state, the fear of treatment, of stopping drinking, is so much larger than the fear of death, or of losing me. But I know that it is the fear of feeling that causes him to numb his body and mind. I see pain and desperation. In moments when the alcohol has stripped away all the masks, all pretense. I want to comfort him, tell him he is safe. Instead, I must cut off contact, threaten to call the police if he doesn't stop his threats, and even leave the country to keep myself safe.

I can't reach him. I have tried begging, pleading, threatening, dismissing, ridiculing, even ignoring him when he is lost in that world. Start treatment, just go to treatment, please. Please just stop drinking. Please don't drink any more. Please don't talk to me like that please don't be hurtful or cruel. I realize a hundred times that I am hoping for a miracle that will not come. The cycle of betrayal, lies, hope, hopelessness are too many and too painful. I decide I must forget him. Although I love the man he is when he is not drinking, that man is harder and harder to remember. I cannot watch the man I love kill himself. After countless cycles of this, I have to detach myself from any hope of making a life with him. I try to detach emotionally.

All day long I think of David existing in his personal hell, impossible to reach and I wearily send another email, even though I've told myself I'll never talk to him again. I can do nothing but repeat words of love and encouragement: even though I know rationally I can't save him, I can't help but hope with every email: maybe this will be the moment that he takes control of his life and chooses treatment. Maybe right now, this hundredth, thousandth time I've told him that I believe in him, that I know he can get through this, maybe this time he'll find some piece of strength somewhere to seek professional treatment. With each email I send I allow a tiny piece of hope again, a wee dream: maybe he will somehow find a way through the inner terror and hell to choose treatment and to stick with it. How long did I struggle in my twenties with debilitating depression and anxiety and how long have I lived with my own self-destructive cycles? How many times did I vow to never abuse alcohol again, only to make a private deal with the devil?

He *chooses* to drink, people tell me, advising me to forget about him. What happened to people understanding addiction as an illness, one that takes away the choice over whether to use? I visit addicts who *choose* to commit crimes, often dealing drugs to feed their addiction. Why do I *choose* to do this?

I'm reading a biography of an English man incarcerated in a Bolivian prison and the 'hilarious antics' (yeah, right) during his time spent there. He describes one of his fellow inmates as a man they call 'slow mover,' because he moves at the pace of a slug, literally. He is so paranoid from years of drug use and incarceration that he has convinced himself that if he moves in the world very, very slowly, walking ten paces in two hours, that he will avoid detection by ghosts. I immediately think of David – I see him moving slowly, deliberately, trying to avoid detection by ghosts. What are the tricks we play on ourselves, the bargains with the devil. If I drink this bottle, maybe no one will notice I am in pain. If I visit this prisoner to cheer him up for two hours, maybe I can avoid a life of loneliness. If hold him tighter to me, maybe he will feel my love is real and stop drinking. If I love this person hard enough, maybe I will be loveable too...

* * * * *

I am back for another visit to Bangkwang before leaving Bangkok. I am exhausted from staying up late and I have to force myself out of bed, guilt-tripping myself to go see Johann again, even in my hung-over state. Not yet having my replacement passport, I carry to the prison a letter from the Canadian Embassy that verifies my identity. It is written in English, has my photo on it and the official Canadian Embassy stamp. As the guards do not read English, they see the letterhead and assume I am on official business and it is clear no one knows what to do with me. I am taken to the prison's Foreign Affairs' office and shuffled around five times from office to office while different officials open the letter, grunt, then gesture for me to go somewhere else. I am sent twice across the road to photocopy the document, before finally being allowed into the visitor's area.

After five days of closure over New Year's, today is a busy visiting day – hundreds of Thais, including dozens of monks visiting loved ones and friends, and ten foreigners. I meet an American tourist who has chosen a name randomly off the internet and is visiting someone he doesn't know. He is nervous and I talk him through the routine – what we can bring, how to purchase stuff for the inmates, how long we have to talk, etc. I point out a woman I recognize from my last visit who is engaged to an inmate – they met and fell in love when she came as a visitor. I can't believe I am hearing the words 'jailhouse romance' come out of my mouth. We talk about all we have read about the conditions behind the walls while we wait for the procession of inmates looking for their visitor.

Twenty minutes later, the men start walking in procession in the corridor opposite us, a dozen or so inmates, smiling and looking around for a familiar face. A few recognize me and wave. I wave to Liam, the Australian, and to the French man whose fiancée visits him weekly – both men serving life for smuggling heroin. Then Johann approaches and gives me a big wave and we sit down facing each other across the large gap and two sets of glass and metal bars. We pick up our phones. He is surprised that I am here, thinking I had already left for India, and I start to explain about the stolen passport and change of flights, but he is not listening. He introduces me to a young guy about 25 – 30 years old sitting beside him in a red shirt who is waiting for his visitor to appear. 'Show her your shackles,' Johann says and the guy smiles a huge grin, lifts his legs to reveal heavy leg irons and thick metal chains, then drops his feet and sits facing sideways, staring at no one. I don't know what the appropriate response is, but I don't have to come up with one: he is looking away into space. He has been sentenced to death. All the death row inmates wear shackles 24 hours a day. Johann mentions that the first 18 months he was in Bangkwang, he also wore the leg irons.

Johann is frenetic in his speech, agitated in demeanour and inattentive. I remember from the first time I saw him that he has strange conversational habits, but today, conversation is almost impossible. He frequently looks away when I reply to a question, as if bored, uninterested, then interrupts me with a forced smile and a cheery question: "So... How is everything? It's GREAT you're here," he repeats, looking around constantly for escape. It's pretty clear this conversation is difficult for him to sustain – I remember this bizarre sensation from the last time and I don't take it personally – I don't think it's me he wants to escape from. I sit staring at him, watching his mannerisms and his struggles to converse 'normally' with me and something like fear stirs in me. I start and stop conversation a hundred times but he interrupts and yells at other inmates, making jokes with them and I can't help but petulantly feel a bit annoyed that he would rather spend my visit talking to the guys he is locked up with 24 hours a day.

I ask him how the Consular Christmas visit was. Johann mentioned on our first visit to me that the Canadian Consular staff brought him a McDonald's hamburger as a holiday treat last Christmas. I am curious what he chose as his treat this year? He explains that the Embassy was 'too busy' this Christmas. I try to hide my anger at this. Johann shrugs understandingly: he knows how 'busy' people on the outside are. I remember Warren Fellow's describing how being treated like less than human creates a belief in the inmates that they deserve nothing and the phrase 'learned helplessness' flashes through my mind.

We try again to converse about neutral topics, but Johann repeats that he just needs to focus on getting through each day. During a previous visit, he repeated this mantra with a big smile, and I admired his ability to stay positive. This time, when he says this, I see only terror. Later I recognize my own fear watching his agitated attempts to act 'normal.'

A middle-aged Dutch woman is walking up and down the visitor's row, flustered – she can't find 'her' inmate – the young man in a red shirt and leg shackles has disappeared. After Johann makes enquiries on his side, he explains that the guards have removed the young man from the visiting area, having suddenly decided to enforce the policy that death row inmates get no visitors. The young man has been brought back inside. Is this intentional sadistic cruelty on the part of the guards? I wonder. I have heard too many accounts of the psychological games played with inmates, intended to break all hope. In this prison, death row inmates are given only two hours' notice of their execution – another method to keep them in continual fear and uncertainty.

The Dutch woman is pissed off and keeps interrupting everyone to show her annoyance that she has wasted her time waiting for someone who is not showing up. Johann empathizes with her frustration, explaining to me that it is not fair for the inmate to disappear like that, wasting this woman's time. They are acting like this was the inmate's fault. I don't know what to say.

The phone lines shut off abruptly. Two rows of people stare at each other, waving, smiling, gesturing across the gap. Someone explains to me that the visiting time for Thais is finished and that the guards cut power to all phones to indicate this – but phones for the foreigners will be restored in five minutes. We stand and stretch and talk to our neighbour or gesture across the glass divide as we wait for power to be restored. Liam, the Australian inmate, motions to me that he likes the star tattoos on my arm, giving me the thumbs-up. The Dutch woman is complaining that because 'her' inmate is gone and she wants to visit with Johann. The power is restored and everyone on both sides of the glass and metal partitions picks up their telephones to resume conversations. I am thinking about the young guy in the red shirt and shackles, wondering what has happened to him. Johann starts babbling at me with a manic cheeriness.

Suddenly, it's all just too much for me. All of it.

I make excuses to Johann about needing to go to the Embassy to pick up my new passport, tell him I'll write him from India, and I run off, leaving him to converse with the Dutch woman. I buy five packs of cigarettes for Johann at the prison shop and head for the river boat. I am ashamed that I left so quickly and on the way to the pier, I briefly wonder if I should go back. I can't. I keep running. I see Johann's face as he attempts conversation: shadows of fear crossing his face. I see the young guy in the red shirt grinning as he shows me his shackles, then sitting, facing sideways, staring vacantly.

I am angry. At myself. At Johann. Many times in the past weeks, I have drawn inspiration and comfort from thinking of Johann's courage in the face of his circumstances. When I felt lonely, afraid, unsure, worried about my own sanity, I thought of Johann's ability to stay positive, to transcend his worries, and this gave me hope. I am ashamed of my reaction today when faced with Johann's veneer of optimism cracking. I see the fear in Johann's face as he forces a bright smile and cheerful voice and I feel betrayed by his visible struggle. What does this mean about the possibility of sanity in insane conditions? I push all those thoughts away. I busy myself at various Embassies replacing travel documents, trying not to think about my experience and reactions at the prison.

That night, I am talking over drinks to a guy at the guesthouse about my day and I find myself needing to say something – anything – about the intensity of the experience. I have no words – I can't say what I have seen and felt. So I make vague, general statements expressing my outrage that human beings can be treated in such brutal and de-humanizing ways and the ways all of this is normalized.

"What do you expect?" he says. "These people *CHOSE* to commit a crime."

"Maybe," I cried, not wanting to engage on that point. "But people don't deserve to be treated like this, no matter what they may have done. You can see the inmates visibly struggling to maintain any semblance of sanity," I try to explain.

"Incarceration takes a toll on people," he shrugs. "Everybody knows that even if they get out of there, those guys will never be the same again."

He smiles and changes the topic.

EARLY DAYS

My job in Chandigarh, India turned out to be fraudulent and after a few weeks in an increasingly dangerous situation, I made a hasty middle of the night exit from a locked compound, then out of India with the help of Canadian Embassy officials. Back in Bangkok, despondent, totally broke and feeling like a failure, I was determined not to return to Canada empty-handed, tail between my legs. I resumed prison visits at Bangkwang.

TUESDAY, JANUARY 30, 2007

I went to the prison again today. I'm not allowed to visit with more than one person a day, so I picked Zaw, as he is Burmese and has few visitors, Johann told me. Ten years served already, he has a great smile and jokes a lot. He was grateful for the visit and it was mellow. Several times, the road bisecting the visitor's courtyard behind me was filled with prisoners marching in handcuffs or shackles, or by an ambulance or mail truck going into the prison. I'd never seen it so active in there. Zaw told me about surviving without money by cooking for Nigerian prisoners until they were extradited en masse in 2003, or washing other inmates' clothes to make money to survive. He learned that his dad died sometime last year in Burma, and he is has been waiting for months for any confirmation of this through acquaintances who might bring word from Burma. Zaw was illiterate when he arrived in prison at the age of 27, but has learned to read and write Burmese, Thai and English from other foreign inmates. His English is impressive.

I imagine trying to get funding to do educational stuff in these prisons. Although totally unrealistic, I would love to facilitate improv Playback theatre classes, or to offer courses in social sciences, creative writing, or art. It would be fantastic to be able to offer the foreign guys any kind of creative, intellectual, somatic outlet. That is highly unrealistic, given that they don't even have running water. I have a hard time imagining the big trough of Chao Praya river water that the guys say they all have to run to and 'bathe' in at the start of each day when they are let out of their cells. When that water's used up, their only option is to purchase bottled water, if they have funds.

Lots of people at Bangkwang today: Two other Canadian travelers were there to see Johann and he babbled on the exact rehearsed spiel he had given me my first day. His stories change the longer I've known him. He seems proud of the 'bad-ass' persona he creates for the newcomer. I am mildly annoyed about having been lied to in our initial visits, but this feeling lasts only seconds. He doesn't 'owe' the truth to a stranger. I don't care to engage with the stories of inmates' crimes anyway, as I imagine they are all self-serving – I am more struck by what the prisoners think they have to do to get attention or sympathy from a visitor, as displayed today by Johann's antics. Whatever it takes to get someone to come back, I guess, not surprising for a population desperate for company and fearful of more abandonment. I send a package to Johann with shampoo and Kit-Kats and ointment and razors and a letter saying I intend to offer conversation and moral support, nothing more, and I hope he doesn't think he has to perform for me or entertain me in order for me to keep visiting him.

THURSDAY, FEBRUARY 1, 2007

ON THE BUS TO MAE SOT, THAILAND

Today I 'called out' Liam, Johann's friend and cellie, probably due to a curiosity I've had from the beginning to meet him, as he always gestures when I am visiting Johann, giving me a thumbs up on my arm tattoos. I wonder if my meager efforts are not needed with respect to Johann – he seems to get quite a bit of Dutch traffic. He had a Swiss 'meditation teacher' come today. Because Johann had so many visitors, I chose Liam and discovered that today is his 30th birthday – What a fortuitous choice. Liam had woken up depressed that he was alone on his birthday, but I surprised him with a visit.

We had an awesome dynamic talk – moving from fetish and spanking through piercings, sex and gender fluidity, contact visits when he can't bring himself to let go of his mom, bipolar diagnosis and through to the incompetent prison psychiatrist we speculate may be fleeing prosecution to land this gig, to what Liam would design if he made my sleeve for me – my next tattoo. I told him of the crazy experience in India and of the scary escape from the 'employers' who had me under lock and key. We talked about childhood escapades, I told him about my favourite children's books: Arnold Lobel's *Frog & Toad*, and why my friend Jessica might make a great pen-pal for him. Liam did impressive Sean Connery impersonations and we exhausted all our *Chuck Norris* jokes. I bought Liam three notebooks at the prison shop because he says he writes down his dreams – very cool. Inspired me to do more of my own dream-work.

SUNDAY, FEBRUARY 4, 2007

MAE SOT, THAILAND

I am feeling the roller coaster of uncertainty of whether I can make a viable life here that feeds body and soul, always wondering about my struggle to do meaningful work for no money. My budget here is $3 for housing and $3 for food and sundries per day, still very bare bones in this inexpensive country. At this rate, I can maybe stay a few more months, I hope, as long as I can stay to my strict budget. *Don't sell yourself short, Heath.* I just got an email from my friend back home who was thrilled I connected her with a new pen-pal, Liam. I was inspired by her email to create an intention to make my dreams to finance this prison work come true.

I was very low yesterday, wondering if I should just get on a plane, go back to Canada, admit defeat and continue the frustrating life that awaits me there: full of bureaucracy, expensive, useless material things and soul-less conversations. At least I would be with Morgan, whom I miss so much. Shit, I don't know, it is so hard to be without her and yet I am trying so hard to create a different life for us that isn't just working furiously non-stop to barely stay afloat in Canada.

Today, I went for a bike ride in the countryside around Mae Sot with an English and a French guy. We stopped by the river that divides Thailand from Burma, took off our shoes and waded into the gentle current. It is a lovely spot with gorgeous trees and I stood basking in the sun, knee-deep in the river. Two women carrying baskets and a baby were crossing from our side to Burma, and as we stood in the water, we saw two guys with boards of teak lumber strapped together start wading slowly across from the Burmese side dragging the floating wood to our side, where some men were waiting for the 'shipment'. You hear all the time about the teak, drug, human, and gem- smuggling that happens across this border, but it is quite surreal to experience it as a peaceful Sunday afternoon moment in a river, watching people with big smiles who wave as they wade back and forth across the river, bringing items illegally. It was a beautiful bike ride and I feel more relaxed, less anxious about the future, although I still don't know how this will all unfold. But, I keep having to remind myself: we never know how anything will unfold, so I just need to embrace all this.

Din, a Burmese refugee friend just called me and is pressuring me to 'sponsor' her, her husband and her young daughter to come to Canada. They seem to think that all I have to do is show proof of a bunch of money in a bank account in Canada and they can go. I know am incredibly privileged compared to them, but it's hard to explain that a low-income single mom in Canada living below the poverty line is in no position to 'sponsor' a family of refugees. It just doesn't work that way. Still breaks my heart, though.

* * * * *

9:30 pm and the moon is full and bright orange. The military police are everywhere and I don't know why. I am so glad that I managed to get off cover letters and cvs to three different ngos tonight – proud of having pushed through self-doubt to accomplish this. Now that the documents have been sent, I feel somehow more legitimate, more credentialed than I did a few hours ago when my same intentions, work experience, skills and education had not been quantified.

WEDNESDAY, FEBRUARY 7, 2007

BANGKOK, THAILAND

I took the overnight bus from Mae Sot, deeply ambivalent about leaving. Coming to Mae Sot was fear based: having run out of money, I desperately thought I could work with grassroots organizations involved in combatting sex- and human- trafficking, or providing refugee or migrant services, but of course, they are mostly volunteer-run. I left feeling useless: what am I contributing of 'worth' in Mae Sot? I am not visiting prisoners nor do I having paid employment. Always the game of credentialing. I felt strangely ok about the interactions with Din

trying to explain with care that I was thinking of them while assert-
ing my boundaries repeatedly that I cannot personally sponsor anyone
to go to Canada. And that the information they are getting from the
refugee camp is an understandable but tragic combination of misin-
formation, desperation, and pure invention. Fuck, it doesn't make me
feel any better about their situation or their options. The reality of the
majority of the people in the Umpiem Camp is that they is that they
will be waiting many years, not weeks, for any small chance of being
sent to a third country.

FRIDAY, FEBRUARY 9, 2007

Yesterday was actually a good birthday. Alone and lonely on my birthday,
I woke up late and hung over and decided to go to Bangkwang. I left the
prison elated, and I was happy to get a birthday singing message from
my daughter, sister and mom as well as very thoughtful and caring
messages from my ex-partner. I know that regardless of potential job
rejections by ngos, or difficulty in securing funding, that what I am
doing visiting and supporting prisoners is valuable and not self-defeat-
ing, not crazy. I am looking around at teaching jobs in the North, and
will work today on a spreadsheet of the inmates and visitors, to start
organizing all this properly.

I reflect on my first time at Bang Khen Women's prison on Wednesday. On this day, I have chosen a South African prisoner, because she is
the same age as me and has an eleven-year old daughter. I am unsure of
how Carolina will receive me, and find it odd that I am so much more
nervous about this first visit with her than with meeting a new male
inmate. We are only allowed twenty minutes together, and as I walk
towards the small area where dozens of prisoners are shouting across
chain-link fence at their visitors, I wonder how I will recognize her. In
the midst of the noise and confusion of a crowd of visitors and inmates
shouting their messages at each other, I see a tall woman jumping up
and down waving furiously at me with a huge grin on her face. She
leads me to a booth, where we can sit and talk to each other through
our microphones, and not once through the entire twenty minutes
does she stop grinning. Her joy is infectious and we talk easily. She tells
me that she woke up this morning, praying someone would come and
visit her and that her prayers were answered when I showed up. Our

conversation flows easily, we talk about love and appreciation of small moments of joy in our lives, freeing ourselves from negativity. She insists that the gift of my visit to her, should be reciprocated with a song. In a clear, strong voice, she sings about God's love that sustains her. I am looking across two sets of metal bars at this woman leaning into the microphone, and I am humbled by the immense and unconditional love she sings about, filling her, spilling onto me. Tears are falling at her beautiful gift to me.

I will never forget the image of her jumping up and down with excitement when I arrived, nor her song.

FRIDAY, FEBRUARY 9, 2007

Today, I see two women inmates at the prison together because the officials didn't seem to understand that I wanted to see each woman separately, in succession. We three women stand awkwardly and the two inmates are curious as to why this Thai woman and this Nigerian woman have been requested together by an unknown Canadian. I tell them that I am here to offer support and they break into huge smiles – amazed that a stranger would come to visit them. Polly has been in nine years and Songma for five. Songma gave birth in prison and gave up her child to her British boyfriend's parents, who took him back to England to raise him, when the baby was two months' old. Her boyfriend is in the men's prison and both are serving life sentences after being arrested at the home of a drug dealer, Johann, on their way through Bangkok to England. *Guilty by Association*, this crime is called in Thailand.

Today I saw Liam – "How is he?" I was later asked by a friend. How would I know, really? We both put on our 'visit' face – both so happy to see each other – what are we going to do, bitch about our lives? No, we can leave that to the safety of our letters, where we probe more intimately our darker thoughts and struggles.

He looks good. His small grey eyes still very intense – I hear his bitterness, note his laughable attempts to prove to all that he is evil. Today he wears his Satan t-shirt, such a contrast from the gentle, loving person I know. Is this another form of the bravado I see in Sergei – the tough guy pose these guys adopt – is it for each other, for survival inside, or is it only for my benefit? What does it give them to 'perform' the peacock for a woman? I want to ask about this prison culture of men who cannot show emotions, except stoic toughness, hardly a new phenomenon, or original, but still, I'm endlessly curious. He seems to speak to hardly anyone – like me, Liam has closed himself off from most of the world.

I know it's a small thing, but I wasn't even allowed to bring grapes in today. 100 baht those purple things cost, and the guards confiscated them. I talked again to the American missionary and learned that bible study classes have been conducted inside the walls of the prison for over 20 years, by a man and woman, and my hopes rose. I want to appeal directly to the King to get permission to access more inmates, to teach social sciences, English, creative writing, theatre, anything. I wonder for the hundredth time about writing a long letter to the King, asking for permission to help the foreigners do classes or meditation, and giving my academic credentials, references. What do I have to lose? He might consider it a great idea and very good for the benefit of Thailand to take good care of its foreign prisoners. On the other hand, staying under the radar seems like a better option for me.

Today, the suffocating heavy heat descended on Bangkok. Until today, I was thinking: *hey, the heat's not so bad, I think I'm finally used to the heat of Thailand*. Well, bullshit. Today, the heaviness arrived, you know, where the air is a thick, heavy grey blanket and you don't want to move, you don't want to think about moving, and the thought of walking to the post office to send the last package to inmates seems undoable. The heaviness descended on the guards at the prison, too. They were all in supremely pissy moods, denying entry to all food or care items. And, as is customary, they were randomly making up ridiculous new policies on the spot. A Swiss woman I met on Monday entered the prison at the same time as me, and we both secured our purses in a locker, as per usual. As we were searched, suddenly a Thai guard yelled at all us foreigners that we need to carry our passports. *What do you mean?* We already have the photocopies of our passports stamped and authorized before we even get to this part of the ritual. Our passports are locked away in the lockers, with all our valuables, as per their instructions that we enter empty-handed.

The guard yelled at us to go back and get our passports, so all foreigners returned and lined up to retrieve our bags from the lockers and removed our passports. When we approached the same guard to show him our documents, he ignored us and walked away – just to be an asshole. Then they threw away the rice cakes and fruit that is normally allowed in, all sorts of stuff like that just to piss off all the *falang* visitors. I should be used to it, just some days it gets to me more than others.

Athough I hate the taste, I enjoy smoking with the inmates. I've gotten in the habit of palming a pack of smokes and a lighter when I go in, and often the guys will bring their smokes with them. It's an immediate connection, a sense of sharing something tangible across the barriers between us. Sometimes just sitting in silence, each smoking our respective cigarette creates an intimacy far greater than an hour of talking. The guards will probably put a stop to that soon.

Sergei and I are both relaxed today – he appreciates the cigarettes I bought for him last time at the prison shop, he says, and repeats what they've all been insisting: that the actual visit itself is infinitely more meaningful than the food and goods I bring. Today, I believe him. Sergei is young, with a 100-year sentence started at the age of 20 for trying to smuggle heroin with some friends from Burma to China. In most moments, he seems quite sincere, very earnest. He tells me about the pet bugs, frogs, rats and stray cats the inmates occasionally keep. He refuses to learn the Thai language, even though he can't help but understand it, he says. He is not unusual in his stance. I can't see how this symbolic resistance to speak Thai among foreigner inmates will do them any good in the long term, but I can understand his position, not wanting to participate in the language of his 'oppressor'. On occasion, Sergei adopts some macho posturing in his words and demeanour – lots of ugly racist terms directed at the Nigerian inmates. Is this for my benefit, or a reflection of what is required inside, I wonder? It makes me uncomfortable, but I say nothing, and we change the topic. Building #2 houses death row inmates who are only allowed out one hour in the morning and one hour in the evening, so the rest of the time, the area for the non-death row inmates is not very crowded. It means a lot more space for exercising, and Sergei tells me that inmates have set up a room where they can draw and paint, if they purchase the material. Sergei's lucky enough to share his only eight – person cell with a Russian Ukrainian, so they hang out and speak in their common language of Russian, and cook soup together every day. He has no embassy support, but holds on for that very faint hope of a Royal Pardon.

He tells me of another African inmate, Figaro, who wakes up each day of his 100-year sentence, smiling and marveling at the beauty of the day. The men gather around the trough of dirty river water each morning when they are let out of their crowded 50-person rooms to wash quickly before the water is all gone. Sergei tells me many are crying, others despondent, some totally numb with despair, but Figaro sings, celebrating the beauty of the day with a huge infectious smile. Sergei shakes his head in wonder as he recounts this. I leave, carrying that image with me for a long time.

Usually I fall asleep on the riverboat on the way back home, but today I sat next to a Canadian guy: it was refreshing to hear an attractive older man condemn the practice of Western men coming to Thailand to buy young women or men for sex. He mentioned how hard it is to be a single male traveller in South East Asia viewed suspiciously through the sex-tourism lens. I cynically wondered how much that declaration was for my benefit. I declined an offer to join him for dinner, got off the boat at my stop and went for a cold shower to wash off the prison grime.

THE SHITSHOW

Today, another day that leaves me exhausted, full of conflicting emotions, and questions about this work, about everything. It's hard to convey the intensity and absurdity of everything I experience, so my emails contain just snapshots of small moments in packed days.

The culture of misogyny, racism and classism in the prison whirls around my head and I wonder at my responses and non-responses to those unacknowledged layers that permeate everything. I have decided that my priority is to be present with an individual inmate, to listen and be compassionate, to offer myself as a witness to his situation, while treating him with respect and honouring the privacy of our conversations. I am careful to not talk to inmates about each other, trying to preserve the little dignity and privacy they have. I am challenged by institutionalized racism and misogyny, of which I catch glimpses daily, and struggle to understand the prison culture they have to live in.

Then there's the three-ringed circus of the prison visitor culture...

Last night at the bar I bumped into a New Zealander, Travis, who recognized me from a few weeks ago when his Australian friend went to the prison with me. Travis was hoping to visit a fellow Kiwi, but, like everyone going for the first time, didn't want to go alone. I agreed to meet him at the riverboat pier this morning, and we rode up the river together, so I could walk him through the opaque process.

As I show him how to register for a visit, I am nauseous from the endometriosis pain in my abdomen that is badly aggravated by the heat. The prison is a shit-show again today, with dozens of missionaries crowding into the visiting areas armed with bibles and lists of prisoners they are calling out. Missionaries are allowed five prisoners each, during the 90 minute time-slot (I figure roughly 18 minutes per prisoner) whereas 'regular' visitors like me can only call one prisoner per day and we spend up to an hour and a half with them. I fight down my anger that because of the gaggle of missionaries (or is it a 'murder,' like for nuns and crows?) the foreigners' visiting area is over-crowded and there are not enough phones to go around for all visitors and inmates. The din of a long row of missionaries yammering away speedy bible lessons makes meaningful conversations for the rest of us virtually impossible.

Just two years ago, I would often be one of only a handful of visitors in the foreigner section, but now there are dozens every day. The presence of so many missionaries (do they get free airline tickets?) is excessively frustrating: firstly, because of the impossible racket caused by so many people, but also because if I call a prisoner and he has already been called by a missionary, we miss our visit, and I am not allowed to register with another person until the following day. And, I am biased: I don't think that 18 minutes of bible-reading is really a great way to offer support to an inmate. On some days, I may be the only person visiting a single inmate. When missionaries show up in droves, dozens of prisoners stand against the wall, looking out at us, waiting for their 18 minutes of 'soul-saving' and others who have had their 18 minutes remain in their corridor for as long as they can, chatting with guys from other buildings they don't usually get to see. From there, they get an opportunity to look through dirty glass at the dozens of visitors milling around the courtyard.

Today, I called Zaw while Travis called a fellow Kiwi whose Italian-sounding name he had gotten from the New Zealand Embassy. After going through the standard paperwork, frisking, maze of checking and re-checking our bags, metal detectors and gauntlet of lackadaisical guards (who all greet me warmly now and laugh with me at my lingering road rash from a recent motorcycle accident), we wait for what seems like forever in the blazing sun or stifling corridors of the visitors' area. We hope the phones will work today and I ask the guards to turn on the few ceiling fans. They only do this job 365 days a year, I think, yet wait to be asked each time to turn on the rusted fans to try to bring a semblance of motion to the heavy air.

The visitors wait, exchanging nods and small talk. An Australian man introduces himself: I learn he's called out my friend Liam today, and I am pleased, because it means not only that Liam will have a visitor, but also that I'll be able to steal a few words with him as well. Two days ago, I called Liam on his birthday and a bunch of missionaries and the *British Ladies* gathered around my phone on our side, while a bunch of inmates gathered around him on his side and we all sang *Happy Birthday* to him. "Bad-ass" Liam, who likes to ask the missionaries to lift their shirts or to tell them he's the Anti-Christ turned beet red and tried to disappear into the wall while we sang.

Waiting for the inmates to arrive, I ask this guy how he knows Liam, and he says he was travelling through Thailand years ago and decided to visit a fellow Aussie in prison. He visited Liam and promised him that if he ever came through Thailand again, he'd bring him a carton of his favourite cigarettes. Then he mentions that he's just spent the past five years in prison in England for murder and remarks bitterly that no one came to visit him, so on his return to Australia, he's honouring his promise to Liam, by visiting him and bringing him ciggies. Unfortunately, the duty-free cigarettes he promised were accidentally sent, along with the rest of his luggage, onward to Tokyo, but he's still happy to be able to see Liam for a few minutes before he runs for his connecting flight to Japan. Apparently, he's flying with multiple passports, thus allowing him to visit several countries, even with a prison record. The man sweats profusely, shifting uncomfortably in brand new patent leather shoes as we wait and wait and wait...

Finally the guys file in to the corridor across bars and glass from us and our visits begin.

Zaw and I have a wonderful visit. A Burmese inmate ten years into a 100-year sentence for transporting drugs into Thailand. Like many Burmese migrant workers in Thailand, he says he was given meth to work longer hours in Thai garment factories and was asked to transport meth for his Thai boss. His friend was shot dead at the border by Thai police when they were intercepted.

I ask him whether he gets annoyed at the recent influx of missionaries into the prison. He says he appreciates the missionaries during the slow months when there are no other visitors: "Even the Muslim and Buddhist inmates appreciate a chance to come out to the visiting area to talk to someone, even if all they do is read the bible at you. And they provide free sausages at Christmas!" He laughs and remarks that it's amazing the number of converts to Christianity on Christmas Eve, just in time for the free sausage. We laugh.

"But seriously," he says, his tone angry, "these missionaries do not come here to communicate. Communication happens when people listen to each others' beliefs. They only come to tell me what I should believe. If it was somebody else, and they were to talk to me like that,

I would tell them to 'Fuck Off' but they come all the way from foreign countries to tell me what to believe...!? So I sit and listen and when they're finished I get to go look at the eye candy." He gestures out behind me, indicating dozens of Thai women and the odd foreigner lining up in the courtyard to drop off food and clothing, care packages to their loved ones.

He laughs again.

I enquire about the prescription drugs I got from my doctor in Canada for Zaw's ulcers, carried to Bangkok in my suitcase, and mailed from Bangkok to a Western inmate to pass on to Zaw. Did he receive it? Yes? Success. After a few more minutes of conversation, I realize that Zaw seems ambivalent about taking the pills I worked so hard to get to him at a cost of about $250. I wonder if I have overstepped boundaries by assuming that he would want Western medicine for his painful ulcers that have bothered him for years, but I distinctly remember asking him last year if I could send him this medication. I approached a doctor on Zaw's behalf and paid an arm and a leg for antibiotics, which I mailed to him, but he never received. I remember explaining to the doc about the rampant disease, overcrowding in the prison and asking him whether he'd be willing write a script for a general antibiotic, knowing it is not for me. He agreed, and he said as he wrote it: "Whichever guy gets this will undoubtedly feel better than he has in a long time, no matter what is ailing him." Undeterred by the first failed attempt, I mailed the second batch to Johann. I've learned through experience that the Western guys are more likely to receive their packages with less theft from the guards. This was months ago, I was working 80 hours a week waitressing in Canada, getting the money together for the pills and shipping. Here, today, Zaw doesn't seem very interested. In fact, he mentions that he does not want to take them.

He tells me of contracting malaria working in the jade mines in northern Burma a few years earlier, and how a friend 'cured' his high fevers by repeatedly pinching his skin. He prefers 'traditional' methods of healing – 'holistic' or 'alternative' the hippies on the West Coast of Canada would call it – but my bullshit meter rings loudly, competing with my intention to be 'culturally sensitive' to anyone's beliefs and choices....GRRR. I am resentful at my wasted efforts to get him antibiotics so many people have no access to, but I realize I cannot force him to accept my 'aid' – I have to let go of my resentment. Remembering the doctor's words and the high rates of disease and infection among these inmates, I hope Zaw at least gave the valuable drugs away or traded or sold them to an inmate who could benefit from them. I realize my ego needs to be able to report back to Canadians that I have succeeded in helping to rid a Burmese man of his ulcers in prison and I remind myself that this isn't about me, about my 'successes.' I accept that it has to be enough to provide Zaw an option he didn't have before, and what he does with it is up to him. But it is a bitter pill to swallow, so to speak.

Later in our conversation, he invites me to visit his aunt and sister, who live in a remote monastery in the mountains of Northern Burma. He says he will mail me a letter of introduction so I can stay indefinitely with them.

The unmistakable rattle and crunch of heavy chains interrupt us, and I turn to see inmates in shackles being escorted through the courtyard behind me to their court appearances. No matter how many times I witness that, it is hard to get used to. The guys talk about those heavy shackles that are welded to them for the first year or so as the single most degrading aspect of their experience as prisoners. When the men are sufficiently pacified, (i.e. psychologically degraded), the shackles are removed, except for the death row inmates, who must bear them permanently.

A pick-up truck exits the prison behind me, bursting with huge live pigs, stacked one on top of the other. There is a pig farm inside the prison – where Building 1 is supposed to be – supposedly, the pigs eat the faeces of the inmates, as well as the government rice that is supposed to be the daily fare of prisoners. Once sufficiently fattened, the pigs are slaughtered and butchered, then sold at a profit for the guards running this side-business. Don't know that I fully believe the shit part, but I don't get too caught up in the veracity of most claims – reality here has always proven to be far stranger than fiction.

After saying good-bye to Zaw, I see Liam standing, his back against the filthy wall, looking out at the courtyard, waiting to be brought back to his building. I wave him over to a phone, where we speak a short while until the phones are abruptly turned off. Waves and smiles all around, and the inmates file back to their buildings. We remaining thirty-odd visitors start a new waiting game in the hot courtyard under the glaring noonday sun, while guards re-inspect the packages we've brought to the prisoners, searching for hidden cell phones or money or drugs. Only when they are fully satisfied do we get our slips of paper stamped, allowing us to exit the prison. In previous years, this additional step did not exist, but too many times guards have found contraband smuggled in the care packages. Just a month ago, a woman was caught with pills in the Durian fruit she had brought for her husband. They arrested her on the spot. I heard about it the following day. Every time I hand over my bag of food, books or toiletries for an inmate, I worry that someone has somehow slipped drugs or other contraband inside. It is only very slowly, over years, that my daily anxiety about somehow not being allowed out of the prison has subsided. I only remember that fear now when new visitors comment on it as we wait for the large heavy gold doors to swing open and release us from this crazy liminal space into the regular world.

As we wait to exit, the regulars make small talk, complaining about the heat, the long waits and the gaggles of giggling teenaged missionaries from Singapore. We are all crowded around a small wicket, waiting for the name of our inmate to be called, so we can get a permission slip to leave. The sticky muggy heat is almost unbearable after two hours in the prison. We gossip a little about who may be getting transferred or shake our heads at the Thai girls who come regularly to visit the British guys, hoping to marry a man with a foreign passport. It's hard not to notice the gendered aspect of this three-ring circus of visitors at this men's prison – 90% of the visitors are women, not just wives and girlfriends, but also missionaries and regular visitors like me, who have spent years coming here.

One woman, a Dutch flight attendant, has been visiting for 30 years, using her free flights and days off each month to bring food and conversation to the inmates here. A Columbian woman, Lena, whom I see every Monday and Wednesday, offers to give me a list of inmates who are learning English and would love an English-speaking pen-pal. I readily agree, happy to hook up more people back in my home community in Canada with inmates wanting pen-pals. Her inmate husband teaches English inside the prison, she explains.

She peers close to my face and asks me if I ever fall in love with the guys I visit.

"No," I laugh. It's absurd and obviously an ethical breach in a relationship with this type of power imbalance. And besides, it would be just plain delusional.

"Are you sure? Never? You do not fall in love with them?" Her face is very close to mine, incredulous, searching, peering into my eyes.

"I've grown to care very deeply about some of them as close friends or brothers over the years, I say, but I don't fall in love with them." In truth, I think I fall a little in love with every one of them, maybe just not in the way she means. A few of these men are closer to me than anyone, aside from my daughter.

This highly dramatic woman, who speaks in exaggerated tones and grand gestures, explains that she met the man of her heart, her soul-mate, here at the prison. In her heavily accented English, she explains that she was married to a Thai monk and they had some children and they decided to visit prisoners at Bangkwang. The minute she laid eyes on this inmate, Victor, she knew, just knew (clutching at her breast for emphasis, and rolling her eyes back in her head) that this was the man she was born to be with. She instantly divorced her husband and married the inmate, whom she has now been visiting twice per week for years. She even rented in an apartment overlooking the prison (*Jesus,* I'm thinking,) so she can watch over the prisoners from her balcony. Apparently she was banned by the administration from visiting for several years, but has recently won her bid to be allowed back in. There were other pieces to her long convoluted story about the VERY powerful energy inside the prison and the alignment of the stars, but I didn't quite catch all of it. My mind wanders and I smile and nod, tuning out as I watch her face – bright shining eyes, intense gaze, laugh lines and creases, she is a beautiful woman. She pauses, taking a breath. I can't help but ask her whether she works, privately wondering how such a lunatic can keep a job.

"Oh, I translate between Spanish and Thai, but my main job, the job of my life is to LOVE and LOVE and LOVE him," she sings emphatically. I stand there, absorbing this.

A skinny Thai lady-boy with the largest Adam's apple I've ever seen on any human approaches me in her tight-fitting short-shorts and gushes at me about my tattoos.

"OOOOHHH, she coos, I scared of tattoos, I no like pain."

"Yet you have tattoos on your neck," I can't help but point out the obvious.

"OK, actually, I not scared of pain," she announces, "because I have surgery everywhere: my face, my titties, my pussy, and here is silicon," she says, indicating her hips. "Now I have the perfect body," she says, spinning in order to showing me her features from all possible angles. "Not like you," she says, wrinkling her nose in obvious distaste. She continues: "I am model and I want to work for Victoria Secret. I send them a picture and they say: OOOOOHHH you so pretty, are you man or woman and I say I am a MAN! she shrieks and covers her mouth dramatically, then continues, "and Victoria Secret say but oooooohhhh you so pretty and with perfect body!"

I have little patience today. Everyone is irritating me. I am in a lot of pain from endometriosis, and I am acutely aware that there is no bathroom, no water source to access, should I start gushing dark blood through my pants. I am run down from the pain in my abdomen and lower back, and the dozens of Ibuprofen and Tylenol I have been popping for days do absolutely nothing except burn holes in my stomach. I am unable to bring to Thailand the prescription narcotics that actually help manage the pain, as they are illegal here. While I stand here gritting my teeth, on the other side of these thick concrete walls are 6000 or so inmates, many of whom are sentenced to 100 years or the death penalty for drugs. Each one now has access to all the narcotics he wants, from other inmates or guards, at a hefty price. Meanwhile, I have to wait while some of these same guards check the bag of books I've brought to make sure there are no pills stuck between the pages. Weird.

The guard at the wicket makes mangled attempts to sound out English names and dozens of us crowd around to retrieve our exit permission slips. I push through the crowd, grab my piece of paper and head out. As I am lining up to collect my personal belongings, the aspiring model lady-boy strikes a dramatic pout at me then shoves her phone in my face, that shows a picture of her face posed in exactly the same pouting expression.

I can't think of anything to say, so I say nothing.

I ask Travis how his visit went with the Kiwi inmate – he and the guy really clicked, he said, excitedly, and they exchanged addresses to continue to write to each other. Turns out the inmate was Iranian-born and after living ten years as an immigrant in New Zealand, received Kiwi citizenship. After 9/11, he was subjected to continual racist harassment and interrogation by police in New Zealand, based on his Iranian name. He changed his name legally to an Italian-sounding name, and was apparently never harassed again.

I stop at the prison shop on the way out and buy a carton of UHT milk for Zaw. He requested a wee shopping list of items that would make his life better and I have agreed to get them and mail them in. Some Muesli, some stamps, some A4 paper to give to the guards so that they have no excuse not to print out emails sent to inmates. This weekend, I'm also going to look around Bangkok for a bakery that sells dark bread, and treat the guys to a loaf of bread, cheese, Western food next week. That is one of my favourite aspects of this mission – buying food for the guys that I know they miss and appreciate – fresh fruit, bread, cheese, salad. Most days I bring fruit and cooked food from the vendors outside of the prison, but many weekends, I go to the high-end specialty supermarkets in Bangkok to get some "Western" food that is greatly appreciated by so many.

A man pushing a cart of freshly butchered pig meat and pig faces, covered with flies leaves the prison as the same time as me. He crosses the street, parks his cart and starts selling the meat alongside the other vendors who sell fruit across from the prison gates.

I fall asleep on the riverboat back to my guesthouse, exhausted. It is five hours since I left this morning before I return from one single prison visit. I doze in order to stop the questions swirling in my head, wondering why I am here and what I am doing. The human capacity for predation and degradation and brutality of one another is overwhelming. At times I wonder about my role and I am not sure whether participating in the shit-show at the prison every day is useful.

Then there are moments when I know that this work IS important – that the visits, the conversations, the vitamins, art supplies, pen and food parcels and books do mean a lot. A hell of a lot. Still, everything swirls and I try to make sense of it or put it into a framework that is useful for me.

I go to an internet café and listen to a cheesy video called *Healing the Hearts of Humanity* and it somehow helps me to reconnect to the knowledge that there is more than just shitty-ness in the world.

I suddenly feel grateful. I am thankful for the kind words, for emails that encourage me, for new people I've met here offering support for my work. Like the owners of a café on Samsen Soi 2, who donated ham and cheese sub sandwiches a few days ago that I brought to Ivan and Sergei so they could have a taste of home.

Each of the letters and bits of cash slipped into my pocket to help me buy food and stuff for the guys, and each book and magazine donated makes a huge difference. Nothing is perfect. It's a fucked up place and my small funds allow me to offer only very limited material support. But these small gestures and words of encouragement, make the heaviness and craziness bearable. I know how much it means to the guys, that I am here, but it also sustains me, knowing that the ripples of this work are getting wider and wider and there is a network of people in the world who will not let these guys be forgotten.

THE CORPSE GATHERERS: WHAT IS TAKEN

Tuesday, I had a great visit with Liam. It felt a little more authentic, rather than the recent posturing, bravado and walls that he sometimes puts up. Although a decent conversational partner is not what I expect from most inmates, with Liam, I expect, perhaps unfairly, that we don't bullshit each other. Liam is like a little brother to me. No matter what is going on in our respective lives: heartbreaks, betrayals, sorrows, we are pretty real with each other.

As we talk, a crew of corpse gatherers wearing masks enters the prison behind me, followed a little while later by a truck. The corpse gatherers are a volunteer organization used by the prison to remove dead inmates. We peer out from the visiting area, hopeful voyeurs of the macabre, speculating whether it might be someone we know. Rumours and speculation die quickly, we resume our cheery conversation, a light dusting of resignation settling upon us.

All I know is that another person has died inside, not able to return home to their family, not able to outlast the faint hope of a King's Pardon that keeps most of them going for years. Maybe the guy was happy to die, released from this earthly suffering and ready for a new beginning, as some Thais believe. It is hard not to feel defeated, though, that Bangkwang has won again and the small candle of hope we carry flickers in that moment, diminished. The corpse gatherers are a tangible, sobering reminder that, despite our cheery conversations and the inmates' continual assurances to me that Bangkwang is 'survivable,' in reality the acute stress of that place, the mental illness, rampant disease or suicide has taken another person.

A few weeks ago, Zaw told me of an inmate in his building (of 800 men) who had had a heart attack while his brother slept just across the bars from him. As the prison is overcrowded, and all inmates are locked up from roughly 4pm to 7am in their overcrowded cells, the halls outside cells get used as sleeping areas as well. For 6000 baht (roughly $200) an inmate can purchase a place to sleep in the hall, which affords him a bit more space than inside the cells. One brother in the crowded hallway heard his 40-year old brother call out during a heart attack inside the adjacent cell and die. He was unable to reach his brother, and there is no medical attention available to inmates, no guards who come after lockup.

There is a particular horror that comes into an inmate's eyes when he speaks of death in there – no one wants to be the body that is left bloating in the heat for hours, sometimes days, before being removed by the corpse gatherers. Johann's biggest fear, he once told me years ago, was to die inside and to suffer the final indignity he had seen countless times of being reduced to a lifeless body left, stared at, stepped on, walked around for hours. Other inmates have told me of having to sleeping beside a cell mate who has died and been left by officials for hours or days.

On the riverboat returning from the prison, I sit beside Bob, an older gregarious Canadian from just outside Toronto, who has also visited Johann for years. He spends a few months living every winter in Thailand, in a sleepy beach town south of Bangkok and comes up to the city to see Johann once every three weeks or so. Usually I sit alone on the riverboat, tuning out the heat and prison and the loud roar of the engines sputtering and shrill whistle of the boat crew signaling as we dock at each stop down the Chao Praya. Sometimes I fall asleep. On rare occasions, I debrief with another prison visitor, usually a woman, and we converse quietly about the challenges it takes to offer loving kindness to wounded men, about how to handle their self-pity and their projections, of the politics and rumours of the prison.

Bob is loud and irreverent, he is a caricature – bright pink sun-burnt skin and huge 1984 Magnum P.I. moustache perched atop a bright fluorescent orange wife-beater and shorts. I just want to tune out the day, and rest on the ride back, but soon I am grateful for his distraction from my thoughts – Bob's chain-smoking, loud politically incorrect rants and black humour are a breath of fresh air. Bob is totally oblivious to the volume of his voice and his use of offensive language on a crowded boat full of Thais. Today, I welcome this irreverence.

"I don't know how you can go into that stinkin' rat-fuck-hole every day," he says, shaking his head. "It's all I can do to come here a few times a year." A few years ago, Bob was allowed an 'inside visit,' with Johann, the once per year visit when a visitor is allowed to sit at a table with an inmate for an hour with no bars and glass between.

"It must have been precious to have actually been beside Johann, conversing normally, like regular people." I am deeply envious.

"Precious for him, maybe!" Bob snorts. "Not for me! I fucking hated it. I tell you, Heather, it's a rat-fucking-shit-hole in there and even if they pretty it up with picnic tables and plants for visitors, it's a fucking disgusting rat-hole." He shakes his head. I mention the body that was removed during today's visit, and I tell him that I learned that the corpse gatherers not only remove the dead from Thailand's prisons, but first must ensure that the prisoner is not faking death. In order to do so, they slit the ankles and wrists of an inmate before dragging him out.

"Faking?" Bob shouts. "What the fuck?! Can they not afford a fucking stethoscope? Jesus! That's one practical joke you don't want to pull. Sorry, just kidding, I wasn't really dead. Oh well, now you gotta bleed to death: so sorry!"

Despite myself, I start giggling and Bob and I spend the half hour down the river laughing hysterically about all the possible scenarios of an inmate trying to fake his own death and the corpse gatherers who don't quite get the foreigner inmates' attempts at humour. None of it is very funny, but I am crying from laughing so hard.

We have both read Chavoret Jaruboon's memoir, the now retired executioner of Bangkwang, who was in charge of executing all of Thailand's death-row inmates from the 1970s until 2003. We recall his account of the woman prisoner who was tied against the post and shot by an execution squad five times on the left side of her chest, as per standard practice. A doctor used a stethoscope to determine there was no heartbeat and she was placed in a nearby room to await the corpse gatherers. Suddenly, she flails and struggles for breath and guards realize she is not dead. They grab her and prop her screaming against the post again and tie her in position for another round of bullets. Again they fire directly at her heart, and again she does not die, until the third time.

Later, the medical officer determined that this woman had a rare condition whereby her heart is located on the right side of her body, rather than the left.

"What a practical joker that prisoner was!" says Bob, "I bet the guards laughed about that for weeks..."

THE CORPSE GATHERERS: WHAT REMAINS

I shower off the stickiness and tension and walk around Bangkok, thinking how grateful I am for Bob's humour that diffuses the tension from the prison visits and usually makes me crave a drink. I am reminded of an elderly woman I saw once leaving the prison. As we made our way out, this woman I assumed was a missionary turned to me and said: "Fuck, could I ever use a bottle of whiskey and a pack of cigarettes after that." I laughed and nodded in agreement. Couldn't have said it better myself.

This evening, I am sitting with friends who run a bar, drinking wine. It is my birthday. It is a lonely time of year for me and I miss my daughter in Canada very much. She usually comes with me every year, but now grown, is now living with her boyfriend and I miss her like crazy. Today, I am particularly lonely. A French acquaintance of the bar owners has just returned to Bangkok after a year's absence and joins us. As the evening progresses, more wine flows and the talk turns to my prison work. Gregor, the bar owner, wants to come with me to offer visits to inmates – his wife Tatiana does too, but decides she cannot, as she is afraid of what she will feel or see at the prison.

After skirting around this question for hours, Tatiana challenges me: "Why do you support prisoners? Why not children? Why not orphans or animals or refugees or abused women?" I have been asked that question many times by so many. The subtext is clear: helping innocent people is obvious, but these people are not innocent. What makes them deserving of anyone's help? I am tired, and not wanting to justify my efforts, but I try anyway. I talk briefly about needing to let all people know that they matter. I mention something about when we decide that any one group of people is less than deserving, can be treated as less than human, that legitimizes violence and perpetuates injustice for all of us. It makes no difference whether 'those people' are prisoners or drug addicts or Chinese or gays or women. Violence will never lessen as long as we allow ourselves to view anyone as 'not deserving' and to dehumanize them.

Tipsy, I ramble a bit more about each person's inherent dignity and that no one deserves to be forgotten. I lived in a prison of mental illness for several years, unreachable by others, and my mental suffering and agony was unbearable, and terrifying. I hoped only to be released by suicide, but could not abandon my child. I could not convey to others what my inner world was, but I did know that the rare times that another person was able to reach me and convey that I was not alone were vital. Perhaps that, in part, draws me to this work. I know that we are drawn to what wounds us, and that perhaps for selfish reasons, I support prisoners in the hopes that I would never be forgotten. I speak a bit about human rights, a bit about the need to respect everyone's inherent dignity, but I don't want to talk anymore... I am tired, lonely and drunk and I don't want to justify anything to anyone.

The French man is silent for a long time, then suddenly starts muttering about what a saint I am. He is talking to himself, and staring intently at me: how no one could possibly understand how vital this kind of visit is to someone who is incarcerated. No one. I am used to the categorization of my actions and beliefs into two dichotomous entities – either I am a saint/angel, or I am a deviant demon. This is part of the problem, as I see it. We cannot seem to see each other, all humans, as flawed, imperfect, complex beings with overlapping contradictory bits – either we must be sinners or saints. I shake my head in disagreement at his characterization.

When I start visiting a new guy, he often calls me an angel, a saviour, for the first while, building me up unrealistically, until invariably, I fail to match his unrealistic expectations and ideals he has built up for me. I wonder how much we all do this to each other – have relationships with projections of other people, placing them on a pedestal until they invariably disappoint, or we feel we have to knock them off the pedestal we have built for them.

The French man is staring intently at me, agitated, and continues talking half to himself. He tells me that he was incarcerated for seven years in a prison in Nepal, and would wish that horror on no one. He tells me that what I do is beyond valuable, and is life-affirming work. Coming from him, this means a lot to me, and I am touched by his intense sincerity. Although I get overwhelming responses and gratitude from the inmates, validation from former inmates is the most meaningful outside praise I can receive. I face innumerable challenges and questions about my prison work from detractors, constant barriers and obstacles to funding my efforts, and make regular justifications to people about the value of this work. With no salary, no external pats on the back, I appreciate this rare validation from someone with his experience.

He continues on, speaking louder and sounds increasingly angry. He starts shaking, now shouting at me: Do I know what it is like to be treated as less than human? Do I have any idea of the horrors he suffered? Do I have any clue what it is really like to be in prison in Nepal? "No," I reply to the last question, "I do not." He is spitting his words at me. He shakes his head violently, as if to shake away images and emotions. There is horror in his eyes and words – it is large and fills the air around us. I have seen glimpses of a similar look in their eyes when the guys speak about the heavy leg irons they have been forced to wear, the iron shackles welded on to their legs for the first few years in prison that rub raw to the bone, making it almost impossible to bathe, sleep or change clothing. When inmates speak of the humiliation of being treated like a dog, an animal in chains, I see behind the anger something that I can only describe as raw horror.

The French man continues to yell, now incoherently, to shake his head violently. Caught in memories of his experience, he is shouting at us, as if in a trance. Then he starts describing in a numb monotone things I don't want to hear: violent rapes, degradations and survival in inhumane conditions...

This man grabs my hand and repeats that I must be a Saint, or I must be the Devil. Why did I make him remember these things? He challenges me. Stories flood out of him about his experiences, and I don't want to hear them. He's speaking quickly in French, which the other two don't understand and they drift away from the table, leaving me with this man in an altered state, reliving his trauma. The floodgates have opened and it washes over him and me. For hours this man continues: "Could I possibly have any idea what he has lived and suffered?" He asks me. Can anyone? The agony in his face is excruciating. Finally, a long time later, he abruptly stands up and runs away from the table.

Overwhelmed, exhausted and still somewhat drunk, I want only to go back to my guesthouse to sleep off this night. I pay my bill and wander down the small *soi* towards my rented room. As I near the end of the street, I see the French man waiting for me. He is agitated, shaking with emotion, screaming: "Who are you? Are you an Angel or a Devil? How dare you make me think of things I have never talked about?"

He is no longer here in Bangkok on a street at 3 am – he is in a prison in Nepal and his eyes are wild and he is suffering indignities and degradations that no one can imagine and he does not know what to do with this pain, he is flooded with emotion and images. He is shrieking: "What could you possibly know about prison, you privileged little princess who knows nothing about reality?"

Spitting venom in my face, his violence spills everywhere. He demands answers I don't have. He attacks me with his rage, his agony. I see how big it is and it scares me. I know that it is not mine to take on, but that he will try to force it on me.

I am sobbing and dialing my mobile phone, trying to reach a friendly voice in Canada, while this guy screams and yells his rage at me on a street at 4 am. I am locked out of my guesthouse and I am too exhausted to run, so I sit on the street outside a 7/11 for the next two hours crying as he alternately runs away and returns to lash out at me again. A foreign tourist approaches me and asks if I am ok, as I sit sobbing from exhaustion and fear, but I wave him away. Finally, around 6 am, as the sun rises, I stumble to my guesthouse, where the old Thai landlady finally lets me in.

I am so full of anxiety, I cannot sleep. I want the comfort of another person, and alone in this town of 15 million, I do the only thing I know how to do: I shower, change clothes and go to the prison.

Standing outside the gates, feeling exposed and raw in the glaring morning sun, I register to see Ivan, who is expecting me that day, even though I don't want to see him. Waiting for Ivan to arrive from his building, I see Liam who is unexpectedly also in the visiting area, summoned by his Embassy representative for one of their rare visits. He sees me and reacts instantly to whatever is showing on my face and waves the surprised Embassy officials away. After they leave, he beckons at me to come pick up the phone. I pick up the phone and burst into tears. Agitated, deeply shaken by the nights' events and from sleeplessness and the after effects of much drink, I am hyperventilating. Liam tells me that he is there, that it is not my fault, and that we can just breathe slowly together. I start breathing more deeply and I feel calmer. In this special Embassy visiting room, out of view of the guards, I climb onto the ledge counter that the phones sit on, curl up in a ball against the glass partition and we cry, each leaning against the bars and glass between us.

Ivan walks behind Liam, arriving for his visit with me, then stands waiting thirty feet away at another phone, so I try to pull myself together. Part of my brain is aware that no matter how much I need to blow off Ivan and just get comfort from Liam right now, I should not do anything that would aggravate any tensions between inmates. Ivan is not good with emotions, and I don't feel like it is okay for me to dump personal shit on him, but I am too worn down to put up much 'professional' demeanour. I wipe my face and move away to another phone to try to talk to Ivan. I feel guilty that I cannot hide my distress and just be present for him, but I am too exhausted and overwhelmed to muster up phoniness.

To explain my distress, I briefly mention that I was verbally assaulted the previous night and upset from it. Ivan responds in his typical manner: "You are a woman alone in Bangkok – what did you expect? Just try to smile, you'll feel better." Gritting my teeth, I steer the conversation to neutral topics, asking about his family, but when he instructs me to smile a second time: "Fuck you!" bursts unchecked from my lips. A shocked look flickers in his eyes, disappears just as quickly behind his mask. We manage to get through 45 minutes and I leave, apologizing for 'not being at my best' and promising a better visit next time.

I eventually get home to sleep, re-playing the previous evenings' events in my head over and over. I remember dialing my phone desperately to Canada at 4 and 5 am and saying cruel things to the person on the other side, because of my pain and fear that came out as anger. Just as that man took his pain and fear out on me, I in turn, turned it on someone else. Despairing at the endless cycles of violence: how on earth do we ever stop the violence we each have within us, born of the pain we feel from being degraded because someone decided that we were less than human? If we cannot see that in other people and witness it, then how can we ever stop the cycle?

I know that the evening would not have unfolded the same way had I not been drinking. All would have been kept in check. But the drinking is not the problem – this pain and suffering still exists under the surface.

I don't excuse that man's violence towards me – I just know that in that moment I was witnessing what happens when we put 'prisoners' or any human on one side of a divide and the 'rest of us' on the other side and take no responsibility for what happens to a person whom we degrade, humiliate and treat as less than human, then expect to get back out in society and function 'normally.'

Everyone knows all this already, but I feel an instant ironic clarity as to why I do this work. I can read about compassionate listening and about transforming anger. I have a lot to learn about my own anger and pain and capacity for violence. I don't always know how to stop it within me.

There is more than compassionate listening that is needed here. There is witnessing. At the prison, Liam was able to bear witness to me. And this is what I try to do for these guys too.

In my endless quest to fund this work, I can't write a funding proposal that talks about visiting prisoners as a useful strategy to reduce recidivism rates. It is not about that. It is about all humans needing to hear that they don't deserve this. We can all do better to witness each other's pain and to witness each other as human.

How is one to live a moral and compassionate existence when one finds darkness not only in one's culture but within oneself? There are simply no answers to some of the great pressing questions. You continue to live them out, making your life a worthy expression of leaning into the light.

~ BARRY LOPEZ

HOLISTIC HEALING: BANGKWANG-STYLE

It's April Fool's Day at the prison. Not a prank comes to mind – the whole situation here is already as absurdly surreal as possible.

The cast of characters large and familiar, the ever-rotating bunch of missionaries, family members, do-gooders dripping sweat as we stand around for an hour inside the prison waiting, waiting, waiting for all the prisoners to come out...The guards mill about, checking through large plastic bags of cooked food items in styrofoam containers and the ubiquitous plastic baggies that everything in Thailand is dispensed in – hot meals scooped in, beverages poured over ice, even gasoline can be purchased in a baggie.

I see Shazam, the Sri Lankan missionary committed to coming a few times every week to check in on poorer prisoners and I gravitate to her, loving her smile, her incredible warmth and the peaceful love she radiates. I want to say goodbye to her and she wishes me a speedy return to the prison next year. A small round woman, the inmates have nicknamed her 'the little elephant', because of her size.

We women who visit are all rated and dismissed by our looks, age, our perceived attractiveness. Delores, one of a small dedicated group of regular visitors I long-ago dubbed *The British Ladies* (who in fact are not all British, nor all ladies) is disrespectfully referred to as an 'old lady' by some of the guys. Moved by the situation of the poorer prisoners with no Embassy support, she has visited inmates for years, bringing food packages and visits to those in need. The prisoners all wave to her, then disrespect her looks or her age. I grit my teeth at the sexism as an inmate assures me that, although no longer young, not to worry, I am still beautiful. Yuck.

The inmates seem to experience no cognitive dissonance between my coming to see them, to affirm that they are valuable as humans, and their own denigration of women as second class citizens. Each inmate expresses his personal gratitude that I treat him as a human, rather than degrade him as 'less-than,' and yet each one rates the women visitors on our perceived 'fuckability'. Ok, I get that a sexualized view of women in an all-male environment is to be expected, but I naively hope that some inmates might be able to make a link between the injustice of their treatment and the injustice of such treatment of other groups of people, an ambitious goal that I still unrealistically cling to.

Some days I can't bear the misogyny of this world. I read this week in the *Bangkok Post* – a pile of dead female babies found drowned in China; somewhere else an 'honour killing' of a woman by her male relatives (who make sure they gang-rape her first). In this city alone, thousands of women stolen, sold, bought, traded, raped and subjugated by others for money. First Nations' women in Canada murdered at alarming rates, invisible to most. And I choose to come sit with men who make sexist comments at us women visitors. Fuck, I shake it off, like I have to with everything I encounter here. No way to make coherent sense of any of it anyway.

Ten am and we have been waiting for what seems like a long time – sweat pours off everyone. We stand or sit listlessly, fanning ourselves with whatever scraps of paper we may be holding, sharing news about the prisoners and griping about the daily arbitrary rule-changes at the prison – one day, cans of tuna are banned; the following day, tuna is allowed, but male visitors must wear blue fisherman pants over their own clothes.

Lena, the Columbian woman who visits her husband Victor twice a week without fail, is here with her two youngest children. Aged roughly 5 and 8, these boys accompany her on prison visits occasionally. They run wildly, ignoring all their mother's cautions and orders. I have not seen either look at her or respond to her requests or ever stop banging on things. A few weeks ago, the oldest one marched up to me, grabbed a bottle of water from my hands and guzzled it, threw it down and marched away, a defiant smirk on his face. His mother called after him: "You need to ask before...." voice trailing away feebly. He ignored her and went back to running around the compound. Lena looked at me, sighed and shrugged, as if to say: *What can you do?* I imagined punching her in the head for being so weak and raising disrespectful monsters but I just smiled.

Today, she enquires about my daughter Morgan who I am delighted is spending some weeks with me in Bangkok, and upon hearing that Morgan has been having digestive problems, exclaims in her typical dramatic fashion: "You MUST give her a urine enema!" Oh God, here we go, I think.

Lena claims many professions, I have learned over the years and today, 'holistic healer' is one of them. She steps closer to me, and starts preaching in her odd English about the curative powers of urine. "My boys (indicating the kids who have been banging incessantly on a wall with their fists) NEVER been vaccinated, NEVER have allergies, NEVER been to doctor and NEVER suffer from illness, because I cure them with my urine. EVERY DAY I drink my urine." "You know Heather," she continues, "the human being does not need food, only the urine. It is so POWERFUL, the urine, with it you heal EVERYTHING." Each time she rolls the word 'yoooouuuu-rr-reeeeeen' off her tongue, her eyes roll skyward, and her arms flap about to indicate the magnitude of the magical properties of this wonder-substance.

Lena grabs her oldest son and points to an ugly red mark on his sunken cheek as he stands sullenly staring at me. She explains that a few months back, he cut open his face on a large shard of metal outside the prison registration area. The boys were playing, climbing around a massive pile of debris and garbage behind the toilets. This mass of twisted rebar, broken concrete blocks, drying squid, decomposing pig faces, plastic bags, electrical wires, empty pop cans and dog shit is the usual mix of detritus one finds in heaps in Thailand. On that day, the boys jumped off an abandoned train boxcar into the large garbage pile, and apparently the son who is now glaring hostilely at me split open his cheek from ear to lip on a hunk of rusty metal.

At this point in the story Lena goes off about how the presence of that particular piece of protruding jagged metal at that particular location on that particular day was no accident, but in fact deliberately placed by the prison guards in order to kill her son in a conspiracy to discourage Lena from visiting her husband – but the powers of Justice and Truth prevailed and Lena Herself had the last laugh. I am nodding as she speaks, hoping for an escape.

Continuing on the main story, Lena explains that when her son came running, screaming with his face gashed open, she took him home and pissed on his face. During the following weeks, Lena healed his cheek with carefully applied compresses of her urine.

"NOTHING else, just the urine!" she exclaims. "NOT ONE stitch I put in – I NEVER take him to hospital and look at him now!" She pokes her finger for emphasis into her son's sunken, deformed left cheek and the angry red scar on it. "My boy, he now knows to come home, make pee-pee in a glass and drink his urine after school each day. He's such a good boy." I glance over at the boy with vacant eyes studiously ignoring his mother as he bangs his fist against the glass partition that separates visitors from prisoners and I think: *that explains a lot.*

Turning her attention to the subject of my seventeen-year old daughter, she explains how, naturally, Morgan might be reluctant to try a urine enema, so I should surreptitiously collect Morgan's urine in a bottle when she goes to pee at night for a few days (I'm trying to imagine how Lena thinks I would accomplish this). When I have collected 2 litres of the precious substance, she instructs me to administer the urine into my daughter's ass while she sleeps. (I'm really not sure how she thinks Morgan wouldn't notice this part of the procedure). I am to block the exit port with both hands for as long as I can in order to allow the magical properties of the urine to fully be effective. Lena gives a graphic visual demonstration of the two-handed technique needed to block Morgan's asshole, as the imaginary urine swirls through Morgan's body. I can't believe this lunatic is the closest thing I have to an ally in this prison. I smile weakly.

Sensing reluctance on my part to follow these detailed instructions, Lena grabs me by the shoulders and insists that I try the urine panacea. If an enema is out of the question, she explains, urine has homeopathic properties, and thus if I slip just one single drop of my own piss into a large glass of water and give it to Morgan at night to drink, the single drop will travel through the whole body (full demonstration of the zig-zagging route urine apparently takes to travels within a human body) and cure EVERYTHING.

As I stare dumbfounded, Lena tells me proudly that her young sons drink a cup of their own urine when they get home from school each day. (No mystery why classmates don't come over to their house to play). Lena continues with anecdotes of wise men in India using urine to achieve spiritual enlightenment. I can see that there is a particular clarity of thought and vision derived from drinking one's own urine daily that Lena herself has been benefitting from for years.

I make a pathetic excuse to exit the conversation – suddenly needing to check on something at the other end of the corridor – after assuring her I'll consider the urine enema when I get back to my daughter resting in our room.

I am not even supposed to be here today, I think.

SAFETY & SECURITY

I'm not supposed to be at the prison today.

I said my tearful goodbyes to the guys in the weeks prior. Leaving each year is very hard, as I experience both my own sadness, but also a few weeks of serious acting out on the part of the inmates, many of whom deal with the anticipation of separation fairly predictably, as abandonment: they show anger, hostility, withdrawal and aggressiveness in our visits. With a few others, we share some tearful or wistful farewells, sometimes sharing a song or lovely quiet contemplation. The final weeks are especially emotionally exhausting, and I get pangs of survivor guilt for being able to walk out and away from so many people who cannot.

After months of difficult daily prison visitations, I am finally returning to Canada in a few days and look forward to the cool of the West Coast. It's been hard to integrate a very intense time and rich learning. Morgan came to join me for a month this year and after a relaxing holiday week with her in a quiet Thai beach town, we returned to political protests and bombings in Bangkok. I am unsure how I will re-adjust to life in a world where time is lived differently, a world that reeks of privilege, entitlement and safety.

How safe is safe? What does it mean to be 'secure?' And how safe do you need to feel in order to act? Most Canadians enjoy a level of safety and comfort unimaginable to the majority of inhabitants of the world. Despite this, in Canada, we have elevated our preoccupation with safety and security to a freakish national obsession. Canadians seem to need an ever-increasingly huge 'safety net'. I notice Canadians feel entitled to personal 'bubble zones' – imaginary safety zones that guard between them and the next person – larger than most other people. I notice this in traffic, where a one-foot gap between cars is plenty sufficient in Bangkok, but would get you glares, horns and road rage in Canada. Canadians also spend a lot of time discussing 'financial security,' which means: how much money and material crap have you amassed as a buffer between you and your fears ...of dying....or of being 'poor'?

Despite living in, objectively, one of the richest, most secure and most peaceful areas of the world, West Coast Canadians seem to require also to 'feel safe' before saying or doing anything and often demand that the people around them create an 'emotional safety' bubble zone for them, avoiding conflict in conversation at all cost, and avoiding anything that takes away their 'happiness.' How one creates 'emotional safety' seems to be complicated and the subject of much time, energy and navel-gazing especially on the West Coast, and may entail chanting or other forms of removing 'negative' energy from the milieu.

I wake up to the continual state of emergency in Bangkok – the 80,000 or so Red Shirts have kept up their protests around the clock for five weeks, demanding that the current Prime Minister dissolve parliament and hold elections. They are not leaving and their determination and actions are escalating.

Drinking a coffee at an internet café, I open an email from a Canadian named Bill. He has contacted me from my website to ask for information on how to donate some money to one of the Burmese prisoners, Zaw. I get the occasional email from people requesting information on how to send care packages to prisoners, or whether donating money is a good idea, or mostly, asking for the name of an inmate to write to.

I reply by email that the only way for Bill to get money to a prisoner is to physically deposit it at the Bangkwang prison wicket after visiting him and only on his allotted visit days. The following day, I receive another email from Bill requesting more 'specific information' on how to get money to an inmate. I write a detailed description of where the Bangkwang prisoner account wicket is located and how to get there by taxi, bus, riverboat or tuk-tuk. I offer to deposit money for him, if he is not in Thailand to do it himself – as he has not indicated where he is. If he wishes to do so, he can send funds to me via Western Union. Despite having said all the difficult goodbyes this year to each of 'my' regular inmates, I am willing to make one more trek to the prison, through a city shut down by protestors and military police facing off, if it will get funds to Zaw.

Over the following days, Bill emails me half a dozen times to inform me that he's in Victoria, BC, and thus cannot get the money to the prison himself. Could he not instead mail an international postal order or perhaps find another way to get money to Zaw? I am irritated.

Apparently, Bill assumes that my days doing prisoner support work consist mainly of sitting at internet cafes, responding to queries with false or misleading information. I re-iterate in my next email that the *only* way to get money to a prisoner is to directly deposit it at the prison, again it is futile to mail any money or money-like items to prisoners, they will not receive them. I also re-iterate that I have only a few days left here, and I repeat my offer to help, for Zaw's sake.

Zaw is from Burma and has been in Bangkwang for 13 years, since the age of 26. I have been visiting him for five. Reduced from 100 to 40 years, his sentence now has 27 years remaining, which will see him released in his sixties. Usually a cheerful, reflective and thoughtful person, last year, I noticed a marked change in his demeanour. Although he said nothing about this change, I saw and heard the accumulated weight of Bangkwang reflected in him, of the many years he's spent and the many years ahead. This year, I saw him for the first time angry, confused, and bitter.

A month ago, on a visit, Zaw asked me to remove his name from a website that solicits pen-pals for inmates, as he is worried that publicity of his situation will negatively affect his treatment in the prison. It is hard to know what guards take offense to, but as a poorer prisoner and from Burma, Zaw is subjected to the worst treatment inside the prison, and, understandably, does not want to jeopardize further his already difficult situation by bringing attention to himself.

He also does not want any more people to write to him. He seems angry and avoids looking directly at me. He talks about the pain of betrayal of having people show up randomly in his life through letters to be-friend him, then who disappear, never to be heard from again. He has been waiting a long time to hear back from a woman who says she will start an application for him for a King's Pardon – a very faint-hope at release. An application for a King's Pardon is a long-shot, a time-consuming bureaucratic process, impossible for a Burmese inmate to undertake without significant help in resources and work from someone on the outside. Zaw says he is just waiting for her to re-contact him – his eyes say he is resigned to the fact that she will not come through.

I have thought a lot about this dynamic over the years between prisoner and outsider – the manipulations and power imbalance in a relationship where the prisoners are subject to the capricious nature of people on the outside. I hear their tales of devastating pain of lost hope, betrayals, abandonments when people simply vanish from their lives. Unlike on the outside, where we have opportunities to re-connect with or to repair damage in a broken relationship, prisoners are powerless to repair misunderstandings or to question motives or gain new information about people who simply disappear, never to be heard from again. Re-abandoned and devastated by the loss of a precious link to the outside, inmates agonize over every conversation, every written word and wonder what they have done wrong. Acutely aware of this, I reflect carefully on my every interaction with them, careful not to betray trust, nor to create false hope or to make any promises that I cannot keep. Still, in this intense environment, where every word and look and gesture is meaningful and amplified by a thousand, dissected for months and years by the inmate, I am sure I have caused hurt and confusion through careless words and actions – despite best intentions, it is inevitable. But I feel deeply protective of these hurt men and I want to scream at every person who has written to a prisoner once or twice on a whim, then forgotten them.

I am reminded of the words of an American death row inmate, Sunny Jacobs, from her book *Stolen Time*:

"We in prison depend on those we have left outside for our very existence. Without their support and acknowledgement we cease to exist in the outside world. We fade before our very eyes – we feel life slipping away as the people drift farther away from us. It's like being shipwrecked in a hostile land, the land of the lost. And, half the time, the people who supply you with the vital elements of life and hope, get tired, or too busy, or simply don't care anymore. So like the old Eastern adage about the tree falling (does it make noise if no one hears it?), we cease to exist."[*]

As I prepare to leave Thailand, rushing around to pack up my belongings, I stop at another internet café where a new email from Bill questions why I gave him a Salt Spring Island, BC home address for a Western Union reference, if I am actually in Bangkok. He also asks that I mail him a prison receipt for the money he wants to send. I am more than annoyed. Each day for the past few months, I return from the

---

* *Stolen Time*, Sunny Jacobs: Doubleday, 2007.

UNFORGOTTEN

prison more exhausted, carrying with me the cumulative witnessing of men's hopes, fears, pain, suffering, anguish. I have no energy to hold this Canadian man's hand through the 'security risk' of sending $40 to me via Western Union. *What's the worst that can fucking happen to you, buddy? You end up feeling stupid because you lost $40 to a conniving con artist who pretends to support prisoners in Thailand?* I take a deep breath and write a brief email saying that if he doesn't feel 'safe' sending money to a person he doesn't know, I suggest that he not do it. No one is coercing him. I want to remind him that *he* contacted *me,* not the other way around. I mention that there are only 24 hours left before the final day I am able to deposit the money to Zaw's prison account.

I press 'send' and go to the prison. It is 8 am, and thousands of Red Shirts are streaming up and down the street in pickup trucks, waving flags, noise-makers and screaming. It is 37 degrees and I am sweaty, and my daughter is sick, sleeping at the guesthouse. Today I visit Sergei. He is surprised and excited to see me, and I explain that I have a few unexpected days left in Bangkok before flying out. We are happy to have this extra visit. He is twenty-six, has been incarcerated since the age of twenty on drug charges. Sergei is obsessed with Japanese cars, has learned English in prison, keeps prison rats and prison cats as pets and dreams of having a wife and kids one day. Locked up in their crowded cells for 16 hours at a time, the inmates watch a lot of tv as one blares down in each cell, showing mostly Thai soap operas. Occasionally, they can tune in to an American channel. His favourite show is: *So You Think You Can Dance.* His eyes go big as he describes the dancing that enthralls him.

I ask about his mother – a factory worker in Kazakhstan and his disabled sister. He speaks to her every Friday for five minutes by phone – a recent luxury the inmates can purchase at a huge cost from the guards. "She's fine," he says. She says she is waiting for him; she waits for his release. Something flickers in his eyes, as he says this, but he quickly checks it. When emotion threatens, Sergei physically braces himself, smiles and repeats in his heavily accented English: "Vat You Can Do? Is OK." He is always trying to reassure me that he is fine and that things are ok. Often the men try to reassure me that they are ok, to be strong. It's not like I'm sitting there pitying them or asking with puppy-dog eyes if they're ok. The bravado is often to assert their strength for my benefit. Men from Canada, Australia, and Europe more freely express their emotions to me, are more open about their struggles, their fears. Those from Iran, Central Asia and Russia display what I consider a more macho tough 'front,' seen through my cultural lens. I wonder whether it helps them cope to be able to act 'strong' for a woman, or whether it just makes things worse to not be able to express what's really going on for them. How could I possibly know?

Sergei's mother is saving her money – has been for years, to come to visit him. He says he doesn't want her to, as he worries about a Kazakh woman alone in Bangkok. I hear the weight of being unable to 'protect' and provide for his family, the guilt for the pain caused. The sheer impotence, the total powerlessness to provide comfort, security to their loved ones is hard to carry, especially for Sergei and Ivan, as the men in the family from cultures where they feel they must provide. As their mothers send them any spare money or clothing they can to help their sons survive the prison, the men carry a heavy burden for the emotional suffering they have caused their mothers, evident when they talk of devising strategies to re-pay their financial debt.

Sergei tells me he is 'prepared' to spend 'only' a decade in this prison. As a way to sustain hope, he has wrapped his head around the thought of being released when he is 30 or 31. There is no logical or judicial reason for this – he is sentenced to 100 years and his government has no prisoner transfer treaty with Thailand, and there is no reason to suppose a treaty will soon be made. But this thought is what keeps him going – he has adopted a survival narrative whereby spending a decade, his twenties, in a foreign prison is just the gift that has saved him and will allow him to grow as a man into a positive person, he explains to me. Then he quietly laments the loss of his youth, gently expressing fear that at 31 or 32, it will be impossible to have anything he has hoped for – a wife, a family – his youth will be gone and so will all opportunity at a life. Then his frown clears and he smiles at me: "Vat You Can Do? We OK. I OK, Don't Vorry About Me," he reassures me.

In fact, he informs me as he changes the subject, that he and the other inmates worry a lot about my safety.

"You, Heather, alone in Bangkok, is not safe. We, we are safe in here – nothing can happen to us. Even if we have no money to buy food, even the poorest prisoners get government rice. In the outside world, you have to find job, to work. If you don't work, you don't eat. You have to walk in the streets where people can hurt you, rape you, and there are protests, bombings, car accidents. We, in here, we safe. Prisoners are in safest place. We OK. You live in outside in the dangerous world. Inside, we just watch Thai tv."

We laugh together at the irony.

When I meet people and tell them that I visit prisoners in Bangkwang prison, they invariably ask: "Is it safe to go to the prison?" I laugh. I think of the thick concrete walls, the barbed wire and guard tower, the three screenings we visitors must go through to enter, and the dozens of armed Thai guards lounging in the shade, watching us. I have to agree with Sergei – it is probably the safest place I can be.

This morning, more car bombs go off in my neighbourhood and grenades have exploded. I am not sleeping well, with Red Shirt activists screaming, broadcasting propaganda and crappy Thai pop music on loudspeakers all through each night from various locations around Bangkok. Just three blocks from my room, they have occupied many streets and the roughly 50,000 military police have been blocking roads, access to parks, the zoo, government buildings, for weeks now. I take pictures of black military helicopters flying low over the streets as I shop for food. The Red Shirts vow to stay until the government agrees to step down. In a strange symbolic move, protesters have been drawing 10 ccs of blood from their arms each, collecting it in buckets, and splashing the gallons of blood all over the streets, the Prime Minister's residence, and other buildings while the military and police calmly watch the demonstrations, making no attempts to stop them. Bombs go off at least once per day, and grenades have been launched at banks, at department stores, and at government buildings around the city.

Although most Bangkokians, the majority Yellow-Shirt sympathizers, have chosen to ignore the Red Shirts and tolerate the take-over and blocking of all major intersections and business areas without counter-protest, there are limits to everyone's patience, and the tensions are mounting. We foreigners are oblivious to any of the real tensions and complicated history behind all this, and I am all-too aware as we debate the 'issues' nightly at bars, how ignorant I am. I can only observe with curiosity. The local English-language media write inflammatory articles, daily warning of 'impending violence' and 'anarchy' in the streets.

Tourists are leaving and staying away from Thailand in large numbers and several countries have issued advisories against travel here. After a month of this, I can't help but be impressed by the sheer volume and perseverance of this protest. I cannot imagine my fellow passive Canadians flocking by the tens of thousands to our largest city from all over the country and occupying the downtown, government offices and business district for a month night and day, to demand that the current government step down. Neither can I imagine our leaders simply watching as protesters push against riot police, and re-asserting 'everyone's right to peaceful protest without interference.' The leaders of our democratic country that supposedly guarantees the right to express opinion and to protest peacefully would probably order riot police to shut down any occupation of the streets within days, citing 'security reasons.' While I don't agree with their aims, I am impressed with this massive ongoing display of Thai civil disobedience and the concomitant restraint shown by the authorities. But yes, the grenades and barricades are nonetheless disconcerting. Having seen bombings, shootings and other 'unrest' over the years, I am partially accustomed to this here, yet still unsettled.

In the lead-up to the annual Songkran Festival starting in a few days, the city officials worry about the impact of the presence of hundreds of thousands of additional people, military and protestors, in Bangkok during this infamous Thai New Year's Water Festival, when businesses close for a week and much of the country drinks whiskey and beer and engages in a massive water-fights. Already the most dangerous time of the year for accidental alcohol-fuelled deaths, last year's Songkran festival saw Red Shirt protesters and police clash, causing additional deaths and injuries.

Hoping to recuperate financial losses caused by the protests that have scared tourists away over past months, I hear city officials are thinking of extending Songkran by a few days to encourage tourists to come back and see what a 'fun' place Thailand is. Never mind that the tens of thousands of armed Red Shirts camped and living all over the streets of Bangkok will now have even more days to drink whiskey, pop pills, as will the police, military, and Yellow Shirt revellers. Great idea.

But I don't think too much about these things as I head to the prison every day. The inmates may worry about me, but I in turn worry about them. Over the years, I have heard the same message from different inmates, repeatedly: "Don't worry about me, Heather – I am totally safe here. I am in the safest place possible. It is the outside world that is not safe." It always strikes me as odd, given the intensity of their situation and the oppressive conditions. I wonder about the effects of institutionalization on these guys, eventually making them fearful of a life outside their tiny, harsh, yet predictable enclosed world.

On the last night before my final day in Thailand, I go to an air-conditioned internet café to cool off from the stifling heat. I open three frantic emails marked !Urgent! Apparently, Bill has sent money via Western Union to me, and I must respond !immediately! with confirmation that I have received the funds. I can only shake my head, wondering if he has considered that Bangkok is in a a time zone fifteen hours ahead of his and there are fewer than 24 hours before I leave.

The following morning is April Fool's Day. I stop at a Western Union on my way to the prison and collect Bill's $40 for Zaw. At the bank, I receive a free t-shirt covered in pink psychedelic elephants as a promotional gift.

Waiting for the prisoners to be brought in, chatting with the other visitors, sweat dripping down my scalp and into my eyes, my clothes are soaking and I wonder if I'm going to die of a fucking heat stroke.

Johann, surprised to see me again, runs over and says hello – he takes a break from his Dutch backpacker-visitors to update me on his legal situation. He has just learned that, despite their best efforts, the Canadian government cannot revoke his citizenship and bar him from re-entry into Canada, as he was born there and thus is not a 'naturalized' Canadian. This means that when he is hopefully transferred to Holland in the next year (due to a prisoner transfer treaty with Holland, after serving over 10 years), he can hopefully eventually move back to Canada, which is his goal. This is thrilling news. We both cross our fingers that we may one day see each other on the 'outside,' wave goodbye, blowing kisses across the dirty glass.

Liam strolls by and we sneak a quick few minutes joking. His visitor today is a friend returning to the US after 15 months in Thailand and he's saying goodbye to her, so we just spend five minutes renewing farewells and promises to write.

Finally, Zaw arrives. He sits down across from me, we pick up our respective phones and I ask how he is. He starts to say something, changes his mind, and says: "Not good." He stares at a distant place not looking at me. He repeats that he is not well. It's his head, he explains: he can't concentrate, can't focus, hates his existence, wants to run away from his head. He is depressed, has lost hope, and is thinking of suicide.

Pretty hard conversation. The affect is flat: there is no emotion. He just stares off into the distance, speaking slowly. He says he can't even write letters anymore – tries to, but gets confused, loses all interest, can't finish anything. He is shaking his head, as if trying to clear the mental fog he describes. He asks me to pass on his appreciation to his pen-pals in Canada, but that he just cannot write, cannot respond to them. He just wants to 'run away from everyone and go where there is no one.' He talks of going into the open latrines, slitting his wrists and waiting to bleed away, but he is afraid of the pain. He says instead he exercises every day to stay healthy and figures he may last another 2 – 3 years inside.

He outlines his situation in monotone: he will never see freedom, will never get out. There is no comfort I can find to offer him. It's not like his assessment of his situation is un-realistic:

- The long-anticipated prisoner amnesty of April or May is now unlikely, given all the political unrest – and if the government collapses due to all the protests – then it will be more years of waiting for the next amnesty.
- If it were to happen, a general amnesty would only chop maybe 3 – 4 years from his long sentence anyway.
- A King's Pardon is the only way he will be freed: A King's Pardon for a Burmese inmate is less likely than a snowstorm in Bangkok.
- People write and make promises of friendship and to help make an application for a King's Pardon, then they never write again.
- People you trust make promises and break them; they disappoint you; they hurt you; they lie to you; and it fucking hurts.
- Democracy will not come to Burma in his lifetime.
- He will be old before he has a chance of release – he does not want to start his life when he's old. He'd rather die than get ill and suffer from debilitating disease and degeneration inside prison.

I listen in silence. His hopelessness is infectious, and I dare not say anything trite or placating. It is totally unjust that this man will spend his whole life from the age of 26 onward in a foreign prison, enduring loneliness and hardship, with no contact with family. No government to fight for him. No chance for release from this terrible situation. He sees foreign prisoners from Western countries get transferred home after 8, 10, 15 years of fighting for release, having received support and lobbying from fellow citizens and their Embassies. He wakes up every day knowing that he will spend his entire life here, simply for the reason that he is a poor Burmese man in Thailand.

Zaw lifts his head, looks at me and says ruefully: "After thirteen years in here, I still sometimes think that this is all a dream and I will wake up."

My gut clenches. I cannot begin to imagine what that experience must be like. I can't hug him or hold his hand – I can do nothing but listen. Our phone cuts out – signaling the visit time is up. I wave to Zaw across the dirty glass and leave, feeling helpless. Telling him I deposited $40 to his account seems pretty hollow.

On the way out, I give the pink psychedelic elephant shirt to the guards for Zaw, courtesy of Western Union. I stop at the Post Office and drop a prison receipt into the mail to reassure Bill in Canada that his money is safe.

JOURNAL 2011

Talking to a friend a few days ago, he touched on the new buzzword 'resilience' in the environmental movement...forget 'sustainability', he said: we need to think about environmental 'resilience'. This hits me hard as I think often about inmate resilience. I used to ask them: "What sustains your hope?" Now I am reflecting more about their personal resilience and the varied resistance strategies to insane conditions.

APRIL 2011

Been thinking about what draws me to people's suffering, to liminal spaces others find hard to inhabit. In witnessing people's fear, suffering, loneliness, struggles and doubts, I open a little space for mine. When I see in someone the ability to overcome and soar and I can encourage them to do so, I wonder if I offer myself a little more distance between my own dark places and the shadows that threaten to swallow me?

NOVEMBER 22, 2011

It's impossible to maintain my 'humanitarian face' in the prison every day. Although I write papers about the 'humanitarian imperative' – the need to alleviate suffering and to uphold dignity in an inhumane system, I am still human. On good days, I maintain that I have spent six years developing a polite, respectful relationship with the guards at the prison, and that it matters to try to build bridges and to not see them in an adversarial manner.

Then days like today, where the sheer obtuse idiocy of the prison system makes me want to scream. Today, another arbitrary rule change that I cannot challenge, but must accept with a tight smile that feels like it will crack my face open. Every day before today, if I arrived at Bangkwang by 9:10, I would be registered for the 9:30 visiting time. This year, they've changed it to a 9:45 visiting time, and I have arrived with plenty of time to register, as usual. The visits are so short and I am allowed only one per day with a given inmate of a specific build-ing only, so all must be carefully planned and choreographed, before I rush to the next prison across town with its own bureaucracies, idiosyncratic rules and challenges. I am ready with paperwork and documents to deposit this into the small wire basket as I have done hundreds of times before.

I wait with all the other visitors (today I am the only foreigner) as they process our paperwork and finally, at 9:40, the guards call us to enter for a 45-minute visit. The days of 2-hour visits are long gone. I stand in the overcrowded waiting area, acrid black smoke of burning plastic in the air – I try to breathe through my mouth in order to avoid the usual mix of dog shit and fish guts, raw human sewage, and various foods deep-frying on open burners, but today the burning plastic scorches my throat.

I watch an inmate walk by me, identifiable by his blue shorts and blue shirt, holding a broom, a pair of pink rubber gloves and a bucket overflowing with black water in one hand and a clear plastic baggie containing two steaming cooked corn cobs in the other. He crouches, setting his lunch and gloves on the concrete ground by an open gutter in front of the toilets, and empties the bucket into the gutter, splashing black liquid on the bag of corn in the process. He haphazardly sweeps cigarette butts and garbage into the gutter, then picks up his baggie of cooked corn and his pink plastic gloves and moves on.

I wait until all the other visitors have filed into the prison before enquiring politely about my paperwork. The guard looks sullenly at me, then says something in Thai to his co-workers, who all laugh. He points to the sign indicating the 10:30 visiting time slot. There is no reason for them to delay processing my paperwork, except to show me that they can do anything they want and, *by the way, Fuck You, Foreigner, you can't say or do anything about it.* So I stand for another 45 minutes, dripping sweat as dozens more Thais crowd in and fill out their paperwork, carrying bags of chocolate bars, chips, cooked chickens, rice, and other assorted food items, each sweating in its little plastic baggie.

The stench from the two toilets is overwhelming, and when I can't hold my full bladder anymore, I enter one and gingerly perch myself over the hole, splashing urine on my ankles, shoes and the leg of my jeans. A second open hole is brimming with human shit, and I gag as I rinse my fingers under the trickle of water coming from an old faucet near the ground. I hold my purse in my teeth, and a notepad is wedged under one arm, as I flap ungainly around, trying to pull up my pants without letting any part of my body or possessions touch any surface of this stall. I exit into the waiting area, and the smoke from burning plastic rips my throat again. I spend the next half hour staring blankly at every prison guard who walks by me, acutely aware of this passive-aggressive adversarial game we play: they change the rules randomly to fuck around as many people as possible, daring the Westerners, who, with our notions of 'rights' and 'justice', like to bitch and moan about 'fairness' until we realize that it is futile. The game ends when we realize and accept that they hold all the cards – that there are no 'rights' or 'justice' or 'fairness' here... I *know* this already but it doesn't make it any easier to swallow. And this, in a week where guards have removed 90% of the foreigner inmates to far-flung prisons in other parts of the country without informing Embassies or families, ostensibly due to the widespread flooding. I spent hours waiting to see an inmate on Tuesday that the guards knew perfectly well was gone. Not the first time, and not the last time. I recall other days in the prison, waiting hours, melting in the stagnant heat, only to find out, that the inmate is dead, and won't be joining me. As I leave, the guards laugh and smile at me as usual, and I grit my teeth and grimace in an attempt at a smile.

On Tuesday last, as usual, they smiled blankly and let me sit for hours like an asshole – worrying, wondering what the fuck is going on with Liam, until another inmate who recognized me motioned to me to pick up a phone (much to the disgusted look of his visiting girlfriend). He informed me that Liam was transferred two weeks ago to a prison in Songkla, down by the border with Malaysia. Hundreds of people have lost contact with their loved ones – with no idea of their whereabouts. Letters mailed to this prison will no longer reach the transferred inmates.

"I'm surprised they didn't tell you," this inmate says, referring to the guards who let me register and wait for an inmate they knew was no longer here. Surprised? Why? Because the guards would actually do something that is helpful, rather than wielding their little bits of power like bullies at recess, taunting and whacking the shit out of the other kids with their sticks. I know this is nothing compared to what the inmates deal with every day but even just five minutes of this today, and I am ready to explode and rip somebody's head off. But I must stay cool.

On other days I am the one trying to calm down a foreign visitor who can't understand why all the food she brought for her brother is being unilaterally rejected. "Yesterday I was allowed to bring meat and fruit', she complains. "Yes, but that was yesterday, and today is today.

Any change of rules is just to piss us off and to show us they can." Just smile and accept it, to save their face and your own, or it will be worse for us, and even more so for the inmates.

Another day, I arrive at the prison and a guard waves me away dismissively: "YOU, Go, Go! Every day you come." I smile politely and thank him, and turn around, get on a sweaty bus spewing diesel fumes and ride an hour to my room, wash off the grime, pollution, frustration, only to try again the next day.

After years of seeing the same faces in uniform each day, I now wave and smile at some of the guards. There seems to be a less overtly hostile attitude towards me, which I attribute to familiarity. On days when I exchange small jokes or pleasantries with some guards, I am tempted to think I have been 'accepted,' but this delusion is quickly smashed on a following day when the same guard who was smiley the previous day stares blankly at me and denies me entry. While a few have made their antipathy clear, and one or two try to woo or flatter me – a very awkward and uncomfortable situation in moments – most are relatively friendly. Despite the rare sudden violent or hostile eruption from any one of the guards, much of what I take away from my thousands of interactions with the prison officials is the normalcy of these working people doing their repetitive quotidian grind.

Today I wait, frozen grimace, worried about Liam as the voice inside me repeats the mantra, like a broken record: "I hate these fucking people, what the fuck am I doing here, I hate these fucking people..." but of course, that's what this is all about. They don't want me here, and they don't want to make this pleasant or easy.

My mind plays back phrases like: 'cultural sensitivity in humanitarian work' and mocks me for my attempts to be a peace-builder in my interactions with inmates and officials. I ask inmates not to use profoundly racist or sexist language around me, and explain why I find these offensive. In this very moment, dripping sweat and seething with hatred, I have to laugh at my hypocrisy. I see clearly what this tiny incident has done to me and I cannot even begin to fathom what it must be like for the inmates who have absolutely no say, no power, and are at the mercy of the arbitrary bullshit that the guards and larger judicial system decide. Every aspect of their mobility, their freedom, their ability to do anything: when they can shit, eat, sleep, and what they can access is determined for them – whether they can have visitors, whether they can purchase food....They tell me of the humiliation of waiting in long lineup under scorching sun and being made to jump around and act like a monkey to get a weekly treat of two boiled eggs from the mocking guards. Too many stories, all manner of humiliation and degradation, each moment an acute reminder of their total powerlessness as inmates, sub-human. "No you cannot see a doctor. No, I will not post this letter for you. You must pay for a light-bulb that burned out in your cell."

Today, when I finally see Ivan, he tells me that effective immediately, guards have stopped letting inmates receive packages by mail – the only contact foreigners have with people in their home countries. This seems designed again to punish only foreigners, as Thai prisoners have relatives in Bangkok who can visit and bring in goods by hand. I cannot begin to fathom this new twist in the game. I try to hold in my anger, but Ivan laughs at me, delighted at my outrage. "You see, it's easy to hate these people," he rationalizes. It's not 'these people' I hate – it's injustice and systems that are designed to break people's dignity and spirit. But I see how easily that can become twisted to hate the face of the oppressor. Or really the face of each worker who himself has no power but comes to symbolize the oppression. Yuk. I hate all this today.

At least I can leave, scream in frustration away from the prison and return the next day to try again.

Is there any point to this? Does it really matter for me to visit a handful of foreign inmates year after year? It is the smallest drop in a vast ocean of human need, but it does matter. I guess this is why I cannot give up, and why I must return: to carve out something elusive called 'humanitarian space' in the midst of such fucking idiocy, inhumanity and injustice.

Some days I realize that the lives of guards aren't so shit-hot either and that it is always better to build bridges than to burn them. Today though, I just hate these fucking people.

Zaw has started his own business in the prison. He cooks and sells roti each day to other inmates. A British guy, JR, an electronic wizard, fixes all manner of gadgets. Last week, Ivan and JR acquired a broken tv from an Israeli inmate, who was moved to another prison and had to leave behind all his possessions. JR inspected the tv and ascertained that the main circuit board was the problem, and when I next visited Ivan, he provided me with the model and serial number of the Toshiba part and I agreed to order another one from Toshiba Thailand. I contacted their parts' department by email and asked them to ship me a new main circuit board, using some of Ivan's funds from his art sales that I was holding for him. Most of the money from his art I had already deposited into his prison account when I arrived in November and just in time. Ivan had run out of money and was living on credit and the kindness of other inmates – having sold his mp3 and anything else of value in the previous weeks in order to buy food. But he asked me to hold back some of his money, for odd requests, such as this tv part.

A few days later, the package arrives, and I walk over to the post office with excitement, so happy to be able to help Ivan and his cell-mates to have access to their own tv. I pick up the package and rip off the address, and carefully re-address it to an X---- Y--- Z-----, as per Ivan's instructions. He has arranged with the guards to watch for a registered package addressed to this name and for a price, the guards will allow the tv component through, Ivan explains. It never ceases to amaze me how much money the guards make off the inmates, whom they are supposed to be providing a minimum of shelter, water, food, sanitation and medical attention. Instead, all basic necessities are for sale, plus the extras.

So I re-address the box, pay to ship it into the prison, cross my fingers and wait the few days until I see Ivan again. So far this has cost Ivan: 1,700 baht for the part, 100 to ship it to me, 57 to re-ship it to the prison, and whatever amount for the guards to accept the package for him. I didn't ask and he didn't volunteer the information. Despite being insatiably curious about some of the details of their quotidian existence, I refrain from asking certain questions – like the exact price exacted for each tool, letter, pen, plate, bottle of water... I hear about beatings, about petty rivalries and other features of their confined days,. so familiar after six years with many aspects of their existence, yet I have no idea the exact fee Ivan has to pay a guard to pass me a letter.

Today Ivan explains that they moved all the guys out of their rooms last Friday in order to check them for contraband. They do this about three times per year, he says. In addition to obvious contraband items such as cell phones, drugs, and cash, more importantly, all the inmates' cooking utensils, frying pans, hot water makers, rice cookers, tvs, dvd players, mp3 players, watches, anything of any value are also taken in these raids that are done in greatly publicized moves to 'clean up the prisons.' Anything other than clothing, books or letters, is confiscated under the guise of being 'illegal,' even though it is the guards themselves who sell all of the above to the inmates, so they can cook and survive in the prison. Three times a year the prisoners try to find inventive ways to hide their few possessions and utensils they have amassed, as the guards comb through the prison and steal back the items. Without any means to cook, to entertain themselves, or to run their small businesses, the inmates are forced to re-purchase the items from the guards.

Ivan is laughing as he explains this to me. Finally, he has a main circuit board for a brand new flat screen Toshiba tv, but no tv. He laughs and laughs, and I can only shake my head. It is too much for me – every day I witness brutality at the prison, and today, this benign, silly piece of news has me crying, because Ivan is laughing so hard and refuses to be defeated by this new absurdity.

DECEMBER 15, 2011

Bangkok feels a little crazy today... some days I realize I get too complacent, and forget that this place is a bit edgy. Last night, shots were fired at three am in the street below my guesthouse. Deep in alcohol-induced slumber, I barely registered the events, but got the update from all the locals and expats in this close-knit neighbourhood.

After prison, I returned to my guesthouse exhausted, sticky and showered off the prison grime before heading out for lunch, a 25 baht *somtam* at the corner street vendor. I met a French couple from Strasbourg and I discussed with them the bizarre coincidence of discovering today at the prison that there is one inmate from Strasbourg as well. I played up some New Agey hocus-pocus to tell them that this was a 'more than coincidence' that I should meet them and 24 hours later, discover an inmate from their home-town of Strasbourg who needs visitors. I got them: I expect to bring them to the prison in the New Year. I don't mind manipulating some people's flakey spurious reasoning to bring support to inmates. Our discussion turned to the racket at three am, which had awoken them as the shots were fired just outside the window of their room. Later, as I had a coffee, Nit, the Thai owner of the coffee shop explained that the guy "who owns that truck right there" came back drunk from Khao San Road, where he sells trinkets to the *falang ki nok* ("bird-shit foreigners" – the backpackers with smelly dreadlocks or travellers with ripped, dirty clothing who, in blatant disregard of Thai social norms don't bathe and often insist on going shirtless in the street). This vendor was putting away his stuff for the night when another drunk Thai apparently cut him off with his motorbike. The first guy pulled a gun and shot at the fleeing other guy and the whole neighbourhood woke up.

DECEMBER 19, 2011

Today was very hard. A lot of new information to process. Some of it too private to share here. One incident, though, sitting with me weirdly:

I saw Miriam, the wife of one of the Israeli inmates. One of the regulars, we see each other every Monday and Wednesday, as she visits her husband, bringing home-cooked kosher meals to carry him through the week, as well as taking care of her two small sons, the youngest of whom was born the day her husband was arrested when she went into labour from the shock (I know, you couldn't invent this shit if you tried).

Today, she approaches me as we wait to enter the prison and asks if I am buying anything for my guy at the prison shop. I said "No." She asks if I would be willing to buy something for one of her guys (she supports three Israeli inmates). One of the rules of visitations is that you cannot buy something for a prisoner if you are not entering to visit a guy. One purchase per day. Since I am not using my purchase privilege, I agree. We fill out the form for two cartons of cigarettes and a case of Coke and I wait patiently while the guards studiously ignore us at the wicket, eating their meal. It never ceases to amaze me how Thai employees at any occupation are always eating a hot meal at work no matter what time of day, and always, the work part is put on hold in order to fully devote attention to the meal. Finally, the guard processes my order and I pay for Avi's cigarettes and Coke which will be delivered to him later.

In my visit with Ivan, I casually mention that I bought stuff for Avi, and Ivan says that the guy is his cell mate. "Quite a nice guy," says Ivan, "weird that he butchered his wife into tiny pieces," he adds, laughing. I freeze – and realize that over the years I have become so accustomed to most of the guys being in there on drug charges, that I forget that there are a guys in for much more serious crimes.

Ivan is laughing his ass off, shaking his head, as if to say: "Who does that, anyway? Who kills his wife, then cuts her body into tiny pieces to try to hide the evidence?"

I feel revulsion: this offends and violates every cell of my being. I have spent my life actively opposing violence. Murdering and butchering a woman is *NOT FUCKING COOL*. I sit there, staring at Ivan, not really knowing what to do or how I feel about all this. I'm not ok with buying this guy cigarettes.

I decide that if Miriam asks me to buy the wife-killer cigarettes again, I will say: "I am not going to help you again buy him stuff – I don't feel ok buying Coca-Cola for someone who butchered his wife."

Ivan sees my frozen look and realizes he has probably created some problems for himself in giving me this information. He sobers up and asks me to not share with anyone that I know this about Avi's crime, because it would fall back hard on Ivan himself.

Thanks a lot, I think. Now, I feel I am in caught in a shitty situation of wanting to act on this new information, i.e. by not purchasing that inmate any more goods, but I need to agree not to say anything to anyone, because I don't want consequences for Ivan.

So I start pondering:

1. Consent of information: even though what I discuss with each inmate is confidential, I feel that I should have some right to not hear information I might want to act on, without first consenting. If someone is going to give me information that may change how I view someone, they need to ask me first, because I did not consent ahead of time. It's too late for me to undo this knowledge – I can never not know anymore that this man freely admits to having killed and chopped up his wife ten years ago.

2. I don't know how I feel about this. Ivan has another cellmate who murdered a woman, then raped her. Although I may feel personal revulsion, I am not here to condemn them – but I am allowed to not support them materially. I think that's an ok position to take. Or is it? What happened to the principle of impartiality?

Ivan's assurances that this guy is a nice guy raises questions of how I judge who a person is...by their most heinous act? or by their most recent one? And...why do I need to judge in the first place? Apparently, Avi has been one of the friendliest, gentlest inmates Ivan has ever known. Is redemption just a matter of timing? I think of Ivan's crime of armed robbery and felony murder (being involved in a crime where someone is killed, but not actually killing anyone) and the ten years he has spent since then, doing art, reflecting, growing and trying to undo the damage of this action. Are we forever defined by the best action we've ever taken, or the worst, or just the most recent? How many 'gentle kind' actions as a friend to Ivan does it take to mitigate the brutal act of killing a woman ten years ago? Or mitigate it enough to 'deserve' a case of Coca-Cola in prison? I feel hypocritical and petty for denying a prisoner a beverage because I feel morally repulsed by the facts of his crime.

On the way out of the prison, as we wait for our packages to be inspected, an elderly agitated man grabs me and tells me of his many frustrations in that he has been unable to contact a Burmese inmate and that the prison officials have been singularly unhelpful. I murmur empathetic responses about how frustrating and unfair it is, and collect the slip of paper that permits me to leave the prison. I start to leave, but the man keeps talking at me. He repeats the same three incidents he has just recounted: replete with all the now-familiar characters: the abandoned Burmese inmate; the poor family desperate to locate this man and to make contact; obtuse prison officials and an intransigent bureaucracy, and this man's inability to make any headway despite repeated efforts. He wants me to share in his outrage at this terrible injustice – and I am apparently not suitably outraged so he keeps repeating his stories, as if it is a failure on my part to comprehend the tale – rather than habituation. I am numb. This man will get on an airplane in 12 hours and return to his home country defeated and angry. I will return to the prison tomorrow and just don't have it in me right now to muster the appropriate anger or outrage at the multitude of injustices played out every day against so many people.

DECEMBER 21, 2011

Today, Wayne, a regular Australian missionary tells me that if I want to visit Liam on Thursday, he will generously allow me his visit day because, as he explains it, he has only two weeks left at the prison before returning home and he wants to concentrate on a Russian inmate, Dmitry because thinks he can he can save his soul in that time. I wait for the punch-line or a smile, but I realize that Wayne is dead serious, and I have to stop myself from bursting out in laughter. I'm thinking: *I didn't realize there was a timeline to 'saving' a soul. What does a saved soul look like? What happens if you are not successful in your two week time frame? Then what happens to his soul?*

A few minutes later, I hear that another 'missionary,' Shazam who also visits one of my guys is wanted by the Thai police for embezzling 8 million baht ($250,000CDN) from Wayne's church. I have known this woman for several years, and we have spoken on many occasions. To hear that this gentle, kind-faced woman had stolen money with the help of her husband, the church's treasurer, and solicited donations from people around the world for years, ostensibly for inmates, but actually to line her pockets, floored me. This time, I did laugh out loud. I couldn't make this shit up if I tried.

Wayne invites me to Christmas dinner in a few days at noon at the Christ Church in downtown Bangkok. Although normally I would run as fast I could from a church dinner, I must admit that I am curious about the assortment of ex-pat missionaries, tourists stragglers and odds and sods that will gather in downtown Bangkok at this Anglican Church for a traditional Turkey feast. Maybe it's loneliness and a need to avoid sitting around my neighbourhood in Bangkok on Christmas day while drunk Thais and Foreigners stagger down the streets, yelling: "Melly Christmas" and crowded street bars packed with stoned revelers that might entice me to join them. I accept his invitation. Later that day, I invite my Muslim Bangladeshi friend to join me with her newborn baby. I hope the event proves to be as bizarre as I think it will.

DECEMBER 23, 2011

Each day I am grateful for so much, and I decide today to practice my gratitude more concretely: to say to each person to whom I feel gratitude, and to write it here. I am grateful for my daughter – for her strength and wisdom and the inspiration she provides me.

DECEMBER 25, 2011

What a shit-show. Two hours in that hell-hole church, sitting at tables in groups of people who don't know each other – a few ancient ex-pats mixed in with shy uncomfortable Thais who have obviously been dragged to their first "Western" Christmas dinner. My Bangladeshi friend didn't come so I try to make conversation with my equally uncomfortable table-mates as we wait for the $30 plate of cold, nasty turkey dinner. An mc shouts out questions at the crowd, a party game entitled: 'What Were Jesus' Exact Words?' *Are you fucking kidding me?* As if anyone here knows Arameic, for one, or as if anything written in the New Testament can be taken as literal quotes ....Argh...So wrong on so many levels. I am seething and annoyed. After hours of waiting, making excruciating chit-chat, I down the shitty cold approximation of a Christmas dinner and leave. Running down the street under 35 degree sun, mentally shaking off the bizarre experience, I am headed for the *khlong* boat that will wind along a polluted canal back to my neighbourhood. Suddenly, my gut sends me a dire warning and I veer quickly into a Starbucks only to explode the nasty turkey dinner all over their pristine toilets. I collect myself, splash cold water on my face and walk shakily out and try to let the whole morning go...although the rest of the day ends up pretty shitty too, as it turns out.

DECEMBER 29, 2011

I didn't go to the prison today. I skipped out and took a mental health day. I spent two hours crying and venting at a friend over the phone in Canada last night, admittedly a little tipsy, until 4 am about all my mixed feelings about what happened with Ivan yesterday.

For the first time ever, I walked away from a prisoner. I was dis-gusted and furious. Ivan was expressing concern about my plans to take Poti, my Bangladeshi friend with me south, away from Bangkok for a few days to get her away from her husband, who beat her severely on Christmas day. I've been hanging out with them, and they are extremely stressed out, trying to get by in a new country on his paltry wages, with a brand new baby, away any family support. On December 25, I insisted Karib, the husband, stay in my small room, to prevent him from going home that night. Earlier, I brought Poti some food to their rented room where she was sitting in pain, covered in welts and bruises. That eve-ning was hard enough, trying to support both emotionally, while my alliances clearly lay with her and I wished I could help her just leave the bastard, knowing she economically and emotionally is not able to do so. I also spent time comforting the distraught and suicidal, weeping Karib who was wracked with shame for beating his wife with his belt. He had come home to find her burning his clothes with a lighter on the floor of their small room to express her sheer desperation at their situation. While I felt sympathy for the stress and pressures he experienced and saw his genuine remorse, I also resented spending my time and energy comforting a man who had just beaten his wife... Merry Christmas!

So it's a few days later when I briefly explain to Ivan that my new Bangladeshi friends are going through a rough patch and that I have invited Poti and her infant away with me for a few days over the holidays when the prison is closed, to get some space away from her husband. A fun little getaway for three. I will get company at the beach, and she will get help with her baby so she can maybe get a little more sleep... and we will have fun exploring the small town near the Burma border together. I really love this woman, and we have a great time together. Ivan listens to my plans for New Years, frowning: Am I going to pay for her to come with me? Of course. But he protests that I don't have any money either. "Well," I explain, "I have enough money to live very frugally here for two more months, so three days with Poti will just mean that I leave Thailand three days earlier to go back to Canada." We will share the room I rent with her baby, so it's just a few dollars for another bus ticket and some food.

Ivan makes clear his disapproval of this use of my money and of my friendship with Poti and Karib, but I don't expect the level of vitriol leveled against my friend. "These people and their culture who can't learn..." and "these people are like animals..." I don't remember nor care to repeat what all he says. I instantly ask him to stop the racist stereotypes and to watch what he says to me, but he does not. He patronizingly explains that I am wasting my time on people who are incapable, due to their place of origin, of ever changing their baser instincts.

I see red. "Really, I say, you are saying this to me? YOU, of all people? Who understands exactly what it's like to be judged a criminal? YOU tell me every day how humiliated you feel, degraded and dehumanized because you are a prisoner. You tell me how important it is that I (at this point I am shouting), that <u>anyone</u> has come to see past the stereotypes and see you as human and to get to know you. You of all people, Ivan, you know I won't tolerate this kind of comment." He protests that he is not judging: it is a basic human fact that Bangladeshis are n-----s, monkeys and incapable of acting in a decent way.

"YOU DARE JUDGE PEOPLE YOU'VE NEVER EVEN MET (I'm not calm here) and dismiss them as animals, as people not worthy of my time and money? Who exactly is worthy of my time, Ivan? Are "criminals" worthy of my time?"

He doesn't know that every day I have these exact same vicious arguments defending him and the other prisoners to people who have never met them, but who don't think that I should spend my time with 'bad' people.

"DO YOU HAVE ANY IDEA WHAT I SACRIFICE PERSONALLY, PROFESSIONALLY, EMOTIONALLY AND FINANCIALLY to come each year to visit prisoners for months at a time?!!!" What it takes to show up every day and bear witness to people, many of whom I don't even like, but feel a duty to support? The countless hours defending my work to random people, the fact that I have no salary, the leaving my daughter alone when she is battling an illness because she knows that I cannot abandon these guys? The other sacrifices I cannot name here has cost me so much. More than any of those inmates would EVER do for me. I know this. He knows this.

And here, I understand that Ivan does not need to know the context of why I come to the prison every day to talk to an isolated inmate... he doesn't know about when I was 12 years old and our house was arsoned – broken into and our beds lit on fire. We had no insurance, and in the aftermath – two days after Christmas, our parents went to live with friends who put them up. My sister went to live with her friends, and my brother at his friends while our rental home was being rebuilt. No one offered to put me up, the youngest, so at 12, family separated, I was put in university residence housing at UBC. I was given a small room in a dormitory for university students and told I could eat meals at the cafeteria. I remember my first experience of what later I intimately knew as panic attacks – at the time, I only knew that I paced a small room, no family, no one to talk to, no friends. Sleepless nights, chest tightening, thinking I was dying every second, talking myself through, pacing the small cell, terrified. I survived as I always did – steely, determined, terrified, just getting through on my own. That year at school a kid offered me a cigarette and I remember the feeling of the knot of terror and anxiety in my stomach dissipating momentarily. Suddenly I wasn't alone and for a few minutes, as we huddled, two kids beside the building of the school, we shared a smoke. I was hooked and smoked a pack a day, usually shoplifted from the local grocery stores. I paced my small cell in the evenings, with no one to comfort me or to talk to. Just a stern warning from my parents who showed up one day to say that there was a known wife-abuser who roomed down the hall from me in the same residence and I should watch out for him.

Fending for myself as a teen, experiencing considerable violence and harassment as a queer woman, contempt as a low-income single mother, my ability to raise a child questioned. Surviving my childhood, and as a young mom isolated and depressed, also gave me a glimpse of the terror and loneliness of surviving with no one to count on. But that is not the business of the inmates I visit. Ivan also doesn't need to know about the grueling, unspeakable year that I just spent and the sacrifices I made to come here because I cannot abandon those who are the most marginalized and have no one to fend for them.

These sacrifices come up right now, as I wonder: *Why the fuck would I go to bat for you? You judge a person you have never even met, based on their membership in a group. I don't expect you to be a saint. But can you not extend a moment's compassion for someone as a fellow human, rather than skewering them without regard?*

That is what explodes in me, and I know that it is not his to carry... it is my shit, my stuff. He has enough to deal with surviving his situation. I am not here to make him feel badly for his prejudices. I don't visit prisoners to 'change them' like the missionaries do. I abhor that. I try to accept them as they are and also to engage with them as the human being that I am and they are. I am here to reflect back to them that their lives matter and they deserve dignity and respect no matter what their beliefs or crimes are. Or at least I tell myself that is why I'm here.

I am angry at myself for slamming down the phone and walking away. I'm angry at the theatricality of it. I hate him also for his patronizing arrogance and for not accepting any of my protests that we humans are all the same in our worthiness of dignity.

If I leave the prison, I am not allowed to see him for another nine days. I know that this will be far more difficult for him than my momentary anger. It is my responsibility to pull myself together and to let this issue go. More so, it violates my most basic principle to not re-abandon prisoners, to 'do no harm'. I have the power in this relationship and I am responsible not to abuse it.

All my actions have a magnified effect on inmates. Each time a visitor leaves, the inmate has no way to know if he or she will ever come back, no power to contact them, or to find out what has happened to those who don't. I see the devastating effects of that on inmates every day who spend months, years agonizing over conversations, letters, wondering why they have been left again. They are powerless over whether they get another visit, unlike my choice to simply return or not. I hold all the cards here. It is far too great a damage to do to him for my momentary anger. Turning this all over in my mind, the answer I keep coming back to is: I uphold an inmate's dignity when I return to engage even when I wholly disagree with this person's actions, attitudes or behavior. He is human, and therefore deserving of respect. I have no right to use his egregious views as a reason to compound his suffering. Although there have been men over the years I have had to stop visiting because of their unacceptably disrespectful behavior to me, I warn them first not to cross my boundaries and then explain to them when they have that I won't be back. I do not compound their powerlessness by leaving them hanging, wondering if and when I will be back.

I walk back to the phone and say: "I don't like your judgment – it is unacceptable to me. I don't like racism, you know that, and I expect you to not make shitty comments around me about people you've never met. I expect better of you and it makes me really angry," I say. I apologize for leaving. He nods and says he understands that I am emotional because I am a woman. I can't handle rational arguments anyway and I don't really understand the true nature of people like Bangladeshis because I use my emotions and not my brain to react. I grit my teeth as he expounds on his greater male wisdom. It takes all my self-control to let it go. Just as he knows nothing of my context, I know nothing of his.

I find myself apologizing to him, because of his incredibly shitty situation – ten years into a god-knows-how-long sentence fighting for his physical and mental survival, and just learning that the Thai authorities have decided that he will never leave. They informed the prison that should Ivan ever manage to get a release date set, or a King's Pardon, (which he keeps hoping for) or wait out enough amnesties that his sentence gets reduced to 14 or 15 years, that they have nine more minor charges, such as possession of stolen property and using a getaway car, all connected to his original armed robbery charge. Should he be released, they will dredge up these old charges and prosecute him to ensure that he never leaves a Thai prison. Apparently, they sent Ivan a letter informing him of this.

He got this news in early October, two months ago, but kept it from me until now, as the ramifications have been eating away at him and his hope for freedom. Now he tells me how worried he is. He hasn't the heart to tell his mother, who waits for him in the Ukraine. Instead, he will come up with a plan to deal with all of this. One thing about Ivan that never fails to amaze me is his ability to see every setback as a new challenge to take on, to overcome...and to never give up fighting for his freedom. Now, he tells me that his greatest worry is that, with this piece of news, I will 'give up' on him and not wait out his struggle. Maybe I will think he is a lost cause. He is so afraid I will abandon him. It kills me to see what it costs him to show me his vulnerability. How do I let him know I'll never give up on him?

He doesn't understand. How do I explain to him that I come to this prison precisely because I don't believe in lost causes. I was one. Every adult who was supposed to protect and love me betrayed me in the worst ways, and I learned that I could count on no one and also that the world was violent, neglectful, and abusive. When I turned to my older siblings for protection, they, having also not learned about love and protection also abandoned me.

At the age of 14, I was consuming copious amounts of pot, MDA, acid, mushrooms, cigarettes and booze daily, working nights at a restaurant serving pizza and beer to university students and in a relationship with an extremely violent, sociopathic man. Our first date was his court appearance on assault charges, for which he received probation. A fearful and insecure person with a very hard outer shell, I slathered on a thick layer of makeup and continued to make an appearance at high school for another year or so, where my teachers told me that I was a 'lost cause'. Report cards I have kept from grade ten say: "Heather is her own worst enemy." When I think of the inner strength and perseverance it took to survive my childhood and then non-stop psychological terror and drugs: *How was I my own worst enemy?* Later, as I raised my daughter on my own as a young single mother, I fought the demons of my earlier years alone, isolated, and still terrified. I have known abandonment and violence, and the struggle for sanity in an insane system. Feminist consciousness-raising and academic analysis of oppression helped channel my trauma and anger towards systemic injustice, but my abhorrence of violence and heightened sensitivity to suffering in isolation is largely what brings me to the prison. I can't give up on people.

So what if Ivan and I don't agree on values or issues? Am I supposed to only be helping people who have the same philosophy as me? Wouldn't that make the world an easy place if I only offered compassion and support to 'likeable' people who share the same values as me? Certainly in my early radical academic feminist days, I felt that way: dismissing anyone as 'unworthy' whose politics and views were not congruent with mine. Today, I advocate for the human community, rather than the narrower communities I used to identify solely with. I see ugliness every day at the prison. I see ugliness every day outside the prison. What makes me think that I should expect more from someone just because after years, I consider him my 'friend'? What does it mean anyway to consider him a friend? What happens to the ethical boundaries after years of knowing an inmate in this very limited, yet extremely intimate way? From this claustrophobic inferno, these men and I forge a fierce bond that is unlike any other type of relationship I know. Is it wrong for me to expect more growth on his part?

Two years ago, a Dutch lawyer visited Johann and was frustrated at his lukewarm reception of her when she arrived. She had been advocating for him for years, and had just travelled to Bangkwang from Holland on her own time and money to try to help him further. When she arrived, he busied himself with other visitors (including me) and made her wait to talk to him. Exiting the prison, she was infuriated — I remember her specifically railing about his lack of gratitude for her help. As she complained, I remember self-righteously thinking: *Gratitude? Is that why you're here? So the prisoners can feel helped and grateful?* In my arrogance, I dismissed her for wanting recognition from prisoners and judged her therefore narcissistic and deluded, while others, such as myself, understood this prison work to be a selfless task. What a bunch of deluded crap. I hope I have learned a little more humility since then.

My anger against Ivan's intolerance towards Poti and Karib has pitted me against my own uncomfortable questions: What do I expect from the inmates? And what if they don't provide it? Those are the uncomfortable questions I don't want to think might influence my work here. And what does this have to do with restoring dignity? Whose dignity am I preserving here? Mine? His? My friends? What is in play here?

Took a break from Bangkok to hang out with refugee friends in the border town of Mae Sot. Interviewed an ex-political prisoner who managed to escape Burma and now exists in the many shadows of this town. Bicycled out to the border today – spent all of five minutes in Burma getting my passport stamped, before leaving. Would love to explore more of this country, if it were permitted. Stopped at Dr. Cynthia's Muang's clinic on the way back into Mae Sot. This woman and her amazing work completely humble and inspire me. Now I'm at a Burmese café for dinner and wine – huge posters about Burma's Women Political Prisoners: "You are not forgotten" slogan on the walls. Crowded tables of ex-pat missionaries drinking water and coke and playing cards while a Burmese guy sings phonetic approximations of American classic rock tunes.

DIGNITY

Our discussion was very rich today. I spoke with an American inmate, James, about dignity: that one of my premises for doing prison visitations is to 'uphold dignity' by reflecting back to inmates that they have intrinsic value as human beings, despite not being treated as such. But what does it really mean to restore dignity? *How does one define it?* Although the inherent, inalienable 'dignity' of humans is invoked in almost all countries' human rights legislations as the basis and justification for these very rights, there is still no definition of what dignity actually entails...and yet I think every person has their own notion of what it means for them to have dignity, and what a lack or loss of dignity might look like, for them. For me, it is linked to valuing someone as having inherent agency and choice in their situation, being a subject of their life, rather than object.

After a few minutes bantering around synonyms like respect, worth, self-esteem, James and I try to pin 'dignity' down by asking what constitutes a 'lack of dignity.'

We come to an agreement that there is no universal example of a 'loss of dignity'. What one person sees as 'undignified' action may not be 'undignified' to another, due to different cultural lens and meanings ascribed to the actions. And the *subjective* experience of dignity is constructed individually though one's cultural, familial, social lens. I ask him: "Who decides if someone's dignity has been eroded, compromised, or diminished?"

He counters with: "Do Thailand's lengthy prison sentences constitute a loss of dignity for the inmates?" I say I think not. One hundred year sentences are harshly punitive and should be challenged, but I don't think represent a loss of dignity for an inmate.

He then relates a story: Two days ago, James was released from his cell at seven am. He and the roughly 700 other inmates from his building walked down the stairs towards the outside, when another inmate came flying, tumbling down the stairs ahead of him. He was followed by a screaming guard who had obviously just thrown the man down the stairs. The guard was beating the man with a baton and yelling: "Crawl, Crawl." The inmate flattened himself on the concrete floor, cowering and crawling as low to the ground as he could, as the guard continued to scream and to beat him mercilessly, and the other inmates filed by.

James asks me: "Does this man (the inmate) have dignity?" My immediate reaction besides horror at the mental image of this situation is that the actions of the guard constitute an intention to degrade this man and herefore to eliminate dignity. The violent act can objectively be seen as dehumanizing and clearly must be condemned as such. I hesitate though whether I can say whether the inmate has any dignity: *Is that my call to make?* Is not dignity something an individual can only claim for him or herself? I don't want to further erode the inmate's agency and worth by presuming to speak for him or his experience.

Is it possible to say then that dignity lies in the human agency to choose meaning for ourselves? When people try to take away our dignity in a situation, they attempt to remove us from our humanity, by stripping away our human agency or power. Dignity can be said to remain when we invoke our human ability to choose meaning in our situation, even if all other choice or agency has been removed.

I am reminded of a passage from Gregory David Robert's novel that always struck a chord deep in me:

> "It took me a long time and most of the world to learn what I know about love and fate and the choices we make, but the heart of it came to me in an instant, while I was chained to a wall and being tortured. I realized, somehow, through the screaming in my mind, that even in that shackled, bloody helplessness, I was still free: free to hate the men who were torturing me, or to forgive them. It doesn't sound like much, I know. But in the flinch and bite of the chain, when it's all you've got, that freedom is a universe of possibility. And the choice you make, between hating and forgiving, can become the story of your life."

One of the inherent qualities of human beings is our meaning-making capacity. In every moment we construct our own meanings and can choose between competing stories, and this opens up a universe of possibilities. We can restore our own or someone's humanity, and

---

* *Shantaram*, Gregory David Roberts: Scribe Publications, 2003.

therefore dignity, by invoking our ability to choose alternate meanings, including by refusing the meaning that someone tries to inflict upon us.

James gives me another example from his world:

Every morning from 7 to 8 am, all the prisoners are required to sit on the concrete ground under the blazing sun for an hour, until the morning Thai National anthem is played, when everyone is required to stand at attention. (Indeed, it is not just in the prison that this ritual takes place; it is illegal in Thailand to not stand during the National Anthem, which is played in homes, and public spaces twice per day). For Thais, sitting on the ground is a normal activity, not degrading. For the Westerners, sitting on filthy ground is degrading, dehumanizing to them and they feel their dignity is at stake. They have no choice in the matter. During the National Anthem, all the Thai inmates and guards stand, but many of the foreign inmates refuse to stand, for several obvious reasons, explains James: refusal to dignify the country and institution that incarcerates them; no sense of patriotism for a country and religion that is not their own; an act of resistance in an oppressive institution in which each inmate has very limited power. This one act of defiance, the refusal to dignify the anthem, is quite important for some of the Western inmates for them to re-claim their own dignity in what they consider a degrading situation. James understands this reasoning, as do I, and yet, he chooses to stand during the anthem. He is one of the only foreigners who does so. As he explains it, "It costs me nothing – one minute of my time, to show some respect for the Thai culture and practice."

This past week, the head guard of the building started yelling at all the foreigners, demanding that they respect the Thai practice of standing for the National Anthem. As the head guard explains it, they have committed a crime in this country, the Thai government provides their shelter during their incarceration and the inmates should show respect to the host country by dignifying the anthem. Many foreigners remained un-persuaded by the guard's argument, reports James. For them, this act of sitting during the anthem remained a small way to re-claim power over their circumstance, thus restoring some of their dignity. So the acts themselves of sitting or standing during an anthem are not what constitute dignity: it is the meaning each person ascribes to the acts.

"So where are we getting with this elusive definition? And what does it mean to restore someone's dignity?" I ask James. We agree that restoring dignity is about affirming the inherent worth of a human, as not 'less than'. What we are doing when we refuse to be a party to the degradation or humiliation of anyone is to affirm the inherent worth of all human beings, including ourselves. So dignity is perhaps always relational, constructed in the spaces between actions and meaning-making?

I think of the guard whose sole job each day is to monitor the visiting area. At the end of each period, he instructs the inmates and visitors to leave. Many ignore him and try to squeeze a few more precious minutes out of each visit. Most days, he has to tell each foreign inmate three or four times to leave, by which time we may have gained another five or ten minutes, and even on occasion as much as half an hour. I tell James about this past Tuesday, when I was visiting an inmate, and suddenly I heard an ungodly racket: this same guard was wildly swinging his baton against metal bars and screaming at everyone to leave a half hour early. Visitors and inmates alike were all pissed off at this new seemingly arbitrary act of power-tripping – the visitors all grumbled about power-abusing guards as we filed out. We joked about how maybe the guard had just got a new baton for Chinese New Year and felt he needs to assert his power by smashing us with it. James offers that this guard gets no respect and his job is a thankless one, where daily his instructions are ignored by foreign inmates and visitors alike. James and I wonder if maybe this guard feels his dignity is compromised. We ponder this in silence for a few minutes.

I share with James Dominique de Menil's words: "*What should move us to action is human dignity: the inalienable dignity of the oppressed, but also the dignity of each of us. We lose dignity if we tolerate the intolerable.*" What I like about this is that human dignity is interdependent – all human dignity is at stake if anyone tolerates the diminishment of any other human. Therefore we are not just diminished by acts of violence against us, but also if we tolerate the diminishment of another. Any other. Not just the ones we care about or are easy to like.

Our conversation is interrupted by shouting down at the end of the row, as the same guard makes his first announcement that it's time to go. James stands up instantly. For the first time my seven years of visiting with inmates, I do not linger or ignore the guard, or beg for 'just a few more minutes.'

"I'm going to leave right away this time," says James into the phone, "and help restore the guard's dignity." We smile and wave across the bars and glass and each walk to our separate exits.

NO ONE MAKES IT OUT

I am sick to my stomach – I am crying with grief and rage. No one makes it out. There's a reason the title of the book written by a former inmate was called: 'The Damage Done.' How can anyone comprehend the psychological and physical damage done to these people? Can anything repair a mangled soul?

I sit with the weight of all of this – all these men who don't make it ... I am powerless and angry, so angry and grief-ridden.

Today I see Liam, my little bro, my Toad. A few years ago, he learned he had melanoma. Unlike most inmates who suffer untreated from the many diseases in Bangkwang, he was very fortunate to have a family who raised necessary funds to purchase medical treatment at a Bangkok hospital. Normally not allowed any physical contact with inmates, I sat with him and held his hand for two days. He was not alone when he went under nor when he woke up from the surgery that cut the cancer from his head, shoulder, and back.

Sitting in the public hospital for hours waiting for his surgery, I never left his side except to walk down the hall to use the toilet or get some snacks at a vending machine. The one guard left us alone except to unshackle Liam from the hospital bed to let him use the bathroom. The first time he went for a bathroom break, Liam came back twenty minutes later exclaiming at the joy of using a real toilet and having running hot water. A new guard would arrive every six hours to change shifts. We lounged together on his hospital bed, laughing and joking. Every few hours, the guard on duty would come in to check on us and would point to small sign in Thai and say in English: "One Man Show, One Man Show". We pretended not to understand. He gesticulated for me to get off the bed. I deferentially sat on the chair beside Liam until the guard left then jumped up onto the bad again. I snuck a digital camera in my purse and stole a few shots of Liam in his pink hospital robe and I making faces. We giggled like young kids having a sleepover. The intensity of what felt like stolen time exhausted us, and I didn't want to miss a single precious second. At times we would fall silent and I would stroke his face gently as he dozed. As night fell, and the sky began to darken, Liam abruptly turned to face the open balcony of his hospital room. He leaned as far as he could and watched the changing sky, an unfathomable expression on his face. A tear rolled down his cheek. Locked inside the prison at 3 pm every day for 16 hours until morning in a windowless room lit continuously by fluorescent bulbs, this was the first time in six years Liam had seen the night sky.

Liam was arrested at the age of 28, an addict trying to bring heroin back to his native country from Bangkok, and as we got to know each other over the years, he prided himself on telling me he was clean inside the prison, despite the easy availability of meth, heroin, alcohol, ecstasy, and more. I did not always believe his claims of being drug free, but his behaviour and our conversations always seem relatively sane. So many crazy moments when I saw him 'lose it,' and I tried in my limited way to understand and the contexts of what he lives in his tiny cage, anguished... other moments when we can discuss hope, futures, dreams, and how he can sustain himself through this institutional life he now exists in.

One day, a few years back, I arrived at the prison profoundly shaken by an extremely distressing incident the previous evening. I had been conversing with a man affected by his years in a Nepali prison and he became very agitated, threatening and verbally abusive towards me. It was a long and traumatic night, the effects of which could not be hidden from my face and demeanour the following day at the prison. Liam and I spent twenty minutes with our faces pressed against the glass and bars, as I cried into the phone, fear and shock still overwhelming me. He comforted me until I had to tear myself away to visit with the inmate I was intended to see that day.

The following day, I called Liam again, even though I was supposed to see his cell-mate Johann, an unforgivable breach which took many months to repair in my relationship with Johann, but I felt I had to check in with Liam, to de-brief what I had unloaded on him the day before. Liam, a so-called 'hardened criminal' deemed unfit to participate in society, arrived for our visit, sat down, picked up the phone and started singing to me:

> Lay beside me/tell me what they've done
> speak the words I want to hear
> to make my demons run...

I recognized the song (*The Unforgiven II,* by Metallica). I looked at this man across from me, sentenced to incarceration for life, and now existing among thousands of other men, away from his country and his family, his face pressed against rusty metal bars as he sang softly to try to comfort me.

> *Through black of day*
> *dark of night*
> *we share this pair of lives*
> *the door cracks open*
> *but there's no sun shining through...*

We sat for a long time, both crying. I left this man deemed unfit for society to return to my guesthouse, where I was to finish an essay on the humanitarian effects and impacts of my work on these inmates. How do I tally what this man has just given me?

* * * * * *

In the two months since I arrived to Bangkok prisons this year, I have only seen Liam twice – I arrived to find he had been removed to a prison in the far-flung southern provinces of Thailand, along with hundreds of other inmates, ostensibly because of imminent flooding, but in reality a convenient move by the Thai Department of Corrections to disrupt drug activity in the prison. After inmates were moved, the guards confiscated the inmates' belongings including pots, pans, cooking supplies, food, and other 'contraband' that the prisoners buy at great expense from the guards to make their lives more bearable.

The two times I manage to see him, after he is finally returned from the southern prison, Liam is evasive, uncomfortable, paranoid, and speaks angrily about conspiracies amongst his fellow inmates to label him a heroin user. He complains of being ill to his stomach for weeks and of losing weight – he doesn't want visitors, including me, his family, nor his girlfriend, who has been a regular visitor for years. He rejects all attempts to connect. This is the first time in six years he doesn't ask me to return as much as I can to see him. I am worried but respect his wishes to leave him alone.

This week, his family has flown in from Australia – they have special permission from their Embassy to visit him daily all this week. As I visit other prisoners, I walk by and wave a quick hello. He avoids my gaze; his facial hair is heavy and there are dark bags under his eyes, his cheeks sunken and drawn. My heart goes out to him as another part of me screams at him: *You fucking bastard!!!!! You spent six years clean in here – you have ONE YEAR to go – you're on the home stretch – you are getting out of this godforsaken hellhole because you are one the few lucky ones who has an Embassy that will fight for you to be transferred to your home next year; you are lucky enough to have a caring family who visit once a year and provide financial support to you; you have a sweet girlfriend who is waiting for you; you have friends to visit you and support you; you have the end in sight; vastly more so than many people in this place – WHY WHY WHY the fuck are you throwing away your life, sabotaging your relationships with people, choosing oblivion and drugs???* But addiction has no logic and I know this — intimately.

This doesn't stop me from railing against this fucking prison that offers nothing but oppression, violence and drugs every day...every fucking day. Who am I to judge? Seven years in that place... would I have lasted? Who knows?

"Not all humanitarian goals are sustainable," I read in my course work that I attend to each day after the prison. No fucking kidding. I think of how every inmate I meet tells me repeatedly of the importance my presence plays in his life, his survival, his ability to hope, to make it through, and yet.... Let's be fucking honest here. No one I've met has survived. I am ostensibly doing an assessment of the work I do, the 'impact' on the inmates. I reject the jargon of 'accountability' and 'results' in international humanitarian discourse. I send yearly reports to my Board of Directors. Who am I accountable to? What are the results of my prison work? It depends on the goals... Long-term? Not so good. But that's the framework humanitarian agencies always use — 'the work means nothing if there's no long-term impact.'

One major problem: every man I've met so far, despite resilience, optimism, fight, determination, is beaten by the prison. So 'objective' long-term goals don't look good. Each year I return and I see many people more depressed, darker, a little less connected to what we on the outside might consider a rational way of interacting with the world. Of course they are thrilled to see me and are grateful for the support – the impact is tremendous, but how to quantify this?

I offer a chance to exercise their sense of agency in our interactions – by giving and respecting their choices as people, which they have had taken from them in all other aspects of their lives... but the new 'normal' they must adjust to in a profoundly abnormal institution erodes their sanity, despite best attempts to survive, to cope, to thrive.

Liam's visible erosion: another glaring testament to the crushing power of this juggernaut and to the seeming futility of my efforts to mitigate the effects. I am absorbing all this slowly as the inmate I visit that day makes a request: a cell mate of his has never in ten years had a single visitor, and would I consider adding him to the list of people I support? This happens rarely as appreciative inmates usually try to keep my support to themselves but occasionally an inmate will want to offer up others they see in need – the need is great but my time and financial resources are finite...I write down the new guy's name and say that I will do what I can. But I am just one. The lists of those waiting are so long, an ever-expanding spreadsheet of all those I've seen over the years and where they are now, who writes to them, who visits them, added to daily by people writing from overseas to my website about their brother, cousin, or friend stuck in a Thai prison.

The weight of all of these men's needs and all of those I cannot reach sits heavily on me as I ride the riverboat back to my guesthouse. Who takes responsibility for this? For what these institutions do to humans? I can write papers romanticizing the resilience and coping skills and tremendous human spirit I encounter in the prison from these men...all true...but only part of the story. No one survives...I don't see anyone thriving – I don't even see people surviving.

Where do I scream about these lives lost, the damage done? Today, I cry all day after returning from the prison. Grief pours out of me as I go for a massage to release the accumulated tension, and tears spill over my dinner, and into my wine. Evenings, I try to forget and unwind from the daily stress at a local bar, but often this is when I find myself surrounded by tourist men questioning why I would support 'prisoners', the word spat out as if the non-value of criminals were obvious. Sometimes I manage to say that this attitude is exactly what permits violence done to people, the horrific effects of which I witness each day. Other days I can only try to ignore.

Today I can't contain my sobbing. Various ex-pats from the neighbourhood walk by the café this evening, see my flowing tears, approach and sit momentarily, and speak at me, telling me about my moodiness, my hard day, my emotionality as a woman, speculating about my time of the month, dismissing without ever hearing about the grief I carry for forgotten people, lost lives and injustices. I can only marvel at the inability of most people to just sit and be present with another person's pain and grief, without trying to excuse it, fix it, or dismiss it. So many people exist and react only in fear, and try to throw whatever they can onto other people.

I grieve for each man I have met inside the prison – because the fact remains that he will not make it out alive. The damage done is too great. I think of the supposed success stories – the two inmates released over the now seven years of my coming here – finally gone home – something the other men dream about every day. But there is no freedom, really, for them, the years incarcerated here have taken a toll so great that each has sunk under its weight. I cannot even write about what that tragedy looks like for each of them.

No one deserves this.

PAEDOPHILES & BANANAS

I brought three visitors in the past two days with me – each got to visit an inmate, so in two days, we visited 5 people at Bangkwang. Today, I went with my close friend Jay, who recently arrived in Bangkok and agreed to visit an inmate. Visiting new guys can be a tricky process, in part, because I don't have the time to add a new person to my roster until one of my guys is released, dies, or otherwise doesn't need my support anymore. I want to reach out to as many as possible, but have to keep clear firm boundaries about how many and how much I can take on. Many times, I facilitate contact between an inmate who badly needs a visitor, and someone willing to bring an hour of conversation and some food, and many of these connections have lasted over years. I no longer visit new inmates without first checking with at least one other trusted inmate that the prospective visitee isn't a complete sociopath. So last week I made discreet enquiries about an Indian man who was contacting me illegally from within the prison on a contraband smartphone to find out what I could from other inmates before trying to recruit a visitor for him. No one could say much, except that he was older, and frequently bullied and picked on by the guards and other inmates.

Jay agrees to come to see this man today, and as we ride the riverboat North to Nonthaburi, we discuss expectations and boundaries to set ahead of time:

"I don't offer to get involved in anyone's judicial process," I said. "I tell them I cannot give money to them." I explain to Jay that I try to head off an inmate's usual initial assumptions, making clear: a) I am not a Christian missionary and am not trying to convert him; b) I am not one of the crazy women who come to the prison to try to find husbands and I am not going to be his girlfriend; c) I do not give money. (Of course over the years I have made many exceptions to this last rule, at my discretion and I spend considerable amounts purchasing food, when I know a guy has nothing and needs some chicken or fruit or a shirt, but I have to quash immediate expectations of financial help). What I can do in addition to support visits is facilitate contact between the inmate and family member or Embassy. I might also email a friend for them. I might also deposits funds to a prison account on behalf of a family member who is outside Thailand. I remind Jay to be clear about his own boundaries and to set them firmly.

We arrive at the pier #30 Nonthaburi, and a young white man exits the boat alongside us. *He's going to the prison,* I think. Over the years, I've become an expert at spotting the tourists who include Bangkwang prison in their schedule of 'must do's' in Bangkok. Jay and I stop at the street market and I buy some corn on the cob, boiled eggs, apples, cookies, and fried chicken for the Indian inmate.

At the prison, I see the young man filling out his form to register. "Who are you here to see?" I enquire, hoping it is not either of the two men we intend to see. There is nothing more frustrating than making the long journey each day to see an inmate, only to find out that a random backpacker has already registered to see him. It is extremely frustrating for both inmate and regular visitor – a waste of my time and the inmate has to suffer through sharing the short visiting time with an unknown tourist who wants to satisfy his curiosity, grilling the inmate: "How long is your sentence? What are the conditions like? Is it really as bad as I heard? What was your crime?" The backpacker then leaves, taking away a great story to tell his friends about how he went and visited a criminal in the infamous "Bangkok Hilton". "Banana visits," the inmates call these types of visit – a tourist bringing bananas to the monkeys in the zoo.

The young man answers with a name I recognize instantly – a difficult inmate – who is always being visited by backpackers from his country, as he is currently the only person from this particular European country in that prison. I know that most tourists assume that all the foreign inmates are here on drug charges, which most Europeans dismiss as unfair and cruel sentences for a 'minor' crime. This particular inmate, however, is convicted of paedophila, something which I can tell this backpacker is unaware of. I hesitate and wonder, not for the first time, about whether I should say something. Is it my place to give out this information? Paedophilia is a crime I, like most people, find particularly abhorrent, and brings up strong emotions. When I initially started visiting inmates, I specifically asked the Canadian Embassy to not put me in contact with any convicted paedophiles.

"No, No," the Embassy worker laughingly reassured me, "they're all there for drugs."

Over many years, I routinely meet inmates convicted of other crimes – murder, armed robbery, fraud – even though a significant majority are there for drugs. This issue has come up for me several times this year and I have mixed feelings about how best to deal with this.

A few months ago, I was contacted through my website by someone who was planning a trip to Thailand and asked me for the name of someone from his country he could visit in the prison. This is not unusual. In that case, the visitor was from the same country as today, and the inmate was the paedophile. (Notice how I have reduced his identity to that of the crime for which he has been convicted). Yet I struggle with this and I wonder how to proceed. I finally replied to the email by giving the name and building of the inmate, and explaining how and what day to visit him, explaining the prison rules and procedures. At the end, I included a sentence stating that I thought they might want to know that his conviction is for paedophilia.

On the one hand wanting to be impartial, I also figure that potential visitors would want this information to make their own decisions. I would want to know before meeting a new inmate that he has been convicted of paedophilia. On the other hand, I worry that because this type of information is not neutral, it can be used to further marginalize an already marginalized person. The next day, I received a reply informing me that they decided not to visit a paedophile and thanking me for my 'help'.

Today, I am explaining this all to Jay as we sit and drink water in the registration area. I mention that my thinking was further challenged about this issue when, a few weeks ago, in this very area, I met a man, Richard, who lives in Thailand and regularly visits the paedophile. Richard lives in a town a few hours south of Bangkok, knows the man and saw all the man's friends disappear as soon as he was charged with paedophilia. The inmate claims that his charges were trumped up, and that he is a gay man who likes adult men. I am instantly more amenable to supporting him, knowing full well the discrimination and persecution faced by queers. Not that I am ever persuaded by anyone's claims of innocence, and the support given is not contingent on people's guilt or innocence. Richard discloses that this individual inmate has a difficult personality, frequently makes decisions that are not in his own best interest, and is frequently suckered financially by others in the prison. Although his life as a convicted paedophile is much easier here than it would be in a prison in his home country, where he would be targeted for violence by other inmates, he has nonetheless been abandoned by his family, former friends, and Embassy due to the nature of the charges. Richard explains that, while supporting this inmate over the years has been challenging on several levels for him, he himself a parent, it is the right thing to do. I am impressed by Richard's determination to stand by his acquaintance, even as he himself is ostracized for doing so. He is a better person than I, to choose to stand by a convicted paedophile because he knows that no one else will and that the man, difficult and irritating as he is as a human, still deserves support.

As I am relating all this to Jay, Richard, of whom I was just speaking, arrives at the prison, and we greet each other warmly and shake hands. I warn him that there is a backpacker from his home country who has registered already to see the same inmate as he. His frustration and annoyance are evident, as he has woken up in the wee hours of the morning to take a four-hour bus ride to get to the prison to see his acquaintance and now has to share the times and visit with a 'banana visitor,' looking to put another notch in his *Lonely Planet* backpacker belt. The tourist wanders over to us and I introduce the two men and they start to speak in their own language. Soon enough, it is time to collect our papers and Jay and I enter the prison.

Today I see Ivan, who is pre-occupied with fear and worry that I will abandon him in the future. I try to gently bring him to the present, for us to appreciate the here and now of this visit, this conversation, rather than focusing so much on worry, but he remains very agitated and stressed. So I listen to his fears and let him know that I have no intention of leaving soon.

After a short visit where the guards hustle the inmates out quickly, we visitors stand around waiting half an hour for the return of our slips of paper with an inmate's thumbprint on it, that shows they've received the food and goods we left for them, and that also releases us to leave. As we wait, in the thick heavy air of the prison courtyard, Jay and I discuss his encounter with the Indian man, to whom I also said a brief hello. He is 52, has three grown children, has been in the prison for five years, and has no support, financial or otherwise. Jay agrees to email his Embassy to request some medication for the inmate's heart condition and says he will also facilitate some contact with his family, as well as provide occasional visits with food. This inmate is routinely harassed and picked on by the other inmates and guards, and his life is quite hard. He thanks Jay for bringing the food, but says he will get very little or none of it, after the guards and other inmates help themselves to it.

We watch a Thai film crew and camera equipment escorted into the prison and as the guards lead them past us to the inner gates, I get a overwhelming impulse to try to slip in with the group and to try to pass myself off as part of this crew.

I see Richard and ask him how his visit went. He tells me that the tourist got cold feet at the last moment. Apparently, the information about the nature of the inmate's charge, combined with the reality of actually walking into a maximum security prison to meet an inmate, were sufficient to make him reconsider and he turned and bolted. We laugh. *Good riddance.*

Jay and I ride the stinking bus spewing black diesel fumes through the mid-day heavy traffic for an hour back to our neighbourhood, where we collapse at a café and order food. As we eat, he tells me that he is happy to take on the case of this Indian inmate and to follow through on the commitments he made to make contact with the Indian Embassy, and also to try to get him some pen-pals and perhaps occasional visits. I am grateful, as my roster is so full. This inmate's situation is not unlike that of other foreign inmates from the poorest countries: there is vast disparity between the daily lives of the richer inmates and those at the bottom of the pecking order. The latter often work for the former and/ or beg for food to survive, as well as get preyed upon. Jay and I discuss what he wants to do, what he should do, and what he can do and I realize I have amassed a certain amount of expertise on the logistics, ethical pitfalls and limitations of supporting inmates.

As I dig into my chicken baguette, I tell Jay of a Burmese inmate who a few years ago started getting many letters and support from Western pen-pals I had introduced him to. Initially, the guards harangued him: Who are you to get letters from Canada? Why are you getting letters from Western countries?" Gradually, the abuse stopped as his Western friends and support gained him a more elevated status inside the prison.

Jay and I ponder this for a moment in silence.

"So, basically, Jay finally says, the first few letters I send to this Indian guy, he'll be getting beaten by guards or other inmates for receiving Western letters? Maybe in the first letter, I should include some Herman comic strips to ease the pain. I'll write: 'I hope this letter finds you well, but probably you're being hit as you read this...' "

We glance at each other and giggle nervously.

MARCH, 2555

Dozens of silent people, sitting on blue plastic bucket seats, hearts heavy, eyes lowered, waiting to see loved ones. My eyes scan, taking in a new sign installed in this waiting area. Flashing red words *Welcome To Bangk-wang Prison*. A second later, a digital Pacman appears, moving across the screen from left to right, eating the previous letters. I want to vomit.

PART II: CANADA

FISHING I: LETTER TO JAMES

JUNE 30, 2012

Hey Smiley Friend!

First of all! Congratulations! YAY YAY happiness for your imminent transfer to US! Just a couple short months or weeks to go! I can't imagine what you must be feeling. Does it even feel real? I'm so excited for you. Your family must be getting excited, too!

Me: been so incredibly despondent, discouraged, and talking myself through a lot of low moments. I didn't buy the business I told you about because the price was too high, and it didn't seem right to attempt to borrow so much to try to make a go of things in a shitty economy – payments too high given what I would have been pulling in. So that was really disappointing, but totally the right decision. That leaves me still unemployed, scrambling for work, well into June, July... so the business owner says she'll hire me as her helper, and I get a total of $45 worth of work from her in the past two weeks, 'cause business is down everywhere on the island, the country, the world. Trying to get anything else I can, but economy sucks everywhere and it trickles down to us lowly workers who usually can make a living serving the rich people on the island in the summer. This year, the rich folks are squeezing their belts too, trying to get rid of their third homes on Salt Spring and not interested in paying people to maintain their gardens or pools or build a new roof, take care of their kids or clean their toilets. Unemployment and constant rejection I find very demoralizing, no matter how much I keep telling myself it's the economy and not personal. It's still humiliating begging for work, being willing and capable to do anything and yet scrambling just to barely scrape by.

Meanwhile I feel farther and farther away from the prison work and that kills me – it is so hard to be cut off from so many people who count on me, and who I care about and support, work that feels so critical to them and to my soul. And missing people I love. So discouraged about the total disconnect between my two worlds: from the energy and momentum I have when I'm in Bangkok, with the reality of trying just staying afloat in Canada and trying to expand and fund the continued support for prisoners.

I am cheer-leading myself through, 'cause I know I have so much to offer the world and yet feel ground down by rejection, no paid work, no home, no heart connection to share my dreams with...but, self-pity sucks, so I am just plugging on, and I keep smiling, staying positive and focused. Cannot let the thoughts get to me of how many years I've been working so hard to get Morgan and I through, and staying 'strong,' and never getting any- where. Really: financially and career-wise are the only domains in which I 'get' nowhere. Long ago gave up many aspirations, like being a human rights' lawyer, specializing in sex/gender issues (sex trade, trafficking and transgender issues). If I use a different barometer, a more humane one, I can see how much I do as an amazing mom, a compassionate witness to men's lives in Bangkwang, and the many, many ways I am a warrior in the world, and someone who lives with intention and compassionate engage- ment with marginalized people... but on the scale of what the mainstream world rewards, I'm getting nowhere. And it feels shitty, 'cause despite my living on the margins and my values not meshing with those of the 'real' world, I still must negotiate a world that is geared towards greed and con- sumerism and self-interest. And, as people rightly keep telling me: no one is going to look out for me. The longer I live close to the edge, the scarier that feels. And the more old shame surfaces.

The 'help' I've been getting from a friend of mine now has strings attached, and gets subtly grosser. I kick myself, saw it coming, but ignored it because I wanted to break old patterns. Here, I thought I had been devel- oping a new skill: *You don't always have to do everything on your own, Heath, it's ok to accept support from someone and learn to trust that people can be supportive, without ulterior motives.* So I accept his old car as a gift, hoping that it is the kindness of a friend and that should be ok. But no, once again, I am treated as though I 'owe' him because of his 'support' that I never asked for. Subtle, then not so subtle and gross. Today, although I have exactly $3 in my wallet, no idea when the next cent will come in and only a bag of nuts, one banana, and some plain yoghurt left, I go to his house, drop off the car and say: "This doesn't feel ok. I'm not for sale. I'm not your whore" – type of spiel. I leave, feeling clean and clear, relieved, and I am walking along the road back through town and up the hill, grateful I have a place to sleep at my good friend Shasso's for the next few weeks. Gotta get used to walking and hitchhiking everywhere again and how that slows down the pace of everything. The thought crosses my mind that if someone finally calls me to hire me, I may not be able to take the job without wheels. And now I can't just go pick up Morgan and whisk her away for tea when she calls me feeling sad and down, and needs her mom. I can't let this get to me, I keep hoping things will get better. I have applied to a teaching psych position at a college in Van (3rd year course on group processes, social psych and 1st year intro psych) as well as to every possible job on Salt Spring, and am constantly monitoring the overseas humanitarian sectors. No bites anywhere. Occasionally a job I'd love to do and am over-qualified to do comes up in Thailand, and they advertise that ex-pats will get paid as local staff do on the Thai-Burma border, so I can expect a salary of $250/month. Who do they think they'll recruit to do that? Wow...global economic crash sucks. I am walking along the road, proud of myself for getting rid of anybody in my life that doesn't feel healthy, including severing any contact at all with my alcoholic ex-, when my dad calls me from Vancouver, suggesting that I move to Saskatchewan, because he's heard that there is a boom in the prairie provinces and I could probably get a retail job out there. He's heard that Canadian Tire and Wal-Mart are hiring.

I can't seriously believe that this is what my dad is telling me: me, fiercely passionate, committed radical Heath, fighting for social justice my whole life, forging my own path, speaking my truth, and working my ass off to make sure that I live a life committed to paying attention to my inner voice, to embodying alternative visions of being and doing, a sex/gender radical who has taught life-changing somatic playful courses practicing ethical negotiation of power in intimacy, who raised my kid to be an independent and critical thinker, and to always speak up against injustice, to pay attention to her own shining wisdom and never accept others' judgments. I have taken care of others many times in my life and now it's my turn to live for me. It's a pretty low point when my dad is suggesting he lend me the money for a Greyhound bus ticket to move 3000km to apply for a job as a cashier at Wal-Mart in the prairies. I've been in the work force since twelve, waitressing, dishwasher, taxi-driving, general labour, any and all grunt work, as well as social science research, teaching, and lecturing in psychology. I can do lots, will try anything; I'm not above any kind of work, I just can't believe this is where I'm at, at age 40 with a Master's degree, unable to fund my soul's work helping prisoners. His call feels pretty patronizing, as if I'm so incapable of even figuring out for myself how to get a Wal-mart job and shouldn't aim higher. I feel pretty bleak. But wallowing is counterproductive. All of these issues are just details, they are not the important ones in life.

As I'm walking along I hear a loop in my brain, *Creed* singing: *I'm six feet from the edge/and I'm thinking/ maybe six feet ain't so far down/.* I really don't know what comes next or where I go from here, James. I've been at this place many times before. This is old shame getting triggered. I can only put one foot in front of the other and smile even as I'm crying. Is this just my ego, my pride that's humiliated? I don't feel like I get to shine in all of who I am and live any iota of my immense potential. So what? Who ever gets to? The world is set up so rich people get richer, and poor people stay poor, and shit happens and all we can do is be grateful for each moment, keep smiling and go forward with positive intentions, and keep laughing and dancing in the margins...

My identity and self-worth aren't defined by the employment I have, or the size of my bank account, I know this. But, I am still human and need some external validation, some pats on the back, some recognition, some money to pay bills and to eat. I am so unbelievably frustrated. I know my value doesn't come from external rewards, but it really does batter my self-esteem to not get financial compensation of any kind for the important soul-work work I have done for years (parenting & prison work). Never mind the incredible stress of always being fucking poor and the shame at not being able to provide things for my daughter and for myself I want to. This is a human universal, so what am I complaining about? I am still living in a privileged part of the world and not living on a garbage pile in Bombay. I always manage to scrape by and to bring support to others, too. In my core I am solid, just incredibly discouraged for an instant, and I turn my thoughts to the positive again. I have to.

I feel great about my decisions these days – none of them include numbing my thoughts and emotions with wine – and I keep reminding myself that as long as I have people dragging me down or treating me less than I deserve, then I am not allowing myself to soar. So I am alone. So what? I am free to soar. I am proud of myself for staying true to my inner voice, not compromising my values. YAY! I think of you telling me to keep smiling – you are the only person in the world who could say that to me, James. No one else I've met lives it the way you do. I have seen you approach other guys with the biggest smile on your face that diffuses any potential tension in a situation and it is quite remarkable. (And that's just the tiny glimpse I witness in the visiting area). You radiate positivity and that brings immense goodness to many people in your wake. I admire your ability to smile hugely as much as you do, and it gives me great comfort. I am smiling through my tears, remembering that I have my health and my perseverance, and I am grateful to be right here, right now looking at beautiful puffy white clouds in the blue sky. I walk along the road, unsure where to go or what to do next, just knowing that I have to keep going. Each moment is a gift. I am grateful for all that is wonderful, and staying positive about all that challenges me! Hey sky, hey puffy clouds, I am open and available to abundance!

I start singing and remind myself that I have my health, my integrity, my passion for life, an incredible daughter, and that's huge. And I say a silent prayer to the universe that since I have gotten rid of all that drags me down, this opens me up to new possibilities! Bring it on! As I walk and sing, my friend Shasso calls me to tell me that we've been accepted to work on a boat tuna-fishing that leaves in two days. For four weeks I'll be with three guys fishing down the BC to California coast. We will be watching ocean sunrises and sunsets, reading books in the down time, working hard, and hopefully banking money. YAY! YAY! YAY! I leave in 48 hours.

JULY 1, 2012

HAPPY CANADA DAY!

I just read your letter from early June. My sister brought it to me today from Van. YAY! Thank you for writing me and it was great to hear from you. Hmmmm. What do I say? Can I truly understand your situation? No. Can I relate to being despondent, to hitting emotional lows and re-bounding? Yup. Glad to hear you doing ok, James.

I love your 'attitude is everything' motto. You inspire me in how you live that. I admire that in you. You rock! Me, I try for a 'gratitude is everything!' ☺

To respond to the 'serious' part of your letter: when I said in a previous letter that I don't like people trying to change me – I'm talking about people who don't know me from a hole in the wall, instantly putting me in a box that fits into their little pea-brain, and then trying to mold me into who they think I 'should' be. I personally think that all of us contain within ourselves the wisdom to access the best possible us – but often this knowledge or wisdom is obscured by self-doubt, by fear, by addiction, or lack of paying attention to our inner voice, and a multitude of other barriers, outdated survival mechanisms or habits, often obstacles we ourselves have put in the way (as well as external/ societal ones, obviously). I try to reflect back to people the positive in them, their strengths, and support them to listen to their inner voice. I assume we are experts on our own lives, even as we also need mentors, more tools and support. I would not presume to tell someone right off the bat what they 'should' do with their life (unless they specifically ask for my advice on a matter), when I know nothing of the complexity of their lives or situation. I do, however, frequently encounter people who, within five minutes of meeting me, tell me what I need to change about myself or do differently with my life, with no other knowledge of any of me. I think that happens to woman way more than men. I bristle at that and find it paternalistic and presumptuous.

I WASN'T referring to a fantastic human being (YOU!) whose opinion and judgment I value, kindly expressing his concern about a self-destructive drinking habit I have.

Don't worry about me jumping down your throat, James, no need to worry about what you write to me. I wanna hear what you gotta say. About anything and everything. Even though and especially because we see the world so very differently. I respect you and care about you and our friendship and am very happy if you want to write me. Anything that ever comes up between us, any misunderstandings or conflict, I will assume we can resolve with good intentions, honest communication, and big smiles! I have strong opinions and I express them, and I am aware that I am frequently experienced as too harsh and abrupt with people. This is totally unintentional. I still cringe when I think of how I jumped on you in our first conversation about the Christian stuff. I hold that mental image of your turtle neck retreating back in its shell. I am sorry that I am too harsh at times. It is a constant challenge for me to try to soften my overly prickly exterior. So glad you told me at a way later date what an ass I'd been (although pointed it out to me in a very gentle way). I like to get called on my shit. BTW, I'm never gonna totally curb the cursing! ☺

Hey ...guess what? Seeing as my new non-drinking self is in her infancy, I was concerned about the whole hard-working/hard-drinking fishing culture on the boat – me and three guys and hoping they'd accept me as a non-drinking cohort. The Universe dropped this lovely gift into my lap: it's a DRY ship, no booze. I'm profoundly relieved. And, Shasso is one of the guys, so he can show me the ropes on this first trip – he only wants to do one tour, 'cause he has a six-year old daughter and doesn't want to leave her for the whole summer, understandably – and I can stay on for future trips, until the end of the season, if they accept me.

I'll be mailing this letter after I get back at the end of July, hoping you aren't in a Thai prison to receive it! But it sounds like maybe a September/October release for you.

Wow...is it starting to feel real? Getting transferred to the US after five years. Flying home. Duty-free dreams sound cool. How very pragmatic and a great metaphor. I am so incredibly happy for you!!!!!!!!

I miss seeing you! I hope your American-from-Japan buddy was a good visit – although it will be long ago by the time you read this letter.

So I leave tomorrow morning: Three meals of yoghurt and nuts today and weed-whacked a neighbour's place for an hour and a half for $50, bought t-shirts & sweats, and books at the thrift store. Slim pickins' though, so I had to choose some fiction. The astrology and self-help section was massive – no thanks ☺. I'm stoked to get the chance to read on the open ocean for pleasure. I DIDN'T read the running book – I am mystified as to where it is – it disappeared somewhere between Bangkok and here and I'm disappointed: was looking forward to it, especially since you went to the trouble to get it to me through prison channels. I still run 5 km every day at the gym and think of you: still have that weird fantasy that I am running inside the prison to win your freedom and Ivan's (whacky little brain of mine).

JULY 4, 20121 AM

James!
HAPPY whatever you guys call your USA DAY!

I am lying on my bunk on the *Gaffe*, a seventy-foot vessel, fourteen hours into this new adventure. I've never been a deck-hand before on a commercial fishing vessel, and it is exciting. The owner of the boat picked up Shass and I at 10:45 this morning, and drove us up to French Creek, about 150km up the Big Island (Vancouver Island) where the boat is. He bought $500 worth of rain gear and gloves for us, then we met the captain, George, friendly, old-school, about 65 – funny, political, so we ranted a bunch about Free-Trade and the Conservative government and how Canada was going to Hell in a Handbasket. So, Shasso and I the two deckhands, George the Captain, and the fourth guy, the engineer, is called Mak. He's from Fiji, a massive, friendly Christian dude. I like that they're both older, got kids, and there seems to be no weirdness about me being there – we're just all happy to go fishing. We jumped into a truck and headed down the highway to a Costco and spent two hours and $4000 buying massive amounts of food. We loaded the boat, storing all the canned goods in one area, then went to work on deck. I bleached out the metal containers for storing food, then organized and put away all the fresh fruits and vegetables, bottled water, pop, bread, etc. into cool holds on top of the big freezer below for fish that is also where we keep our frozen goods. For the next two hours, as the guys did all the rope work and we set out for Victoria, I unwrapped packages of meat and put pork ribs, beef ribs, stewing beef, thick rib-eye steaks, whole fryer chickens, chicken thighs, chicken breasts, pork tenderloin, pork roasts, whole hams, packs of salami, black forest ham, sliced turkey breast, hot Italian sausages, smoked turkey bratwurst, ground beef, perogies, cheeses and more into plastic freezer baggies in generous 4-person portions, then into milk crates, and passed them down to Mak, who stacked them in the minus 40 degree hold. We are gonna eat like pigs! They pay for all of this while we fish, and we bank all our pay, 'cause we got no expenses on the boat. YAY!

The money is contingent on us catching a whack-load of fish and selling it within a few weeks to the Japanese. George explained that we catch and freeze sashimi-grade Tuna, meaning we bleed it then freeze it before rigor mortis sets in (< 30 minutes), hopefully fetching top-dollar. We set out to international waters tomorrow, after fueling in Port Angeles (WA) and will take 4-5 days to get to the fishing grounds, catching along the way, and then there should more intense heavy-duty, non-stop weeks of fishing. The deal is we stay out until we fill up our hold – 91,000 pounds of Tuna – then we come back and unload and sell in Victoria or Vancouver. And get a cheque. That's the theory.

I am already loving every bit of this experience. I LOVE learning anything new, new skills, new ways of being, and I love the simplicity of the fishing world. Leaving my other woes behind, I get to be on the ocean and just be and do. I thanked the boat owner profusely for giving me this chance, as I know I won't disappoint. I am such a hard worker, no matter what job I do, and easily adaptable. Guys have been expressing concerns for my ability to cope: "Heather, remember, if you get seasick, there's no going back. If you get bored or grumpy or claustrophobic or homesick or unhappy, there's no turning back..." I am not a princess or a delicate flower, so it will go well. Apparently, the mental part is the hardest part for newbies. Many physically capable guys go ape-shit from the solitude or lack of land or boredom or long grueling hours. I am stronger mentally than most people in challenging situations. I don't do so well in "normal" life. That's where I go squirrelly, trying to navigate a world with values anathema to my own. I am the person you want to be with when the plane crashes in the middle of nowhere, or the guy next to you loses it and cuts off his arm with an exacto knife. Those types of situations, while stressful, don't faze me in the slightest. OK, granted, drastic examples, but I feel they are more 'authentic' in the sense that our humanity is in the forefront and I can deal calmly on a human level: there's no game-playing or artifice in those moments. It's the weird social status power games, consumerism and gender games, chitchat, and superficial bullshit that masquerades as our mainstream culture that I can't handle. I get all stressed, as you can tell from my letters where I rant about the 'stupid' people around me just doing vapid, vacuous, shallow, selfish shit that passes for 'normal' life, and worse still, trying to make me conform to their reality. The marginal spaces that other people find difficult is the stuff I get drawn to and thrive in. More authentic. But fishing is hardly marginal, it's just open ocean, hard work, albeit dangerous work. Fun learning, so far. Mak showed me how to splice ropes for the Scotchmen (I just learned what a Scotchman is). Before we got to the boat, I asked Shasso to remind me what side 'port' and 'starboard' are, as I am completely ignorant of any and all nautical terms.

And, lots of time to think and maybe some stolen moments to write to buddies ☺ and to READ, to contemplate life without tv or internet or constant distractions or urgent responsibilities all sound like wonderful things to me, not hardships, like what the guys keep warning me about. I love being alone...my loneliness is not related to whether I'm around people or not – it's more related to lack of people I can really connect with. Well, that and to old grief. I enjoy being alone, and in fact I'll be in close quarters with three other people, so that will feel much more crowded than normal for me. Only three. It must be so challenging for you to deal with crowded pressure-cooker dynamics in small spaces. Your big smile gets you far, I imagine, but what a difficult and constant tension! I have no idea, I'm sure.

I'm in my cramped wee upper bunk beside the engine room right now and I should sleep, but I am way too excited. Hopefully, the thick hot air, heavy with the smell of diesel and oil and the roar of the engine will lull me to dream-space. I am so incredibly excited about this opportunity! One thing you cannot say about me is that I shy away from challenges, new adventures or travel...I want to experience EVERYTHING in life! YAY, James, I'm a fledgling Tuna Fisher! Who knew?

I am thinking of you, sending happy happy happy happy thoughts and hugs!Bye for now...xo

JULY 4, 2012 11PM

Last Saturday and Sunday, knowing that we were heading out two days later on this job and would be off the grid, I knuckled down and put the finishing touches on a pretty kick-ass term paper about mapping social space in prison, 'building' identity in relation to architectural spaces of oppression. It features a lot of Ivan's sketches as examples. I would really like one day to expand on this paper and to discuss it with you. AND, when I sent it off, I was FINISHED my last assignment of my post-graduate degree! Four days early. YAY! Proud of myself.

I wonder if you ever catch a glimpse in my letters the silly, playful side of me: I'm actually a big goofball in addition to being serious, intense and super passionate about everything I do. I actually do spend a lot of time laughing, not just ranting.

What are sides of you that are harder to access/ express where you are? Going to sleep now....

JULY 5, 2012

It's 5pm, I'm sitting in the galley, alone listening to music as we head through the Straight of Juan de Fuca, on a gorgeous sunny summer day. I just finished prepping dinner: chicken and veggie stirfry. I have bowls of red & yellow peppers, onions, asparagus, broccoli, zucchini, and fresh chicken breast all cut up and ready to go. It's a little early for dinner and Shass and Mak are napping so I am enjoying the quiet, the moment to myself to write. Munching on cherries. We all woke at 5 am, fueled up after passing US Customs and Immigration, and got oil and water, and then set out at about 10 am for open water. Our boat has a shower (!) and a water-maker, so we're pretty lucky and can use as much water as we want. I learned a bunch of stuff today, as we set out from Port Angeles and put out our fishing lines. Mak is quiet for the most part and doesn't offer info to me, so I ask him questions, and it's a pretty easy-going atmosphere and lovely little group of us. I made George coffee and a salami, cheese and veggie sandwich at lunch and went and spent a few hours with him in the wheelhouse, learning all sorts of cool stuff, like his navigation programs, and all the GPS programs he's got running that overlay where plankton is, water temperature, depths, etc. so that we can pick best tuna grounds and head for those. The cool thing is he doesn't really get computers, so I was troubleshooting software issues for him with his GPS that kept going off, as well as his email and that gave us lots of time to just talk and get to know each other. He instantly nicknamed me 'Red', for my hair. It gets really faded and reddish over months in the Bangkok sun, so I bought a box of medium brown colour from the store to get it back to my regular colour, slapped it in the night before we left, but it made my hair way more red, which I hate, instead of brown. After the first morning, seeing me emerge from my bunk, George added 'Rooster' to my moniker. So I'm 'Red Rooster' now. Shasso thinks it's hilarious. I like Mak too, but there isn't the instant comraderie and ease that I have with George. He's growing on me though. Doesn't talk much.

I don't have access to internet, but the ship has got satellite email on the navigation computers, so we can email other ships in our Tuna fleet to keep each other apprised of where we are and where the fish are. So I snuck into his system and wrote Morgan a wee email just telling her I'm ok. I know she's worried and missing me. Shasso said she sent him a text, saying: "Please take care of my mom" as we left the island. I can't let myself feel guilty that I'm leaving so soon after getting back from Thailand. I have to go anywhere there's work. The whole time she was small, up to about age 14, I never took any work that would take me away from her – I always did school work or research contracts where I could work from home to be there with her. In part because I couldn't bear to leave her, in part because I couldn't afford any childcare when she was small. No matter what we do as moms, though, there's never enough time and always guilt about not doing enough. Even though she's struggling emotionally right now, I have to let this young women live her own life: It's no good for her to see her mom unemployed and demoralized either. (Wow – did you notice me justifying my choice? Yes, guilt comes with the territory of motherhood.)

I learned to tie five types of knots today and was running up and down between the engine room and the bow, with cool weird tools as I filled the water tank for an hour. We will each have to do night watch shifts at the wheelhouse, starting tonight, so I was grilling George about exactly what that will look like, in terms of safety and every possible scenario that could come up. If I stay on for the season, I'll be with Mak and George again, so it's nice seeing us all fit already into a rhythm, a lovely way of being around each other. Group dynamics are potentially the worst or best part of any work/live situation (not that you don't experience that!), so I'm really happy about our wee group and learning how I fit into it. Mak hates cooking, George doesn't cook as the captain, so Shass and I will be sharing the cooking/cleaning in the galley, which is great. I LOVE to cook, and it makes me feel less useless right now that I can be preparing meals and cleaning when there's still tonnes of stuff I don't know how to do, so I'm not just standing around watching. (Most of the stuff I'm watching is engine repair, so I'm not supposed to know that anyway as it's Mak's domain, but I hate not doing anything when other people are working). Shasso warned me that the deep-hold stacking job gets given to the newbie, as it's the shittiest grunt work. I expected to get tossed down there right away into the claustrophobic deep-freeze of minus 40 F. Luckily, Mak LOVES that, and told us that as long as he never has to cook, he'll do all the deep-freeze stacking. YES! Of course I want to learn all the jobs, but I'm pretty relieved that I won't be down there all the time. I put on the heavy-duty winter gear and went down to check out the deep freeze on the first day. Down the hatch and metal ladder into a series of dark, cold rooms. Door has to be closed above you to keep the cold in. Moving slowly in the numbing cold under the heavy weight of four layers of protection, stepping carefully as the boat rocks and heaves from one tomb-like room to the next, I had a flash of a horror movie moment where you yell at the screen for the woman to get the hell out before the guy with the pickaxe steps out from around the corner and she can't get up the ladder fast enough and the hatch above her closes with a snap, barring her exit. So, thank you Mak for taking that job, I'd rather not hang out down there.

The galley's pretty cool, the size of an apartment kitchen and we have tonnes of food – all the spices, sauces and equipment I need, so I can make great meals – not the beans and toast and burnt steaks I was envisioning. The guys have been asleep for a few hours – me, I took a nap at about 1 pm – couldn't stay awake after all the work. My salami sandwich coaxed me into my bunk and dreamland. I tried to read my book, but made it only two lines.

I'm reading an anthology of 'dangerous ideas' by leading scientists and philosophers from 2007 – what some of the world's great thinkers consider the big ideas of our time that they themselves may or may not be investigating, as governments, funders, donors, universities and the general public often do not support work into the 'heretical' ideas of our times, favouring instead politically correct ones that don't lend themselves to great paradigmatic upheaval or moral quandries, including the discussion of whether there is actually such a thing as a 'dangerous idea.' I'M LOVING IT! Gotta go cook dinner now!

10:25 PM JULY 06, 2012

Just had a 3-minute hot shower to get blood and guts off me, jumped into wee bunk exhausted. Gotta be up at 4 to fish, so I won't write long, just tell you about our first real day:

1 am – 4 am my watch on bridge, monitoring radar and horizon for ships (none), and trying really hard not to fall asleep. I run in place to keep my body from dozing off, but my mind is hallucinating as I'm forcing my eyes open: I see a woman bowling in the wheelhouse with me, a dog barking and a guy standing outside the boat. Yikes.

4 – 6:30 am sleep

6:30 – get up, pull on fishing clothes in 3 minutes, whip up scrambled eggs with onions, peppers, bacon, & two kinds of cheese inside flax seed pita pockets and coffee for the guys. Tea for me. Dishes, winter clothing and head down to the horror-movie hold for more frozen food: pizzas, more meat, cheese, etc. to restock the fridge and freezer in the galley. I pull out a huge bag of beef chunks for dinner.

Fish all day. We have 12 lines heading off the stern and we pull the Tuna in by hand every time a line jumps. This is harder than it looks. I spend the first hour cutting up rubber tires, and sewing this together with thick needle and rope to create some rubber hand protection for on top of the regular gloves. My 'gloves' end up looking like something Slipknot would be proud of. First fish I pull hand over hand, and finagle him up and out of the water, swing him on to the table behind me where I slit its throat, grab and remove the hook, then slide the poor guy down the tube, where he will bleed out. We need to accomplish all this within seconds, but so far, I keep losing my fish at the last moment, to everyone's chagrin. We are not in fish ground on these first days, so we stand there and catch a total of 56 fish big fat tuna today between 6 am and 10pm. The only break from standing there monitoring the lines is when I go to the galley and cook up a beef curry at about 3pm that I let simmer for 3 hours, and we take turns going in to eat between 6:30 – 7. Mak's not much of a conversationalist, and I enjoy silence and my own daydreams as I take in the spectacular ocean, clouds and occasional whales in the distance.

Shasso is not happy about the silence and lack of alcohol and very sporadic fishing... sometimes hours between fish. Me, I'm cool with it, but pretty disappointed in myself about not getting the technique down yet. The guys watch me struggle and struggle to get a total of three fish onto the boat out of a potential six – the rest were on other people's lines. It's my first day and I know I'll get better, but it sucks being weaker and smaller as well as less experienced. Oh well, I'll get it soon enough.

Sending super duper happy thoughts and magical sunsets over the ocean! xo ☺ Sleep awaits, more fishing in just a few hours.

JULY 7, 2012

Up at 4, and pull on sweats, sweater, hat, rubber coveralls, rubber boots, winter gear and heavy gloves. Out on the pitch-black deck, from 4:10 to 4:45, we load yesterday's fish from the plates, where they lie frozen and pass them by hand down to Mak to stack in the freezer. 50 fish down, muscles screaming, many thousands to go. Then we take ten minutes to grab a mug of tea, and set up the lines as the sun rises, a red ball of fire at the horizon. Another 18 hours of fishing, and I'm determined to do better. Waiting for bites, we unload a box of bait (anchovies), one of 35, 50-pound boxes we loaded on in the harbour. Shasso's being really helpful, knowing I'm a bit stressed about not being good at pulling in fish yet – and it doesn't help having Mak and George breathing down my neck, yelling at me that every fish I lose is like losing a $50 dollar bill. Shass rigs up a gallon jug full of milk to a nylon line and I practice. How to get a thrashing, 30-pound Tuna on the end of a line exactly where I need him in 3 seconds and pull him up, flip him on the table behind me. They've shown me the technique a million times, and I don't feel like I lack strength, it seems just to be an issue of always losing my grip on the slippery nylon line, struggling constantly to regain it as it slips repeatedly until the fish manages to jerk free. Suddenly, after about an hour, it clicks, YAY, and the procedure goes from being a panicky ordeal each time, to easy as pie, and now I'm stoked! I get excited by each fish, and pull hand over hand, yank the dude up and flip him behind me, slit his neck, throw the lure back in, send him down the tube and rinse the blood off with my seawater hose. All these maneouvres executed on the constantly rolling boat so as not to tangle lines, get caught in a rope, lose a knife or an eye. We release the fish from the tube to flop on deck every 15 minutes or so, hose them down some more and stack them on freezer plates. So far the fish are very few and far between.

Very long days, mostly standing or sitting, waiting, watching, occasionally running in for tea or a pee. A few hours in, we're sitting there, chilling out at the stern, layers of clothes buffering against the incessant wind, drinking yet another mug of tea, and watching an albatross follow us. Poor guy swoops down and bites one of the lures, and now we've snagged this massive bird. As Mak pulls on the line, we watch the giant bird flapping and struggling, yanking desperately to free himself as we drag him in. Mak manages to grabs his neck to get the hook out of his beak, but the poor bird has drowned. We release him, and he flops once or twice, trying to revive, then succumbs. Funny how I feel sorry for him, but not the fish. The rest of the day rolls pretty slowly and I am lost in my thoughts, looking out to sea, enjoying seeing not a thing in any direction, except greyish blue ocean and the barely perceptible curvature of the earth splitting the world in two: rolling grey ocean and heavy grey sky. It's really quite remarkable...I can see no evidence any-where of anything human-made. Anywhere. Not even other ships. The roar of the boat's engine, and the metal on which I sit remind me that I am not free-floating, but besides that, there is only vast ocean and sky in all direction, all 360 degrees. I've never before been out on the ocean away from the slightest hint somewhere of a distant silhouette of land or a boat. It is really spectacular. Do you ever go sailing?

I don't nap, 'cause I'm the cook, but I get a relief from 'fishing' (actually sitting on a milk crate or leaning against a table for hours on end, trying to stay warm, hoping for fish) twice a day when I remove my bloody, stinky coveralls and cook meals. It's a whole other pleasure in the galley, making food. I love cooking for people – it feels creative and nurturing. By 1 pm, I've been up and at it for 9 hours, would be nice to chill out or lie down for a sec, but everything is go go go, even when there's no fish biting. I surreptitiously grab some of my grubby clothes and scrub them in a bucket and hang them up on a rope on deck, getting a 'Chinese laundry' comment from George, who growls at me for being too 'girlie' by washing clothes. Apparently 'real men' never wash clothes or shower during the entire trip, but his grumpy comments vanish and he's jovial after I feed him. The water-maker is on the fritz, so no showers for us after all and anything must be washed by the deck hose that runs ocean water. No big deal.

I'm out here again, waiting for fish. Shasso's napping and Mak's fixing something in the engine room. I love the solitude, watching the huge open spaces, and I start wondering about the horizon. How far is it? With no object in the distance except ocean and sky, what is the exact distance the human eye can see before all turns into horizon? Who measured that? And how? Obviously a human eye can see objects that pop up from the ground that are very far away, say a mountain 50 km away or a tree 500 metres away. But in the absence of any land features, anything vertical at all, what is the limit to our vision, the horizon edge our brain creates? I ask George in the wheelhouse and he says: approx-imately 2.5 miles. (Incidentally, he radios another captain to confirm the number). I think of the people who first crossed oceans, and who thought, understandably, that they were the center of the world, and that the Earth was the centre of the universe. Here, in this moment, I really understand that literal perspective. Right now, I am exactly the centre of all that is visible to me at every moment. Although we are always seeing from the perspective of 'behind our eyes', the world 'out there' usually takes varying limited distances, shapes and relationships. Here, now, all is exactly a flat plane with a domed roof. There is no: "Hey, that tree is nearer or farther away, or, am I closer to this wall than to that bench?" Instead, on this ocean, no matter how far I travel, I am always exactly in the centre of a vast grey-blue circle with a radius of about 2.5 miles and a semi globe of grey-blue sky above me. Why that distance? Nature uses only a few select patterns and ratios, repeatedly, and all seem to have an evolutionary purpose. Like the 20/400 vision infants are born with that allows perfect focus from boob to mama's face. I start to wonder if there's a relationship between the ratio of me to my horizon and a pupil to an iris, as the ocean and sky remind me of a giant grey eye. I start to trip out on the atmosphere being like the cornea, and the clouds as cataracts. Ok, It's not quite the same if you're not here....good thing I don't do drugs! ☺

I don't talk for hours, even when Mak returns to join me back here and blasts his reggae superloud, so as to be audible above the roar of the engine and the compressor. I am so happy, not worrying about things like where my next paycheque comes from or whether I am wasting my potential in life...those thoughts are gone. It's amazing how having employment curbs my existential fears. I realize I haven't worried once of Morgan or my Mom. I am right here, right now, on the ocean, loving it and learning new skills and marveling at life. I'm having a new adventure and making money. I can't complain. It's pretty cool. And it will get me closer to getting back to the prison to support the guys.

I'm grateful for these slow fish days to get used to the work rhythm and pulling fish before we go ape-shit in a few days with non-stop fish. At 5pm, I head in and make garlic mashed potatoes with Yukon gold potatoes, garlic, onion, butter, cream, and parmesan mushed in and chicken thighs in garlic, basil, and oregano mushroom sauce to pour over the potatoes. I also steam some wee broccoli for veg. The guys go crazy when I call them in for dinner. On slow days we can eat together-ish, unlike busy days where we will eat in rushed shifts, or not at all, they say. I like that they appreciate real food, 'cause I don't like processed stuff, so I make everything from scratch, salad dressings included. I was happy when we were shopping that George was all about buying the real ingredients, like olive oil and balsamic vinegar, and all the spices and stuff I need, instead of bottles of crap or packages of powder sauces. Man, I'm eating a lot.

Now it's 8:30 and I have to admit I'm fading – been a long day and there's a long night ahead. I told Shass and Mak I was going in for a wee sit-down, cause I didn't get a nap today, but I'm bagged and I grabbed my laptop to write a bit to you. We gotta fish 'til 10 pm, then close up everything, then I got another three-hour watch overnight, sometime, and up at 4 am to start tomorrow. Not sure when I sleep! It's long hours, but I'm loving it, mostly. I should go and not look like a slacker.

I spent a lot of daydreaming time, travelling in my mind, planning and imagining, wondering when you'll get to go to Miami to windsurf and to enact all your plans and dreams too. Soon, I hope. I send you big, big hugs! xo

It's ten minutes later and the ship's gone haywire – I'm giddy from lack of sleep, and Shass and I are laughing so hard, I'm peeing my pants. Everything is so serious all day long, and heavy-duty, and now we're all tired, and I am so acutely conscious of the dangers and how when we get tired we can make little mistakes, even of footing, and fall overboard or whatever. All day long I am regaled with stories of previous deckhands: so and so who jumped from the boat to the dock when it was 6 feet out, thinking he could make it, slipped and got flattened like a pancake; or so and so who went squirrelly and hung himself; or so and so who slipped with scissors on the deck and punctured his lungs; or so and so who dropped a frozen fish on Mak's head and cut it open, requiring stitches; or so and so who fell asleep on the night watch and missed the fire in the engine room; or, what's her face who got air-lifted by chopper to the hospital by US Coast Guard and only just made it... you get the point. With the heavy gear, wet decks, long hours, lack of sleep, constant rolling of the ship, and weary legs, I'll admit that I am pretty conscious of how easily a serious or fatal accident could happen here. Our goofiness belies the constant vigilance required. Just now, Shasso came in for his third snack after dinner, cause we're so bored and cold standing there monitoring the fish lines 18 hours per day that we eat a lot and we're thinking that we're gonna roll back to shore having gained 50 lbs each. Glances at me sheepishly, and we burst out laughing. Check on the other two and realize that George has fallen asleep at the wheel and is 'steering' the boat passed out, and Mak is also sleeping while supposedly 'fishing'. Now I'm not so worried about looking like a slacker.

Mak jumps awake and dances around to tunes we've got cranked, air-guitaring a shovel like a maniac trying to keep warm; Shasso is compulsively stuffing his face with peanut butter and jelly sandwiches; and we're killing ourselves laughing. Giddy from fatigue, I'd say. We crack up with the stupidest looks or silliest nonsense or situations. I'm slowing getting used to Mak's silence, broken by occasional highly repetitive stories, and his fantastically loud boom of a laugh that often startles me. It's infectious. I'm appreciating him more as we share stories and spend long hours staring out to sea together. He commented on how speedy I am: I move quickly, I learn quickly, I speak and read quickly. "Everything you do is fast."

"Yup, everything except making love," I answered. He roared with laughter and gave me thumbs up.

I hope you will come to this part of the world one day –it would be cool to show you the West Coast of BC. You could ski or snowboard Whistler.

Ugh. 10:30 pm, stripped off nasty clothes, rinsed face, put on cozy jammies, to pretend I don't feel stinky and gross, smelling of fish guts and blood, sea spray. My face is killing me – fat lip, bashed nose. After 5 hours of staring at rolling waves with no fish, in the final 15 minutes, a whopper of a Grandfather Tuna jumped on one of my lines and I wrestled him in, and as I got him against the boat and was leaning down (wondering how the heck I'd get such a massive fish in the boat), Shass saw the size of the beast and grabbed the gaff to spear his head. As he reached for him, the fish ripped free of the lure. We were leaning over the side of the boat, me holding the fish by the line, and when he broke free, my fist came up and smashed my nose and teeth. Hard. We stood mutely staring at the ocean where the fish should have been– me, tears streaming from pain – when George came running out of the wheelhouse and yelled: "I SAW THAT!" He keeps an eye on each fish via cameras mounted above our heads. More pissed off than he that I lost a huge fish, I said lamely: "It wasn't a Tuna, it was a whale shark." At least they laughed.

Now, though, as I'm typing, he's cataloguing my errors of the day (lights left on, fish lost), and I'm nodding and typing and he's mostly yelling at Shasso about batteries and stuff. "Don't forget I'm riding your ass," he said. I won't. He's a decent guy, plays the role of the gruff captain hard-ass, but he's a softie. He just announced we're getting a break tonight, no watch, we'll just drift and not run through the night, so I get to sleep straight through from 11 to 4. YAY! It won't be a problem dropping off to sleep, lulled by the rocking of the ship. My dreams have been really cool. I wonder what you dream of, what you hope for. I was really struck by the sentence in your letter: "my biggest activity is imagining or remembering, planning and hoping."

I notice how much Shasso talks about missing booze.

Me, I miss a glass of wine as I cook dinner tonight, and miss throwing white wine into the mushroom and chicken sauce, but only for a half second. Really, I think about how easily I could accidentally die on this boat, and I wonder how the hell fishers do this insane stuff while drinking whiskey and beer all day long. Stories Shasso shared from previous years included loading up pallets of beer and hard booze with cranes along with a few steaks and potatoes. I'm extra grateful to be on a dry boat. And determined to make it back safely to Morgi.

SUNDAY, 8 JULY

4 am is November dark and cold. Layers and layers and we freeze our butts off for hours, groggily waiting for fish. Shasso is getting grumpy and panicky about us not finding any. Me, I figure we're only four days in and we'll be out on the water until we get a boatload, so why worry? It is brutally chilly, and layers of wool, fleece, rubber and hoodies don't seem to buffer it. We're so cold that Shass and I snack on at least 5 meals in the eight hours between getting up and noon. Then, I waddle my extra full belly into the galley to make grilled cheese sandwiches and chicken noodle soup for lunch. After Mak eats, he goes out, and relieves Shasso, whose turn it is, and we're joking about how repulsively full we are from boredom, cold and compulsively eating like crazy. I wonder if it's also the alcohol lack and I gotta watch it, so I start chugging even more bottles of water so that I don't eat every minute of the day. Mak returns to the galley and stares at me gravely and declares that I'm the best cook he's ever encountered. This pleases me. Already, he's been giving me huge thumbs up at each meal, and he's stopped pouring ketchup automatically on everything I put in front of him. He is accustomed to

hating the cooking on the boat, and usually drowns all his meals in ketchup – even ice cream, I kid you not. He is practically weeping as he describes in detail to Shasso the 'toast with butter on the outside and delicious cheese' and how he's going to take the recipe home to Fiji and eat 12 of those a day. Apparently it's his first grilled cheese sandwich ever. I just cleaned up and prepared the pork ribs in a homemade garlic mustard rub and stuck them in the oven. I can hardly keep my eyes open, so I'm sneaking off for a nap for an hour, 'cause there's still no fish and we're all just bored and exhausted.

I called Morgan at 8 am and talked for four minutes on a satellite phone. She sounded very very low and hardly responded. She said she started her anti-depressants yesterday and I just told her to hang in and that I ʋed her. Shitty feeling.

I wonder what you're up to. Do you play cards? Are you allowed to? Probably not, as I know they won't let us play in cafes in Bangkok. Shass and I play crib when we can. Mak doesn't want to learn, but he's always watching us, so we'll keep inviting him to join.

I lay down, but couldn't sleep. Too much thinking. Or feeling, really. I knew this would happen, and I knew as I wrote the line about compulsive eating that it was time to face the music. Now that I'm not drinking daily, or distracting myself from my own pain by helping others or dealing with an ex-partner's psychosis, or care-taking sick family members, things come up. I'm glad I'm here, on the ocean. It's time to actually feel pain I've been trying to numb for years with booze. It's ok to write this now, 'cause it's hours later and I know all this is healthy and good. A few hours ago, though, lying in the bunk, grief wells up and engulfs me: my heart feels as if it's ripping and I am crying old old pain into my pillow, and it doesn't feel good. The well of pain feels bottomless. I believe that we are drawn to what wounds us, and I know that much of what I do in the world revolves around my invisible grief, pain at loss and the human need to be witnessed. This is, in part, why I go to the prison, because I can't bear that people suffer invisibly, and I want to reflect to them that they matter in the world. That no one deserves degrading or humiliating treatment; that they are beautiful, no matter how they are treated. I know it's now past time to feel my own stuff, to let myself actually grieve. Easier said than done. Who knew fishing could be so powerful? ☺

Today: A few more fish, day goes faster, more fun, less sleep, lots of intense, crazy, wonderful, tedious, grueling and sweaty moments... thinking, being, feeling, drifting on waves, staring for hours at the ocean, twenty-foot swells rocking us constantly, fish coming in, grabbing, pulling, dancing to music cranked for hours: Fleetwood Mac, Bob Dylan, Ween, Bob Marley, CCR, Michael Franti are especially popular. Belly laughs, fish guts and bloody spray from hair to toes, daydreaming, being, just being... loving it...and hoping a fat paycheque comes at the end of this.

Two more very slow days: only a handful of fish each day. Tensions starting to rise – the guys vocalizing stress and worry about whether we'll find the fish this year, or whether this is all for naught. Apparently, the Americans broke our longstanding treaty with them: they are no longer allowing Canadian fishers into their waters for the first time this year as Tuna stocks are WAY down, but of course they still insist that they can fish our waters indiscriminately. This is why we are farther out than usual, past 200 miles, as we are now banned and they're patrolling the edges as if we are potential terrorists. There are no fish out here so far – water's too cold. Shasso and Mak are especially stressed, but I can't get worked up about it. As far as I'm concerned, whether we worry or moan or stress or blame, the objective reality doesn't change — we're here, we'll be here for a month, and we just gotta go with it and hope for fish a plenty. I have faith that all will be well. We're still laughing a lot and keeping ourselves busy cleaning out the galley, disinfecting stuff that hasn't been cleaned for years. I take pleasure washing and hanging out my pink bras on the ropes on deck so they flap in the wind. Except for the first day, the weather's been really cold out here, it's hard for stuff to dry in the cold salty mist.

Talked to Morgi last night around 9:30 pm. She's sounding ok – getting work cleaning houses for a few hours per day. She and her boyfriend moved into a cute cabin on July 1 and I had dinner at their new place the evening before I left. I brought them pink lilies and after dinner we watched a movie (Wrath of the Titans—it was cheesy enough that we all yakked through it). First time we three hung out together for several hours and it felt relaxed and great. She reported to me the next day that Matt told her he enjoyed the time with me. Yay! Small victories. It did get awkward for him when the topic of anal sex came up (how did that sneak into the conversation as we watch Liam Neesom as Zeus getting thrashed by his betraying son? Oh right, the Greeks). I forget that I'm the "mother-in-law," and it is weird for Morgan's boyfriend to think that I could possibly have any sexual side to me – Ewwww, gross! Anyway, Morgi's ok and she says summer's finally hit Salt Spring: 30 degrees and she jumped into Maxwell Lake yesterday. Sounds heavenly.

George's mis-pronounciation of Shasso's name provides constant amusement. How he can pervert a fairly simple, while unusual name, pronounced SHA-SO, into countless variations. So far he's trotted out: Ya-Zoo, Jack-so, Wa-zoo, Jackson, Zazzo, Jacko, Yasso, Yazer, Zak-sui, and Shampoo (!), and so on. Shasso's used to it and it doesn't bother him – people have been messing up his name his whole life. I'm feeling pretty grateful for my friendship with him. We love each other's foibles, and quirky irreverent goofiness. An actual friend. I don't want to jinx it by saying that. But it's been a slowly deepening 12 years, so I feel pretty damn solid about it. He's not very emotionally expressive though. Very smart and not macho in the slightest, has no problem disrupting conventional gender and social norms, playing at their absurdity, which to me is very appealing in a person. His ex, the mom of his kid, whom he was with for many years is a funny, loud, crazy, fiercely intelligent, outspoken woman, so he is used to and not intimidated by strong women. YAY. His dry, oddball sense of humour can be very off-putting to people – they often don't know how to take him. In fact, he almost didn't get his first job fishing eight years ago because he wore big earrings, and spoke unlike the other fishers. (He doesn't sit around referring to women as 'bitches' or 'old ladies'). The owner of this boat rejected his initial application, probably thinking he was a 'fag'. I was working that summer at the Salt Spring Harbour Authority and in a weird coincidence, Shasso and I went out that night for drinks and saw the owner and his whole crew getting drunk before heading offshore, and as we drank together, I convinced them to hire Shasso. He then worked for several years doing Tuna, Halibut and Salmon, and quit when his daughter was born to spend more time at home. This year, knowing I was desperate for any work, he got us both on this boat. Nice full circle. It would definitely be way less fun here without him.

Night watch: 12 – 3 am. Drinking tea and snacking on granola bars to stay awake. Random dreams and hopes, no particular order:

Getting back to the prison asap; springing Ivan outta there (I know, just a rescue fantasy, because his country has got no prisoner transfer treaty with Thailand); getting financial support to do more prison work. Also wanting to make a doc about finding Sergei (perhaps another rescue fantasy). Writing some academic pieces and doing art to externalize silent grief I've been carrying around like invisible lead weights on my heart. I dream of having a safe space to call my own in trees where I can garden, grow sunflowers and offer a peaceful sanctuary for Morgan to come to whenever she wants to chill out and snuggle with her mama; having a studio space to facilitate physical, somatic, spiritual, playful, juicy, healing workshops. I crave more of that. Also skiing, kite-surfing, skydiving, Morocco...and more. I'd love to teach courses in Bangkwang – even social sciences. I am never satisfied to do just one thing – I want to have more non-specific adventures, that is, have unexpected opportunities and leap at them, as long as I get to learn and experience new things. A lifetime ago, when I would do safe, sane, consensual ethical sex-play explorations with other queer folk, the culminating event often included each of us getting a turn to choose a fantasy that the others would enact for them (after negotiating specific acts, do's, don't and safe words, of course). Someone would pick a fantasy of being a naughty school-girl, for example, being disciplined by teachers (I wouldn't have dropped out of highschool if I had a group of hot teachers who disciplined me like that...but I digress) or pick just a scene of a specific act – like spanking or a healing meditation, or whatever. When it came to my turn, I would always ask to not know what was going to happen to me – I prefer the excitement of the unknown. As long as the larger parameters have been negotiated before so there is psychological safety: Very exciting! I suspended that part of my life so that Morgan wouldn't get the backlash of people vilifying me for my sex-positive stance, but it makes no difference, she gets told daily that I'm a freak, so in some ways, I should have just continued my heart's work. Anyway, I don't want to just tick off a 'bucket list' – although I do have some specific 'bucket' items, like going to the World Music Festival on the sand dunes in the desert of Mali one January. More importantly, I want to explore the unknown, and I want to share experiences with someone who also wants to challenge themself and grow as a person and experience new adventures and be goofy and PLAY!

Since I'm making a wish-list, I'd like a sweet person who loves me for me and I love them and to revel in the simple moments together. I also crave a shoulder to lean on. In Bangkok last January, I paid a guy in my neighbourhood to let me lean on his shoulder for five minutes. He was a huge American dude who had done 22 years in prison in the States. He was sober and chatting with me in my usual Book Bar, about to head out for a night of Meth and hookers, he said. We had talked previously and he was a decent guy, just on an unfortunate track in life. It had been a particularly brutal and hard day at the prison for me, and I asked him if I could lean on his massive shoulder for 5 minutes and I'd pay him to just be there. He didn't have to do anything or say anything, just be a shoulder. He agreed (probably thinking I had an ulterior motive, but I didn't) and I leaned on him, and as soon as I felt my head rest on his shoulder, a floodgate opened and I sobbed for 5 minutes until a part of my brain told me I'd better rein myself in before he got too weirded out. I thanked him, and he declined the money and left quickly and avoided my neighbourhood after that. I guess a human moment is just too much to handle for some. Meth is safer.

I wonder about the parts of myself I've neglected for too long, shutting myself down to appear as 'safe' as I can for the past decade and a half for Morgan's sake, without totally compromising or selling out all of who I am. Or wondering how much I have sold myself out, my values, my politics that got so watered down, beaten down, really, so that I don't even blink anymore at the misogynist, homophobic crap all around me: wrote my thesis partly on that in 2000-2003. I fantasize about just leaving and hitch-hiking to San Francisco, and immersing myself in the queer/political/sex-gender play community (yes!), but grass is always greener on the other side. It's not a perfect community either. Far from it. I think about 'starting over' anywhere, everywhere. But I can't leave Morgan. I want to hike the West Coast Trail. I want to take the Siberian Express from Beijing to Moscow, then onward to Western Europe. I LOVE train travel – so sexy! I'm still super-into all things neuro-cognitive-psych, and I'd love to do a Law degree too. Oh right, I'm supposed to be done with academia. Well, if I win the lottery so I can actually afford to do a Phd. I'd do one – the hard part is picking which field. Everything's so interdisciplinary these days, that it hardly matters anymore (in the social sciences that is, not the hard sciences). I'd like to explore Eastern Europe: Turkey, Croatia and explore their little villages by the sea... ok. enough.

Do you like roller-coasters? I love them. One thing I never need to explore is space travel. No interest in outer space. What about you? If you could take a free trip on a space shuttle, would you? I wouldn't. Not even if you paid me.

I don't get sea-sick. I get exhilarated by movement, by storms, by wind, the raw primal energy. The guys are talking more and more each day about how hard it is to stay out on a ship for long and how people go squirrelly not being near land. I haven't experienced a twinge of that. I committed to the experience and I want its full flavour. I just started reading a novel: "Spanish Fly" by Will Ferguson – set in the US during the depression. Loving it unexpectedly and totally want to pass it on to you, if at all possible.

8pm—not sure what day. Another no fish day. 5, actually, all day. Steering went on the boat about 2 hours ago and we stopped the engine, pulled in the lines and have been attempting to fix the hydraulic pump that controls the pilot steering. Lots of swearing, kicking, more cursing, running around yelling for tools and spare parts that may or may not have been properly stowed on board. After two hours, it looks like we're getting somewhere. It crosses my mind that this whole trip may be a bust, but I appreciate whatever this experience will turn out to be. Life is cool that way. No idea what comes next, no matter what we plan or hope for. We're drifting, three days out from land, and Mak and George are running around like chickens with their heads cut off, but I figure I have weeks of food and I know where I'll be sleeping as long as I'm here, so I have nothing to worry about. Much simpler and more immediate, concrete out here, away from all the other busy life in the 'real' world. We'll see. Anger and frustration levels getting higher in the wheelhouse and engineering room, but I'm kind of floating on a cloud, thinking all this is just cool. Whatever happens, it's just life. Meant to be enjoyed.

Do you ever personally do any cooking in Bangkwang? Or are you perpetually the sandwich guy? Do you have a minister at your church? Or do you do bible study-type groups? Regular services?

11 pm. Wow, tensions are really high. The two replacement pumps on board didn't work either, and we are drifting, unable to steer. The rudder indicator is also gone, and, not responding to attempts to fix it

or replace it. Unbelievably, even though it's a totally unrelated issue, the connection to satellite which allows email and phone are gone, too. I have been working on that for a few hours, but nothing. A storm is on its way, we have no radio to call anyone (we do, but no one is within radio distance), no means of communication and George is swearing a blue streak. It's actually making me laugh how foul his mouth is. Lots of blaspheming that gives me all sorts of interesting mental images.

I'm kind of impressed how we humans with all our technology and savvy can be so easily stranded in the middle of nowhere, without warning, no land for hundreds of miles, no means of communication with any other people or ships at all, rudderless and unable to steer a ship. The waves are picking up, rain is pouring and we have no clue whether we are still in the path of a large storm that was forecast for tonight, as we have no access to weather reports, or even to call other ships way up the coast and see what's up, nor means to get the heck outta here. It's a bit humbling. Hmmm. Nature's way of reminding us that we are insignificant little specks in a vast ocean, literally. I have this laptop that is useless, except as a typewriter – if I ever make it to shore to print out this letter. There's not much else we can do tonight but ride it out until morning and see what comes next. I am strangely calm as these guys get increasingly loud and crass and stressed. It's amazing how racist George is getting as things keep going wrong. Shasso and I are cringing at some of the stuff coming out of his mouth – yikes. Highlight of this day has definitely been the fact that I was able to read an entire novel that I thoroughly enjoyed. What an amazing luxury, to have the time to read for pleasure, and to immerse myself in a parallel world and get lost in it – how decadent. I'm near finished, and I will put you down to dive into the last 30 pages. What a treat.

Well, good night my dear. Sleep well. I hope you are dreaming big dreams for your future. Big happy thoughts to a super guy! And a big hug! Hope your family is well, too. ☺

Morning, we sleep late until 5. George has got manual steering working and we put out the lines and steer towards Emilia Mount, a piece of ocean somewhere 100 miles south of here that is 500 feet less deep than the surrounding area, so it may be fertile Tuna grounds. Despite the expensive sonar equipment, I realized after the first day that finding tuna is more about intuition, gut feeling, luck and perseverance than science. Get out on the ocean, drive around, hope to bump into some fish. Also, the skipper is as superstitious as they come, ascribing the catching of each given fish to random spurious acts, like unplugging the coffee machine. So we occasionally get orders to switch all the lures or to unplug all sockets or to jump up and down flapping our arms, in the hopes that this will bring the masses of fish we need to fill the boat. Not superstitious myself, I nevertheless can't help but wonder at the death of the albatross, notorious holder of bad luck for fishers, on the very first day fishing. It has been mentioned a few times by the others. Mak prays to God for fish. Me, I ask the Universe. George curses. Shasso just eats.

Large waves are rocking and rolling the ship non-stop, and I stand on deck, marveling at the spectacular sight. It is breathtaking out here, and I am entranced. Manage to make breakfast and put on tunes and stand staring out to sea as our wee is ship tossed about. Nothing about the daily business of life feels important or real, mesmerized as I am by the immense power of this ocean. Heavy black clouds and bright sun make large shadows on the waves that are throwing us around continuously. I am electrified by the churning, crashing water as we pound into the surf, spray spilling over the bow. The raw energy sweeps the remaining cobwebs from my brain, electrifying me. A few grinning porpoises swim alongside us, darting and dancing in and out of the waves, then move on. This is pure magic.

Ninja cooking in the heavy swells, as everything flies around. Even as utensils and devices are strapped down with bungy cords, still the constant motion sends everything crashing into walls and cupboards. With oven pans full of hot food and cooking pots with scalding water sliding all over, it gets a little dicey. Sharp knife and me get thrown from our chopping station clear across the room. I have black and purple bruises all over my hips, shoulders, arms and legs from days of continually bouncing off walls, tables, doorways, and more. Cooking becomes as much of an art of survival as of culinary skills.

Day 10: Still no pilot steering, and no fish. At least the rudder is back on and we can manually steer – old school style. Not great. George starts to make mutterings of heading back to shore if we don't find fish soon. It will be what it will be. Mak and Shass are mumbling lots about it too. Worries creep in about this just being a two-week experiment that leaves me in the same place when I get back. Broke, unemployed.

What's the point in thinking this? I am here, living this, right now. Stay positive. Come on Fish!

Read another book: "Left Neglected" by a neurologist – about a woman who has a car accident, brain damage that makes her lose the left side of her field of vision and perspective. Even though her body and vision works, she is unaware conceptually of having a left side to anything. Interesting medical condition, and usually I like reading that neurological stuff – like anything by Oliver Sacks, M.D. This book, however, is a novel, and was written too much like a cheesy Harlequin. All is great at the end as she is forced to stop working and spend more time reconnecting with her kids. She and her husband leave their high-paying corporate jobs with excellent severance packages, sell their million-dollar Boston house and move into their summer Vermont home to live a 'simpler' life and they all appreciate the real meaning of happiness now that they've traded their Blackberries and business suits for small-town life. Oh right, and her illness allows her to mend her estranged relationship with her mother before she dies. Yikes.

Lots of hours waiting for fish means getting more creative in the kitchen. Shass and I are alternating cooking days, and we're baking our own bread now too. Might as well. I am a pretty good cook, but I can't bake bread to save my life, so my attempt at a Rosemary French Loaf comes out a dense football. Shasso impresses me – making decent hamburger buns and great loaves of bread from scratch, even though he's never baked before. Me, I make a mean blackberry pie. Maybe one day, if you are ever on the West Coast for a visit in August, I'll pick Salt Spring blackberries and whip up a pie for you. I'm glad that George is persevering, still heading south, even without proper equipment – I don't want to give up. We all want to work our asses off and make money. We just need to find fish.

I am getting perspective again. I am the luckiest person in the whole world. I sit, reading on the stern while the skipper curses our lack of fish and constant breakdowns. We hope to dodge the massive storm that lurks... somewhere near – if only the satellite weather gear were working and we could pinpoint its location. Alone in the wheelhouse an hour ago, steering erratically as George ate his burger below, I used the time to make a call to Morgan on the occasionally working satellite phone. She was in Vancouver, having sushi with my sister, and her voice perked up when she heard me. I heard the unconditional love in her voice and total faith in me as she peppered me with questions: Am I having fun? Am I loving the adventure of it? And how she misses me. My heart squeezed realizing how lucky I am to be blessed with the greatest gift of this wonderful relationship. What the hell have I been complaining about? I am the luckiest person in the world. I look up from my book and take in the scene and inhale deeply: the evening sun makes the waves shimmer luminescent and I am totally happy.

I am grateful, so grateful to have met you, James, and I wish only the most wonderful things for you each day, each moment. Big smiles. Big hugs.

Sitting for hours, staring off the stern, mesmerized by the huge surging waves. I am looking West, across the ocean towards you. Arms outstretched, I look out to the horizon, and I know you're just over the bend of the earth away. I yell Hello! from me, 500 miles off the Northern California Coast, sending out love to you rippling across the Pacific, into the Gulf of Thailand, up the Chayo Praya, hop off at Nonthaburi and over the wall into Building 4. I hope this finds you smiling and doing something you enjoy! You are wonderful!

Another day, staring out to sea. No fish. Shasso's just called me in for lunch and I munch my grilled cheese sandwich. A warm break from standing staring out as the incredible surf and whipping wind pounds and tosses us about. Rather than feel tiny and insignificant in the face of this ceaseless energy flow, the raw elemental power of this vast ocean instead makes me feel alive, re-connected to the incredible force of all life. An albatross comes out of nowhere and starts following the boat, greedily eyeing our bobbing lures that look like little pink and orange squids. I watch him swoop and dive, then run clumsily across the waves, little feet slapping awkwardly on the water before taking flight again. As he swoops again towards his prey, I plead: "hey buddy, please don't do it – we already killed your cousin and I don't want you to die, too." 500 miles from the closest shore, I wonder at this solitary bird. Where did he come from? Where does he sleep at night? On the waves, just bobbing? Or does he make it across to San Francisco each evening? I know nothing about birds and their habits.

Water leaking on my bed all night, keeping me awake, cold and wet. Got up at 5 grumpy and creaky in the bones, bruised all over. Wind stronger and waves even higher today and still no fish. Cleaned up maple syrup that spilled all over the galley during the night then headed out on deck. Pretty scary out here – one wrong move or jerk from a fish or rope that gets loose and you're out to sea or head smashed in. It's crazy. Nature just does her powerful thing and we need to get out of her way, or just hang on for the ride. I hope each day that I'll be too busy with fish to get moments to write you, but not so far. This may end up being the world's longest letter. Sorry that it's so boring, it helps me pass the time, and I hope it will help to pass yours. ☺

I just spent two hours 'cooking' two breakfasts: sliding precariously, dropping plates that shatter into a million shards of glass on the already greasy floor. Plunging into sides of cupboards, trying to fry an egg on a hot cast iron pan that zigs and zags two feet in all directions, while trying to keep my grip, attempting to shuffle safely from fridge to counter to toaster to stove, but being picked up and thrown willy-nilly. The waves are larger than I've ever seen in my life, crashing over the bow repeatedly. This is the first time I've felt scared on this trip. My fatigued body from the shitty night just doesn't have the same strength to keep up with the constant onslaught, and my mental strength feels lower too. I whimper each time my bruised hip bone slams another corner, or shoulder hits a wall. I'm too exhausted to make Shass and I breakfast after finally getting the other two fed, so I slump here momentarily and try to conjure up all the metaphors of oceans or fishing allegories that I've encountered. The sea as abundant provider and merciless foe. This constant stormy weather is definitely knocking us about physically and emotionally. But nature's storm is different than human life – here, I can face the constant onslaught and understand that it's just reality – no need to take it personally: you win some, you lose some, maybe I'll die today and maybe I'll live to a ripe old age, there's no telling. Nature is powerful.

The world of humans is nastier. When life batters me about in the world of cities and jobs and society, that is people choosing to act in ways that are hurtful, violent, self-centred. We could choose to organize our social worlds vastly differently, to value more humane, just ways, with compassion and care for all, but we don't. That feels infinitely harder. Incomprehensible. Enraging. Please don't say: that's Human Nature. We are all capable of better. Sure, base instincts that tend towards stereotyping and selfishness, but we also have higher moral and rational reasoning that can override them. We could all choose to offer kindness instead of judgment. I know I could do better, to replace sore spots with generosity and dignity. Instead we rape, pillage and murder and poison and fuck over, all for greed and power. We buy and sell things that don't exist, manufacture markets based on image rather than real need, engage in massive games of doublespeak to obscure the inequities that we willingly participate in, allowing a few men to get extremely rich at a huge cost to most of the rest of world's population and resources. And we pit ourselves against each other, everyone trying to get what they can out of it and fuck over the next guy, rather than work for systemic change or for a more just distribution of wealth for everyone. What about kindness, compassion and love? Can we not do better than this? Sorry, I'll get off my soap-box. I dunno James, what say you? Am I hopelessly naïve and idealistic? Am I doomed because I don't want to play those games?

My dreams have been very vivid, working through lots of stuff. A couple of nights ago, I looked up on Facebook (in my dream) an ex-boy-friend from when I was 14 – 15. He was a sociopath, arsoning our house, raping and beating me, but the non-stop psychological torture was the worst. His profile picture showed him middle-aged and smiling, contented. I see him one evening and, fearful of what it will bring up, I get the courage to approach and talk to him and he is friendly, calm. As I listen to him, I wonder: where is all my anger and resentment at him for what he put me through? Where is his remorse or acknowledgement of my pain? Of his brutality? He is oblivious as he tells me of his personal journey over the past 25 years and how good he feels. I want to ask about his sister that he was raping from the age of 11. How did she turn out? How is her life? I look around and she sits there, smiling, holding out her newborn daughter Ingrid to show me and says: "I'm fine, I'm great." How is this possible? I wonder. In my dream, I realize that nothing he did to me – subjecting me to constant terror and violence – was personal. It wasn't about me. He wasn't trying to destroy my power, or me. Doesn't mean it didn't do me considerable damage, but his shit was his own shit. He has no knowledge of the years I spent after escaping him, plagued by nightmares and anxiety, terrified he'd find me and kill me, nor of the emotional damage I've had to work through over years – and still I have a very hard time letting people get close to me. And what about what his sister has had to work through? I want to scream it at him, but then, the feeling passes. That's my shit to carry or release, not his. I have no anger left towards him, I realize. I wake up feeling odd.

Drawers full of tools that are supposed to be secured are repeatedly banging open and shut, sending metal bolts and bits everywhere – strapped down appliances and doors are jumping, pulling against their restraints. Ten minutes of sitting and drinking tea on the bench has rejuvenated me a wee bit. I have no clue how someone who gets nauseous and dizzy on top of all of this could handle it. I hear stories of seasick deckhands who have to get tied to the boat, because they want to throw themselves off, rather than endure the rough weather. An oil spill on deck sends Shass and Mak to clean it, but they can't hold on. Our fishing lines tangle in this weather with regularity and we have to untangle them as quickly as possible, while bracing ourselves against being swept overboard. We keep an eye on each other constantly, as it takes just a millisecond for someone to be overpowered and to disappear into the waves. No one is allowed on deck at night alone, for safety reasons. At night we have to wake someone else up if, for any reason we have to go out on deck. Now I gotta secure this computer as water sprays into the galley. I have a drawer that will hopefully not break or smash open. Bye for now, my friend.

I'm back. I pulled off with great effort and frustration a roast chicken stuffed and surrounded by my special rice (garlic, parmesan, herbs, grated zucchini, onion and carrot) all baking in the oven, with tin cans and stainless steel bowls wedged all over to keep the tray from sliding inside the oven. George is screaming at me that he's starving and doesn't want to wait another hour for dinner. The other two are way more realistic – we three make it a point to be appreciative of all the work each of us puts in, and that we're all doing the best we can. George slams his coffee mug and starts beaking at me again that I'm useless with the oven and why can't I just microwave food, like normal people? He shakes his head and bangs around the galley slamming and cursing. I just let it wash over me. George's initial jovial demeanour on this trip has been replaced with non-stop verbal abuse – litanies, rants, sexist and racist vulgarities.

I never dream of owning a bunch of gadgets, cars, material things, but occasionally I indulge in imagining winning the lottery, and there are so many more things I would want to do – be a philanthropist and create: low-income housing community spaces for single moms; micro-loans for Burmese women; support a million other really cool social justicy, humanitarian or artsy projects get off the ground; travel a whole bunch and try new things; take all sorts of cool courses; play play play, and have wee homes for Morgan and I in several places (like Salt Spring or Strasbourg or Italy) and have a studio space to do art with all the woodworking and metalworking tools I'd want. I'd raid the local dump and create art in my space and have dinner parties and cook for friends. Oh right, I gotta first make friends. ☺ I'd still love to teach my workshops and hang out in prisons; give money away to transform as many people's lives as possible, starting with immediate family and expanding outwards, Burmese friends in Bangkok and on the border... ahhh...day-dreaming on the ocean. Life is beautiful and I am open to abundance – I must practice that, instead of the scraping by and surviving mantra. Yay Beautiful Life! Cool how a $2 lottery ticket can buy days of dreaming.

Do you like reading aloud? Or being read to? I think I asked you that, but I don't remember the answer. I love it... even as an adult, there is a wonderful pleasure in reading a book aloud to/with someone. Morgan and I try to do that still, but it's much harder now that she's grown up and we don't live together. I look forward to teaching Latin, French, science and formal logic to my grandkids, to playing playing playing imagination games, puzzles, drawing, running, skipping. If I'd won the lottery years ago, I would have had five kids. It's truly the space that I inhabit the best – the magical, intuitive world of kids. I am an awesome mom. My biggest regret is that I didn't raise more children. But I am extremely lucky that Morgan happens to be the most wonderful person on the planet. Lucky me!

Day? Week?: Endless days and nights of stormy weather. Chilled to the bone, constantly bouncing in the stormy wind and waves. Tensions high – George yelling at me non-stop last night, taking his stress out on me and I, in turn, bring it out to the stern and throw my stress to the wind to carry up and away. *Don't cry, Heath, it's just fishing.* It's hard to believe it's July. I stand for hours at a time on deck, shivering, bracing myself against the bitterly cold wind chafing my face and the icy spray soaking me. Oil slicks on deck are treacherous, and we three lash ourselves to the deck in the gale to retie the oil barrels and scrub the deck with laundry detergent, in order to stop the homicidal slickness. More and more parts of the boat are falling apart – we wake up this morning to a heavy wooden door ripped off its hinges, flying around the deck, a lethal projectile. Occasionally, I see a flash of fear in either Shasso or Mak's face, and I wonder: "Why are we out here? Oh, right, the paycheque full of zeros from non-existent Tuna." I have to laugh at life. It's pretty crazy. I watch Shasso tumble on deck and just miss going over as the boat flips dangerously close to horizontal at the next huge wave. It would be madness to try to explain to our daughters, Shasso and I, why we risked life and limb to be out here just to make a living. Mak is angry that George's pride keeps him going out further: "This boat is not equipped for this weather," he tells me, "already it rolled once, last year, and the crew was lucky to survive. Normally," he says, "we dock every time the weather is bad like this." Oh great, I didn't want to know this. I was happy to be blissfully ignorant and to assume that even though it felt very precarious, I felt assured that the captain knew the capacities of the boat and was navigating within them. Oh well, nothing I can do to change this. Just enjoy the experience and hope for better weather and an abundance of fish. And keep smiling, as a wise man once told me. ☺

What do you grow in your garden? How do you get seeds? What do you like to plant, if anything? Bruce, the American guy I met in the spring I told you about in Bangkok that I had a few dates with then told me he had a Thai girlfriend keeps emailing me and wanting me to get together with him when I get back to BKK. Too bad, I really liked hanging with him, it was easy and good being with him, and major sexual energy and laughs between us, but I'm not into dishonesty. Nobody wants to be the person at home while your partner says: "I'm late at work, honey," while they're actually out fucking other people. I value honesty above all. Why is it so hard for some people to be honest? Why can't he just say to his girlfriend: "I want to be with other people." Or: "I met someone I'm really into and I need to explore this." Or be faithful, gee, what a concept. I hate deception.

Segue: This spring there was a guy who I approached in the bar to ask the time one night as I took a break from dancing. He responded by quietly saying: "you don't know how badly I NEED to make love to you." Not aggressively, just quiet intensity. He didn't seem drunk or on drugs, just leaning against the wall and looking at the floor. Surprised, I said: "How 'bout we have a conversation first?" He said: "You don't understand, I've been watching you for <u>years</u> – I loved when you had your blue Mohawk and then your pink hair. I've been waiting for that French guy to be out of the picture. I need you." It was a little overwhelming. I'd never talked to the guy before, only vaguely remember seeing him once every few years around the island, sitting alone at a coffee shop or in the background at an event, and now that he mentioned it, he <u>was</u> always watching me. I said that sex was not in the cards that night, but I'd be into having a cup of tea one day and having a conversation, if he wanted. I gave him my number and left. He didn't call. I didn't get weird stalker vibe from him, but a very shy vibe, so I wasn't too surprised. After all, he'd never said HI in the <u>years</u> he'd supposedly been watching me. I told Morgan, she figured that in the cold light of day he couldn't call, lacking liquid courage of the night before. Or maybe he had no interest in conversation. I bumped into him a week later in town and he invited me to his place that evening, after a jam session with his friends. He's a musician, and we have similar taste in music. I brought over an industrial-sized bottle of wine and we spent a nice night talking, laughing, listening to music, dancing naked, and fun sex. Nice guy, surprised how decent and emotionally open he was to talk to. We had a lovely time. I left him sleeping early the next morning and rushed back to work at the organic farm where I'd gotten a few days of farming work. Didn't hear from him again. Didn't call me. I thought: *Seriously, dude? You don't even have the decency to make a two-minute phone call? 46 years old and you can't do the minimum day-after respectful thing?* It just takes one quick call, an acknowledgement, a "Thanks for the evening together." Nope. That felt pretty gross. Days went by, then weeks. I was initially surprised, then angry at myself for putting myself in a situation where I could be treated like that, then got over it and didn't give a shit anymore. Morgan started referring to him as 'the douche-bag,' when I told her that he never bothered to call me after our night together just to acknowledge it. She had been all excited about my date, and I told her we had a surprisingly nice time. Months later, the day before leaving on this fishing trip was the Canada Day Celebration of Life for my dead friend, John. The whole island showed up and told stories and it turned into a huge party, people mingling and drinking. Being Salt Spring, there was a huge cloud of pot smoke covering the southern part of the island, blocking out the sun.

I hitchhike down there, and as I am being dropped off at the event, there's douche-bag walking towards me. First time I've seen him in the 10 weeks since our date. He instantly says: "Uh, I was going to call you but I just figured we'd see each other in town, and then we didn't...and, uh, your cell is long distance and I don't have a long distance plan...and, uh...a million other excuses," he finishes lamely. I almost burst out laughing. Pathetic. "No worries," I say, smiling, "It felt pretty cheap and shitty at the time, but that passed. If you had called, I would have said Thank You for the lovely evening, and that I had a nice time with you." I wave a friendly goodbye and walk away. "Me too, he starts to say, can we..." "No," I say as I keep walking. I'm not a piece of ass in a can to take out of the sock drawer when he feels like it and put away when he's done. I'm human.

Getting emails from the rest of the fleet way up the coast, we learn that the west side of the continent is in this crappy weather and no one is catching fish. We might as well take advantage of the bad weather to get the steering pilot fixed, and hope that when the weather clears, the fish will be abundant. Sounds like just as good a plan as any. So we're heading up towards Victoria, to get to shore and get the many, many broken parts fixed. We're four days away, even if we run 24 hours/24. Mak lies in his bunk constantly now, as he has developed radiating pain down the entire right side of his body. I bring him pain-killers and we make a plan to take him to the hospital as soon as we get in. I call Morgan, tell her we're ok. This whole trip is going totally sideways and I just have to go with it. Wow, crazy.

We run through the night steering in this stormy weather by hand. I do my 3-hour shift and marvel at how cool it is to navigate a ship in a storm by myself, using old-school compass and wheel, directly into waves way taller than us. The rest of the crew sleeps, as I keep an eye on the horizon and radar for ships, while getting bumped and smashed around like a rag doll in the wheelhouse. I'm learning lots. Then an alarm goes off: the engine cooling system has blown. I wake George to watch the wheel and keep us on course and brave the outer treacherous deck in the pitch black. I pull myself along the 10 feet to the entrance of the engine room, ocean spray hitting me full in the face, soaking me and my clothes. I grease the shafts, a one-minute job, then head down the ladder, smashing my head on one of the iron rungs into a swelteringly hot room full of metal machinery, grinding and hissing and screeching loudly. Turn on cold tap water faucet to refill the cooling system. I hope that now's not my time to go, that I won't be pulverized by this engine suddenly exploding, blowing me and everything else into tiny pieces of fish food. Back along the slick deck in blowing wind, gripping whatever I can to steady myself, to the wheelhouse where I send George, groggy and half-blind, wearing just underwear and no eyeglasses, back to his bunk. Every two hours we repeat this ritual through the night. As our water-maker is also dead (the first thing on this piece of shit boat to die), we will run out of fresh water to refill the engine before we get to Victoria, so George decides this morning to try to fix the leak in the engine cooling system, which entails shutting it off, and waiting for hours for it to cool sufficiently to work on it. As we wait, we drift further back in the strong currents, and now, although we all need money badly, we have all but forgotten fish and are focused on just making it to Victoria to re-group and fix the boat, hopefully within three or so days.

As I write this, I hear George cursing from below, and Shass emerges, shaking his head, a weird grimace on his face. Mak has dropped all his wrenches into the bilge, (might have something to do with the fact that the right side of his body isn't working) and George snapped the bolt off the piece he was trying to replace. I don't even want to know. This is madness. Can only laugh and be grateful that we are all still well (ish). Hours later still, thrown about on open ocean, nothing is working, and they've resorted to a bubble-gum solution. Mak and I mix up some grey tar-like gunk and they slap it on a bunch of parts, hoping that will seal things sufficiently for us to limp up to BC. We can't head straight to land from here, as the Americans will blow us out of the water and ask questions later. Or at least stick us in Guantanamo Bay and I don't think I'd do so well with water-boarding. I'd confess to being part of Al-Qaeda in the first two minutes. Although... the warmth of Cuba does sound appealing right now.

The new plan, if we ever make it to Vic is to re-group, fix the boat, then head out for two to three more months of fishing. George asks if

I'm willing to stay on. I say yes. Shasso is not so sure. He is miserable and stressed that we will have wasted three weeks with no pay by the time we're ready to set out again. (We only get a % of fish money, nothing else). I'm not thrilled either, but I'm committed to the season, to really give this a go, not just give up because the first trip is turning out to be a bust. Shasso is loathe to head back to Salt Spring with no money, and to try to rustle up work there, with bills piling up. He quit his plumbing job to come out here. But his kid is much younger than mine, and he doesn't want to be away longer, understandably. So he'll make the decision if and when we get to Vic and get the boat fixed. George tells me that normally there's not this many problems, and that he's never met anyone who took to the ocean and to the work as quickly as me, and he'd be thrilled to keep me on. I am pleased about that. This next run, he says, is his last run and then he'll pass the boat off to a new captain, Cyrus. Although he loves fishing, he's tired of all the other shit that goes with it: boats that break down and don't have the spare parts they're supposed to; politics and bickering between owners and captains; being micro-managed by the wife of the owner who doesn't know shit about our situation but is demanding updates every day by email, etc. Also, George's wife died two years ago, and he says he regrets not having retired earlier to enjoy life with her, rather than always working. He has a new girlfriend and they're gonna do a motorcycle trip around North America. I will be sorry not to work with him. I hope the next captain is as cool. I've heard horror stories from Shasso and Mak about captains that hit them (!) and scream so much they have them crying. Great.

Shit, we're rocking dangerously. I gotta go. This is total insanity.

More yelling and running back and forth. The seemingly infinite seascape of massive ocean swells are just the backdrop to an immediate crisis of a boat that doesn't work or run. 300 miles off the Oregon Coast. Oh well. That's what the Coast Guard is for, right?

My bones and muscles and joints are achy in the cold and wet, and nerves are frayed, but Shass and I still muster up goofy banter, each trying to make the other laugh. Things could be a lot worse. Really, in the grand scheme of things, this is no big deal. An adventure. It's just so frustrating that lack of money, worries about money, the fear of how to support families, pay bills, ultimately underpins all of our stress out here. If not for that, none of this would really matter. So I must choose not to think of that.

Middle-ish of July. Middle of fucking nowhere. Bubble-gum fix finally on, but the engine won't restart. This has become a surreal comedy of errors. I mention that to George but he scowls at me. After an hour of trying, I get through briefly on the satellite phone to my mom and talk to my sister about our latest strategy to figure out living and care options for trying to give my mom the best quality of life and support possible in her dementia, without running ourselves into the ground in the process. My dad's just left for France with his girlfriend for a few months and we haven't yet told him about the legal document, that is, that my mom gave me power of attorney. ARGH! My mom asks me how it's going. I say: "I thought I signed up for the trip with dolphins, dancing girls, afternoon siestas on a sunny deck, and lots of money, not the tour with the broken ship and retarded crew!" She laughs. My heart breaks for her. No choice but to see where the waves carry us next.

Down in the deep freeze this morning, standing on the frozen bodies of our 350 or so fish, I'm scrubbing ice build-up off the fans and plates and my hands are burning from the cold, even through heavy-duty gloves. The cold is so intense, so penetrating, so heavy, it squeezes the breath out of me. I'm hoping I won't have a heart attack and die alone enclosed in the dark cold dungeon and I've exacted a promise from Shasso that he'll open the hatch and check on me in five minutes.

"Ten," he says.

"No, Five!" I insist.

He laughs at my panic. My cheeks feel like dozens of razor blades are slicing them and I force my frozen fingers to run the brush across the metal plates on the ceiling and walls of the dark rooms, coating me in an inch of frost. I hurry the job and get out. We have a running joke about the fact that Shasso told me only to pack t-shirts, as we would be hot while fishing – thankfully, the owner insisted we buy sweaters and hoodies and fleece jackets or we'd have frozen to death. Our clothes and bodies reek from weeks of not washing. I gave up washing clothes in the recent stormy weather. George wears his nasty clothes for a week at a time, then tosses them overboard and puts on new ones. Mak does the same, while Shasso and I don't have extra sets, so clothes just get grimier until we can scrub them again in seawater. Our personal hygiene is good compared to the other two, though, who smell perpetually of dirty ass-crack and wet dog. The foc'sle, the small windowless area where we sleep is like bunking in a hot, sour cum sock. Hot shower and clean laundry are sounding pretty luxurious right now.

I have to admit I have been astounded by the immensity of the ocean – I assumed that we'd see traffic out here: maybe distant freighters coming from Japan and China, the odd cruise ship, as well as other fishing boats. Nope. Not one sign of a human in over two weeks. I also wondered about the huge island of debris from Japan's tsunami that has floated across the Pacific. Already since January, household items from Japan have been washing up on the beaches of BC, further North, and there's a diplomatic conversation happening about who is responsible for the cleanup of an entire Japanese town of debris landing on BC's shores. I was kinda hoping to see bits of houses and things go by but so far, we've seen nothing human-made. Last night during my 12 – 3 am watch, I saw the first vessel. It was a freighter, rapidly bearing down on us and I woke George who stayed up watching the radar for over an hour, monitoring the distress radio in case the captain tried to contact us. George warned me to steer as closely as possible to our course without bouncing around (an impossible feat when steering manually by compass and flashlight), so as not to confuse the other captain. Finally, the other ship veered slightly and passed us on our starboard side, and George went back to bed.

The alarm jolts me from sitting here writing. Our bubble-gum band-aid didn't last 24 hours. The engine cooling system is leaking again. I carefully pull in the fishing gear and secure it and Mak jumps up from his bunk where he's been lying, nursing his sore body. We shut down the engine again and drift back, waiting to try slap on another bubble-gum fix in a few hours when the engine is cool enough. The anaemic sun peeks through the cold grey mist. I think I'll wash some clothes on deck with the ocean water hose and hope they dry. We have had no fresh water for days, as we have to save it to keep cooling the engine. Hee hee! I am smiling, James!

We are getting excited about getting close to shore – maybe only 48 hours away now. I slept a blissful seven hours uninterrupted last night and feel like a new woman. I am grinning from ear to ear, loving this crazy adventure. Today, we are scrubbing the deck and doing as many minor repairs as possible to be as efficient when we get to Victoria – we called the hydraulic guys, the engine guys and others, and have them lined up to start work as soon as we dock. We are hoping for a four-day turn-around, and we'll have washed every possible piece of laundry and bleached every corner of this ship before we head out again. As well as a trip to the thrift store for another baseball cap and pair of pants for me (both lost overboard in the stormy weather), more books and more groceries.

Last night I got triggered as George sat watching a horror movie and the loud sounds of the screams penetrated the whole boat. I can't stand depictions of violence, especially sexual violence against women, which seem to saturate all horror movies. I can't do most crime shows or movies anymore, for the same reason, even though I like mysteries. Most movies and tv shows just love to depict dead, raped or brutalized half-naked women and I just don't need to see that shit. It's unnecessary, disturbing and I don't want to see it. I am enraged by the routine depiction of women as not fully human, but as male characters' pretty appendages to be dismissed, used, discarded, beaten, raped, fucked.

I snapped at Mak yesterday, when he rushed over, as per usual, to take over something I was doing. He regularly physically pushes me aside, grabs stuff out of my hands and shakes his head at me. I hate being treated as incompetent or ignorant. But he clearly assumes women are. He keeps trying to make me stay in the kitchen: to be the domestic girl while he and Shasso take care of the important boy work, and it is infuriating. When I was replacing the brackets on a door, he shooed me back to the galley and said: "You clean kitchen, I work outside." I see Shasso getting frustrated at me sometimes wondering during emergencies why I'm not out there in the dark and cold and wet helping to fix stuff with him and Mak and George, but he doesn't realize I've been ordered back in by Mak who thinks I should stick to the galley, the woman's domain. ARGH! I'll get over it, but it is frustrating.

I will keep smiling, easier now that I'm not totally sleep-deprived. Highlight of today: heating a big pot of sea water on the stove, stripping down naked on the chilly morning deck in the misty cold wind, scrubbing my hair with shampoo, then dumping the pot of hot water all over me, grabbing my towel and running inside before I could catch a chill. Felt AMAZING!

Well, six hours away now. We head down the last channel, the Olympic Mountains of WA state to our right, and Vancouver Island to our left. Grey whales are breaching beside us and ahead, a pod of Orcas show us their tails, welcoming us home. Pleasure boats, fishing vessels and sailboats everywhere. Land looks so peaceful, rocky shoreline and blue-green silhouettes of mountains. No indication of the insanely busy lives running around just beyond the trees. Mak is out on deck, shaving his three weeks' growth and cleaning up for the ladies who will greet us with various propositions at the dock. I thought the whole 'girl in every port' thing was ancient, but apparently, there is a contingent of wharf rats who greet every boat as we dock: an old woman who we will give our empty water bottles to so she can collect the deposit; old guys who will ask us for free fish, and plenty of women who want to 'do' a sailor. I wonder if I count as a 'sailor'? Just kidding. Sounds creepy to me. The last one to proposition Mak before we left was 15 and carried a huge white python with her as she dropped her pants right on the deck and lunged at Mak, according to him. He says he just about killed the snake before sending her scurrying back to her family's boat. Yikes!

If you get this letter, I have made it safely to shore. I hope it finds you well. I won't write after that, as you will hopefully be homeward bound and I will be God knows where, maybe drifting on the high seas. Maybe ringing through purchases at a WalMart in Saskatoon, or picking grapes in Chile, or teaching at an International School in Istanbul or running with the bulls in Spain. Or facilitating playback theatre in prisons or documenting sexual assault cases in Mae Sot or climbing Machu Picchu with a buddy. One never knows. Or maybe I'll have won the lottery and I'll be travelling the world as a roaming philanthropist. Maybe we could meet at Lake Toba in Indonesia for a warm swim in a volcanic lake? What say you? What do you dream of doing? Hopefully, I'll be bringing support to guys in Bangkwang and collecting a real salary for it, kite-surfing and buying a wee home surrounded by trees, where you would always be welcome.

I am happy to be your favourite Canadian, even if you only know one ;). You are my very, very, very favourite American, by far! In your May 5 letter, you wrote that you didn't know what my 'expectations' were about us hanging out. I want to clarify: I love getting letters from you, and my friendship is freely offered with no obligations or expectations. If we see each other again one day and get to hang out, I'd be thrilled! But if you're not into writing anymore or continuing our conversations, then so be it. I would love for you let me know how you are and what you're up to, and if you're safe and well, but I hope you don't feel like you are expected to respond to me if you don't want to.

If I don't see you again, James, just know that I think you are a tremendously lovely person and I'm super grateful for the short while we got to hang. I will always send you big happy thoughts wherever you are in the world and hope that you are filling your soul and heart with all good things and living your dreams to the fullest. Know wherever you are that there is a crazy Canadian who thinks you're awesome and has a huge hug for you.

Big fat love to you, smiley friend, from the luckiest woman on the planet, out on the sparkly Pacific Ocean!

xo Heather.

I MAILED THIS LETTER TO BANGKWANG AND THEN GOT WORD YOU'D BEEN MOVED TO KHAO BIN PRISON! I HOPE THIS LETTER FINDS YOU SAFE AND WELL. I WORRY ABOUT YOU. I SEND YOU POSITIVE THOUGHTS!

FISHING II

SEPTEMBER 16, 2012

James!

I am in Winter Harbour, BC, a tiny sliver of a former village, population 7. It consists of a tiny Post Office, a general/liquor store and a couple of dilapidated shacks that sport fishers use in the summer, as well as abandoned buildings rotting into the sea, evidence of this town's former glory in the 70's and 80's as a bustling Fishery and Cannery town. We are 50 35 N, 128 01 W, in one of the hundreds of gorgeous inlets on the West Coast of Vancouver Island, hiding for a day or two from bad weather. We just arrived this morning, tied up to the dock along side 25 other commercial fishing vessels that are also hiding from the bad weather out there. As soon as we finished tying up, I grabbed my laptop and bought 48 hours' of wifi from the general store for $25 (high seas robbery!). I got on internet for the first time in a few weeks and downloaded your letter from Kao Bin via Yvonne. I am so so so so so so happy to hear from you! THANK YOU for writing!

I have a very short time here, then I'm out to sea again and so am frantically writing a few responses and will send this big letter tomorrow to Yvonne, in the hopes she can forward this to you. I'll include a few photos taken on the boat, but don't know if those will make it. I will respond to a bit of what you wrote in your letter, and send you more of my fishing journal to fill you in on what has happened since I last wrote. I'm glad you want me to write, I love hearing from you too, and would like to stay in touch.

I am very loyal, too, like a dog, as well as highly independent, like a cat. I am also highly sensitive to rejection and absolutely do not want to insert myself into any situation or any person's life who does not want me there, so I tend to err on the side of backing off in case someone doesn't actually want to engage with me. Thanks for letting me know you want to.

First, let's back up. Here is the second installment of non-fishing journal I kept.

On shore in Victoria, I mail my fishing letter to James and a birthday card to Ivan. Hours before we're to leave port, I learn via Facebook that James has been transferred to Kao Bin as the authorities discovered his Youtube video. I am sick with worry and email the American Embassy, asking them to pass on my positive thoughts and wishes to him, should they visit him. I send Yvonne a copy of my letter and ask her to mail it to his new prison. No idea if he'll get it or how he's doing. I am so worried for James.

My cell phone rings. It's [my ex-] David. I am hours from leaving port, and he is at YVR, flying home to France. He asks me casually how I am. The liar manipulator addict at his suave best. It's clear he's not sober: he is only preoccupied by his own shit. I am overwhelmed by learning about James's situation and start crying from all the stress that slams me full force when I hear David's voice. I can't believe this guy is still fucking contacting me, pretending I'm his wife, that all is 'normal' two full years after I left him. He is in an alcohol-fuelled psychotic other dimension. He has no clue I've been out fishing, as I severed all contact with him and have deleted all emails as soon as I got back from France and realized he was off the wagon...again. Done with the yo-yo of his fucked up addictions, I no longer even want to have a 'friendly' conversation if ever he becomes sober again. This man needs to have zero contact with my life. I am babbling in French so that the guys around me don't understand what I'm saying: I scream at him that he has destroyed everything in me and to FUCK OFF. I hang up. I wish just once he could know all the pain he's caused for all the damage he's done. But he never will. Mak is staring at me, wide-eyed – having never seen me hysterical in a second language, to boot. I ask Mak to pray for James. He says he will.

Today was our first day of fishing. We left last night and went through the night (me steering the 3 – 5 am shift), much easier to do now that we've got our pilot steering fixed and all we have to do is watch out for things in front of us and steer around them by pressing a button.

Today we caught a total of 50 fish, all of them after 4 pm. Before that, we were pretty down, trying not to think of another three-week trip with no fish. I was proud of myself for catching the most fish and not losing a single one, but my technique still needs great improvement: I need to be faster at getting the hook out of its mouth, the line untangled and back in the water, and on to the next fish within a split second. I'm still not there yet. I slowed down today to concentrate on improving my technique, as I'm still slipping at the last minute when the fish is against the boat – but at least I'm not losing them now. As I'm pulling one fish towards me hand over hand the skipper, George, comes running out of the wheelhouse and starts screaming in my ear: "Faster, faster, pull you gotta get it faster!" Starts shouting at me everything I'm doing wrong. Everyone's watching me and I'm struggling for eons (mere seconds) to get this fish where he should be without tangling the line in his twitching body. Can't lose my knife as the Tuna flaps violently, splattering blood everywhere. George barks about my incompetence, about how much faster I'm going to need to be when there's lots and lots of fish. I snap: "How about you get us to where there's actually lots of fish and then I'll listen to your theories of fishing?" OOPS. Not cool to criticize the skipper, even if I can't bear his constant berating. He storms off and later, when I go for my five-minute break to gobble down the dinner Shass made, I go up to the wheelhouse and apologize for having been snarky. He says it's all cool.

A blue shark breaks off one of my jigs and the wooden bird that makes the jig bob in the water. The wooden devices that keep the lines trailing on the surface all have different names, depending on the shape: 'mouse,' 'bird,' 'boat' and 'dildo'. The 'dildo' is definitely not something I'd put anywhere inside me. I wonder who named it? There were three or four sharks around the boat today. Gotta be up in five hours to load our fish in the deep-freeze.

Highlight of today: Humpback whale running along side us. Shass grabs his camera and we watch the whale show us her tail and fin as she runs gracefully along side us for about ten minutes. Suddenly leaps straight out of the water not twenty feet from where we stand on deck. She twists her massive body gracefully in mid-air, wiggles her big fin at us, like she is waving goodbye, then turns and swims away. Breathtaking. Shass gets the picture. Mak tells him he's gotta try to sell it – it's a one-in-a million. I look at the pic but it conveys nothing of the actual experience.

194 fish day: Up at 4:30 – stacking yesterday's fish down into the freezer. Three person job, all sweating hard. Brutal on the back and arms.

5:30 am. Grab tea and toast & pb. Fish until 9:30 pm. Muscles screaming. Hitting lows as Mak tells me I need to get a LOT faster and a LOT better and soon! and still I occasionally drop fish. Spray Shasso in the face with drops of anchovy juice not 20 minutes after he tells me that the only thing that ever made him punch a guy in the face was getting hit by anchovy juice. I promised I'd throw the anchovies clear of him as I try to ring our stern with bait. Nothing I did was right. Today I vow to do better. Best intentions, positive attitude, hard work, perseverance, more hard work, and steely determination don't bring the results I want. Really frustrating. Old shoulder injury flares up for the first time in three years. I am now one of those people with an 'old injury' that will dog me. In low moments, when neither Mak nor Shasso will meet my eye nor speak to me, frustration at my ineptitude rife, I look up to the immense panorama of clouds that continues forever and I think: *Be grateful for each and every moment, because this moment will never happen again!* I send that thought out to Morgan, and I hope that she is remembering to love life, each and every precious second, even when it feels so very hard for her. For me, this is nothing. I have lived hell before. This fishing is heaven on earth. Instead, I worry about those who are struggling.

I send love and thanks to James for reminding me to really smile at life, to Ivan who never gives up in the face of challenges and obstacles, and to Liam, for reminding me that I am never truly alone.

Must sleep for a few precious hours. 4 am comes too soon.

Days roll by with very little variation: grateful for days I fish lots; grateful for days I mostly cook, to rest my aching, weary muscles.

I run in and out from galley to deck, back-up fisher: throw bait, cook George ham, bacon, hash-browns, toast and eggs; check lines for seaweed, cook Mak pork-fried rice and pull in fish while he eats; a thrasher shark grabs one of our Tuna and holds on. Immense fin whips back and forth, trying to rip out our gear. I run for the camera, but he yanks the fish off and leaves before I get back.

Baking chocolate chip cookies, bell rings, I run out, pull on gloves and grab a fish off the side bird, slit its throat and it thrashes wildly, spraying every inch of me with blood. Run back inside, peel off gloves and ball up little balls of cookie dough on a cookie sheet and throw them in the oven. Tunes are cranked as we three slam fish after fish onto the bench, wrestle the hook free and throw it back out for the next unlucky fish to grab. These crazy, heady adrenaline-filled moments are punctuated by countless stretches of hour upon hour of staring out to sea from the stern, waiting for any movement, any fish. Sitting on an overturned 20-litre bucket nodding off, sun sparkles off the endless blue and burns my cheeks and nose to a crisp.

Surrounded by other fishing vessels, all vying for the same few Tuna, the US Coast Guard patrolling the border less than two miles from us, daring us to stray across the invisible, yet very real, divide.

Music cranked, sun peeking through clouds, teal sparkles all around, fish jumping and flying onto the boat, we're grooving, dancing and pulling fish...

Lots of grumpy moments each day: exhausted, aching, popping more painkillers, losing another fish, getting screamed at again. Looking out to the clouds and smiling at you, James, I am smiling all the time: this is truly heaven on earth.

Dipping my hands in pure bleach to temporarily rid my hands of the constant stench of fish oil, blood, slime, and to disinfect the millions of cuts.

7 am, the beating heart of a large Tuna falls onto the table and Shasso and I watch, fascinated, as it continues to pump outside the fish's body. Mak reaches over, and pops the pulsating pink mass into his mouth, chews it and swallows. Still groggy from lack of sleep and early morning back-breaking work, my stomach is too weak and I retch. Shasso laughs.

Food is cooked and served, decks scrubbed, fish caught. Tempers flare, sharp words bite and grab and tensions rise then subside, as all things pass and the waves rock us gently to sleep; someone occasionally dozes standing up as we wait and wait and wait for fish. A sudden bite and we all jump up and stare intently at the line.

Worst part of the day: body hasn't fully awoken, between 4 – 5, in the pitch black, we stack frozen fish carcasses from freezer plates to the deep hold, in near silence, grunting and puffing, sweating profusely on the early morning cold deck. Drop the lines in, and fish start jumping. But only a few. Not the 'big fish' we are all preparing for, waiting for, counting on. Long day faces us.

Worst job: Fingers burning from climbing down into the hold, bundled in every available protection against the numbing icy cold. Thirty minutes of standing on, stumbling over and slipping on our dead fish, I scrub the thick layer of frost off large freezer fans. My body moves slower and slower with each passing minute from exhaustion and cold. In this icy dark dungeon, at the bottom of a rolling ship, I fight to stand upright on the slippery bodies of hundreds of dead fish, each one staring at me with one large accusing eye. The commands I send to my limbs to step here or move there are frozen too, executed ever so slowly, and I wonder if I will succumb to the cold and be buried alive. I will myself to continue to move and wonder how long I would lie with these fish before the guys would discover my frozen body. I remember stories of other men on other boats tripping, injuring themselves and freezing to death before being discovered by a crewmate. I wonder if I should climb the ladder before I lose the strength to do so. *I should warm up on deck and continue the rest of the job later,* I think. But my fear of appearing weak or inept is greater than my fear of dying here. I don't want to do a half-assed job, so I continue to inch slowly from fan to fan and scrub the ice overhead that falls on me, burying me in a heavy coating of white powder. My lungs are burning from the cold, my fingers no longer able to grip the handle of the brush. Finally, I manage to climb the ten steps of steel ladder with great deliberation, and throw off the roof of the hatch. The 10 degree air on deck feels like a gush of tropical heat enveloping me in its embrace. Relieved, I finally join Shass and Mak at the stern, but my fingers are no longer working. 6 – 8 am, morale is low as I struggle to get my body to do the tasks required of it. Stabbing pain in my left wrist where I ran into a metal spear earlier makes it impossible for me to lift each fish high enough for my right arm to flip it. Commands from my brain are sluggish and pain in my knees, wrists, shoulders all compete for attention as I try to focus every fibre of my being on the precise series of ten movements required to get each fish in. Quickly, precisely, faster, faster. I can't get my fingers or hands to work and I start throwing my useless left arm around like a prosthetic limb, hoping it can help the process, even while fiery pain shoots up my arm. At the next break between fish, I pop more Advil and Tylenol. I sit back at my post and doubts creep in: Can I do this? Am I not physically capable of this work? Can I face another three weeks of this? Another few months? How will I make it through the next 15 hours of punishing my body? Push through, push through. Individual injuries and strains become a global undifferentiated mass of ache as I push and push and push, forcing my body to just do it. Clench fists, unclench. Clench, unclench. Get the muscles in my hand working harder. I have to have working arms and hands to get these fish in. Ignore the stabbing pain in the middle of my back – it's just a pulled muscle, making it harder to breathe. Visualize the left arm as a pole, swinging the fish up – push through, push through. Creaky elbows and knees get forgotten as I propel my body towards the goal: fish, money. Don't let the guys down. Don't look weak.

Mak stabs each Tuna in the eye (his speciality) and the juice sprays 360 degrees, covering us head to toe. I used to cringe at the ritual eye-gouging, but we notice that it calms the fighting fish a lot to have a blade impaled into its eye, so I've adopted the technique. The knife in the eye also acts as an efficient pivot to spin the Tuna around and propel it nose-first down the tube, so we don't break its tail. THWACK! A dildo snags on seaweed, the line tightens and snaps back towards us like a deadly slingshot, the wooden projectile cracking on the metal boat dangerously close to Mak's head. We glance at each other in silence. Another narrow miss. Pulling, releasing the gear countless times per day, checking for seaweed, for cracks, for tangles. Pull, check, throw out, release the line, avoid tangles. Fast fast fast. Line grabs my boot, wraps around my ankle and for a split second, as I work to free myself quickly from the bight of the line, I see the shark that will suddenly drag me or just my leg out instantaneously.

Doubts dissolve slowly as the day progresses. I can do this. I am doing this. It is grueling, punishing work. Very dangerous. But I am doing it. I am here. I am alive and grateful for the beauty of each moment.

Highlights: Pink morning clouds.

Lowlights: Bullying culture of verbal abuse, constant berating, skipper yelling, demanding, accusing, blaming, shaming the deckhands. We shake our heads and let it wash over, but the "I was bullied by my skipper, so I will bully you" army-style of abusive communication is very draining. George is getting totally unbearable. Accusing, blaming, paranoid hostility. We start to wonder if he's losing his grip on sanity. We deckhands remain at the stern during every waking hour to avoid him. Rock, Paper, Scissors to see who has to report our latest tally to him. Each interaction is horrendous. Mak no longer goes inside to eat meals, preferring to grab his food and wolf it down at the stern.

Two or three stolen minutes of sleep at a time, leaning against a wall, before the body sways too precariously. Second wind produces energy to grab those fish and show the boys that I am equal to the task: the mind and energy is there, but the hands and arms are slow to obey my commands and I am clumsy and awkward, to my continual frustration. I am improving, I tell myself.

Patience is so thin, constant bullying by the skipper is wearing at us. We are finding only 1/5th the 'normal' number of fish. Time and money pressures beat at our already fatigued brains. We are constantly popping painkillers. I'm not so much embracing the adventure anymore, as just trying to get through without major injury, and hoping my body will only get stronger and not weaker during this season. Each ache and stab of pain, I wonder whether the 5 hours of sleep tonight will be sufficient to mend the sprain, torn muscle, etc, as I have to push through the pain and can't afford to be further weakened. 4 am comes too soon and I find myself battered and bruised, not rejuvenated. I do notice I am improving though, but I can't get my body to obey my commands. Today, each limb will seem to only flail randomly in the general direction it was supposed to go in…is this just sleep deprivation and grueling non-stop 18-hour days, or did I suffer a stroke and no longer can control my muscles? I laugh at my paranoia. I am falling asleep standing up, brain fried, and force myself to spring into action to grab the next fish that jumps on my line. I lose two in succession and George is screaming in the wheelhouse. I am acutely aware of the danger of being this exhausted on a constantly rolling fishing vessel, where the slightest wrong move can be fatal. Sounds awfully dramatic until you live it. Although all parts of our being are fair game to sudden injury, we are most mindful of protecting our hands and eyes. A Tuna pops off the line and shoots the jig and hook whistling past us, as fast and deadly as a bullet. In addition to all of this, the waves have suddenly come up and I now also fight to stay upright. Sleep will come easily tonight, but will be far too short.

Highlight: looking out to the endless sea and sky and reminding myself that this will not last forever.

Low moments: Mak tells me of kicking a gay guy to near death because he's gay and Mak hates gays. He knows I'm queer. He laughs telling the story. I tell him of someone I knew who was beaten to death for being gay in downtown Vancouver, years ago. I am sick to my stomach and leave to go cook dinner. Unfazed, Mak tells Shasso (who reports it to me later): "If Heather was my wife, she could cook me my favourite rice: morning, noon, and… afternoon." Wow. Lucky me.

I cannot describe what it feels like to be continually addressed by the skipper as 'bitch.' As in: "Bitch, don't you know how to use an oven?" or "Bitch, did you shuffle the deck properly?" No matter how many times I hear it, I am stunned into silence and cannot comprehend that this person thinks this is an acceptable way to preface each accusing sentence to me.

Shasso is seeing large blue spots in front of his eyes and falling asleep standing up. We are all fried from over-exhaustion, bitter cold, hard work and constant vigilance.

I don't ever mention my fatigue or body pain, just push through each long day and stay positive, joking with Shasso and chatting with Mak. I am secretly relieved when, after stacking the fish in the hold at 5 am, Mak slumps on the bench in the galley and says that his left wrist is killing him. Shasso says that he can't feel his hands. We all suck it up and pop painkillers. Massive waves rocking us about as I stare out to sea on the stern, watching my lines for another 18-hour shift, cleaning gear and jumping each time a fish bites. I comfort myself with the thought that in the ache of the body, there is muscle growing. I am getting stronger and faster and I CAN do this. I AM doing this.

I send love and prayers to Morgan, my mom, my sister, the boys in Bangkwang and to you, James, hoping that whatever your current situation is, it is not too stressful or painful.

Highlight: 5:30 pm. Sun finally breaks through the heavy cold grey fog and reminds us that it is August and not, in fact, the dead of winter.

Americans announce that this year is a record haul of Tuna for them. None of the Canadian fishers are getting any. This trip is starting to look like another grueling waste of time. I remind myself that: if you want to improve your chances of success, double your failures. I borrowed that from *The Drunkard's Walk*, which I just re-read and passed on to Shasso. Beautiful uplifting book on the science, philosophy, history and math of probabilities and randomness in our lives. I want to read it aloud to Morgan. It is the only book I re-read in years. I love that stuff and I often want to teach courses on Salt Spring to the general public on how to critically read scientific studies and understand what they really mean instead of how they are misinterpreted and misrepresented in the media. I think people could really use a basic understanding of probabilities and of the scientific method and of basic cognitive biases and logical fallacies. But I doubt many Salt Spring hippies would show up, even if I offered the course for free.

I'm losing it. I am giddy from mental and physical exhaustion, laughing at everything Shasso says, because if I don't, I'll cry. We are out here making no money, enduring an aggressive skipper from hell, his moronic sidekick and no fish.

Highlight: 9 pm, sun setting on the port side, full moon rising on starboard side, waves reflecting the purples, pinks, periwinkles and teals of the sky, distant puffy clouds on the horizon all combined to make a perfectly beautiful evening sky. I send the beauty out to you, James, hoping you are finding beauty somehow in the place you inhabit.

To Morgan: I am missing her so much. Parenting is a love affair with so much heartbreak as the one you love grows inside you and from the moment of birth separates from you more and more with each passing year. It's normal and what is supposed to happen as children spread their wings and fly farther and farther from the tree to find their own way in the world, but this severing is so, so painful. I wake up and start the day to the full moon still overhead, the dawning day spectacular on the horizon. I send out love, hoping the moon is bringing her peace from the inner storms that rage. I hope she continues to spread her wings and find her passion and follow her heart's dreams.

My heart is sore, grieving so much loss and pain at separation. Do I record these feelings, these moments, or just let them sweep over me, engulf me, then pass… Feeling adrift in the world without purpose or roots this past year, having lost my role as mom, and any remaining chance at salvaging the relationship I fought for years to hang on to, I am now literally adrift in the middle of the Pacific Ocean and learning that being adrift is not so bad. There is learning here, too. And beauty.

Days with more fish and I worry I won't be able to make it through physically. Push through, push harder is the mantra. Days with no fish, my weary, screaming joints and muscles can 'rest' – meaning only non-stop cooking, cleaning and odd jobs for 18 hours before I can finally fall gratefully into my bunk. On these days, it is my emotions and thoughts that overflow, spilling grief everywhere, seeping into all the cracks in my pores.

It is hard not knowing what is happening to you now that you've been 'punished', James. I worry for you. I guess I just have to let it go, and accept. I send prayers rippling across the ocean to you, friend.

Out on the ocean with no distractions, the thoughts and feelings comes fast and furious. It is interesting to observe them, feel them and not be able to do anything about anything in my life. I have no ability to try to fix or change anything that I may worry about, or to even get the information I want, removed as I am from all contact and communication. I have to just accept that whatever is, is. I cannot change or do anything about a single aspect of my life, except my mood and attitude. I just let all wash over me, like the constant waves rolling and washing past, in this churning, powerful and endless, always-moving ocean.

The group dynamics are tense this trip: George has alienated all of us with his bullying and verbal tirades, and now I understand Mak's silence around George. With us, Mak is now talkative, but I miss the old silent Mak, preferring to be in my own thoughts, than to hear his repetitive stories. Mostly, there is silence, though. We hardly talk to each other anymore, each fully absorbed by his or her private fears and worries.

The fish-pulling, the long hours and shitty short sleeps, the stacking and multitude of other tasks and chores are physically intense, brutal, but do-able, sometimes even fun. It is doing all this in close quarters with a tyrant that feels insufferable. Rather than clear, direct respectful communication, there is just verbal bullying and aggressive hostility. I assume that we should have a sense of teamwork, of all helping each other to just get the challenging job done. Instead, George bullies and swears constantly at us, trying to diminish us. It is putting us all further on edge. Mak has mentioned several times that if he were in his own country, he would have thrown George overboard long ago. He is deadly serious and we don't doubt him.

Shasso hits an emotional wall today. Normally easy-going Shasso has reached his limit. He cannot look at or be near George, nor take any more of the verbal hostility and bullying. The frozen silence that follows each one of George's aggressive and totally inappropriate outbursts as we try to process without reacting, is no longer an adequate buffer against the constant onslaught: Shasso wants to kill him. He and I briefly talk about the challenge of being subject to the demeaning, trash-talking culture embodied by George that permeates many male-dominated professions, including the trades and fishing. That abusive style of 'leadership' discourages people like Shasso and I from wanting to stay in those type of jobs. Shasso tells me of working with a new guy on a plumbing job-site last year, where he was explaining what was expected of him, how to do it, and showed the new guy each step. The new guy expressed amazement, saying that Shasso was the first man he's ever worked with on a construction job-site who didn't simply throw him in and scream: "What the fuck's your problem? Just do it, you faggot!" What's with the male culture of homophobic bullying and violence? George's aggressive, confrontational style is so wearying and draining. The implied insult to our characters, to our integrity and work ethic is constant, vile, and unnecessary. The volume of his voice is so high that my ears are constantly ringing from his non-stop shouting: "Bitch, what the fuck's wrong with you?"

Getting harder and harder to see myself hanging in through the season. I was expecting brutally hard, not brutally hard plus no pay-cheque. We are heading North again, looking for fish up by Tofino area. The fish usually don't show up there until September, but we are getting nothing where we are. It occurs to me not for the first time that I may not be physically capable of catching 4-5 times the number of fish we got on our best day so far. If we do finally get to where the fish are jumping, will the searing pain that runs across my right shoulder and down my arm get worse and make it impossible to lift anything? I cannot let doubts creep in. I have to just do it – and concentrate on staying safe and making it back to Morgi in one piece, not maimed. And hopefully not broke.

Please God, can we just get a boatload of fish and get home? This sucks. OK, I finally allowed myself to voice it. This. Fucking. Sucks. But keep going, Heath, appreciate each moment and hope for money at the end. The interminable hours on the ocean with no real purpose and lots of tension, I admit, is getting to me right now. I don't want to feed the negativity. I will stop writing for now, and remember that this, too, shall pass.

It has become clear that Mak and George loathe each other – the tension is horrible. In these close quarters, with the four of us always on top of each other, the shitty dynamics are getting to all of us. AND NO FISH!

Highlight: Hearing Morgan's voice on the phone – she's at Pride in Vancouver with Josée (my ex-girlfriend). She's excited to go hang-gliding tomorrow and I wish her well – so happy to hear her excited. So happy she's spending the weekend away from Salt Spring and around queer, happy folk! YAY.

Staring out from my post for 17 long hours at the endless waves rocking us. Motionless for hours, bracing myself against the whipping wind that cuts through the four layers of clothing and windbreaker, gloves and hats I wear. I occasionally stamp my feet or dance around to ward off the worst of the aches, pains and chills. Hypnotized by the crashing, foaming surf, I am adrift in my thoughts. I thank the Universe for this gift. I realize that I asked the Universe for abundance before this trip and I received it. Not money or fish, instead I got long days filled with nothing to do but to stare out to sea. Here, in this place, I can do nothing about anything else in my life. Mesmerized by the sea rolling past and over us, I cannot receive and fret over unpaid bills; no way to contact James or try to find out his current situation; no way to try to organize a prisoner art exhibit for Ivan's work; no way to search for jobs; no rushing around town, trying to accomplish a million chores in a day; no way to try to fix my Mom's health or finances or Morgan's self-hatred or to control or do. I am forced to just be, for hours, for days, for weeks. What a luxury, what a gift, this abundance of meditation, of just accepting that what is, is. Rather than think about this as a huge colossal waste of time that sets me further back, I realize that this has been another beautiful unexpected gift – and I pay attention to each wave, each curling foaming wall that chases and crashes against our ship, tossing us about. I need to appreciate this, because I will never again have this wonderful moment immersed in Nature's glory. I am smiling.

Making scalloped potatoes, salad and Italian sausages for lunch. Tired of these heavy meals. I crave the simpler, lighter way I eat when not on this ship. I steal a moment to write as we are no longer focused on fishing. There are no fish on these shores. Word is the fish are finally biting 400 miles or so off the coast and we need to get out there. So we are heading south to Victoria, yet again, to replace three batteries, drop off Shasso and George, and then head out for a month of off-shore (meaning way the hell out there) fishing. Mak and I will be with a new skipper and deckhand as Shasso is leaving for school in Vancouver and George is retiring to go motorcycling with his new girlfriend. I call Morgan this morning to tell her. She says: "I'm worried about you out there without your comic relief." Me too. Shasso has been my friend, ally, fishing mentor, and comic buffer against the bullshit. Will the replacement guys resent my presence? Will the new guy be ok to share a bunk with? Are they going to be assholes? Will they hate working with a woman? We have two feet by two feet of floor space we share in which to live, move and get dressed each morning in the dark and cold. It was very close quarters already with Shass, but he and I know each other so intimately that the close proximity was ok. Even as I sit here typing, the shooting pain radiating down my right arm to my fingers worries me too. Well, I'm going for it and hoping it will be ok. So grateful I had Shasso to help me through these first two trips – the next ones will be more intense and harder, but also I have a lot more knowledge under my belt of what to expect and how to deal. Yikes.

Gorgeous no fish day heading down the side of Vancouver Island, sun warming us, blinding light dancing on blue water. Still 24 hours away from Vic. I am puttering around, washing gear, cleaning the galley, organizing the foc'sle, doing an inventory of canned and dry goods to buy. I make a plan to move Shasso's bunk over so that the new guy will not be directly below me, rather ten inches away, giving an illusion of personal space. Spirits are higher as we plan the next trip, hope renewed that this time we'll hit the jackpot. Aches, pains, grueling hours, sleeplessness, wet, cold intense conditions and long hours of work momentarily forgotten as we envision Tuna jumping into our boat by the thousands on the open ocean, and a huge pay-cheque upon arrival to shore. Mak tells Shasso that he's decided I'll make someone a good wife. I decide to take it as a compliment, rather than bristle. At lunch yesterday, he and I shared a moment, talking about faith in God and the prisoners' situation. I had talked to Mak when I found out that the shit had hit the fan and that James has been sent to a new super-max prison as punishment for illegal cell-phone activities. I was a blubbering mess, worried sick, until I pulled it together and now just silently send positive thoughts to James a million times a day.

Mak says he knows James will be ok because of his faith. It gives me great comfort to know that Mak is praying daily for James. I thank him and tell him that his faith in God and James's gives me great consolation for their sake, even if it isn't my own belief system.

Highlight: removing rubber suits, boots and heavy socks, and lying on my back on the top of the hold on deck for a few lazy hours, reading Viktor E. Frankl's Man's Search for Meaning. My sickly pale feet bask in the summer sun and the warmish wind. Soggy toes dry out for the first time in weeks.

Shore just a few hours away: pull in the lines, raise the poles, scrub the deck, pump sludge from the aft-house; organize tools in the foc'sle; shower and shave my pits; bleach out the shower; transfer photos from Shasso's computer to mine; make minor repairs on doors, latches, cupboards; sharpen kitchen knives; wash kitchen mats; throw leftovers from the fridge; dump any refuse overboard before getting into harbour. The energy feels jittery, excitement in anticipation of land. I start imagining the sensation of 'normal' things again: walking on land; seeing people I don't know; wearing clean clothes and smelling nice; walking into a bookstore and browsing; ordering a coffee and sitting at a café with my laptop; riding in a car; seeing Morgan. It's only been a few weeks. I can't help but think about the guys who have been removed from society for years and what it must feel like to them to miss those simple activities of daily life.

TUESDAY AUGUST 7, 2012

FISHERMAN'S WHARF, VICTORIA, BC.

Email from my ex- David today. Apparently he was deported to France at the end of July after causing a bunch of trouble with the cops. That was the phone call from YVR – his one call allowed before exiting the country. I am so unbelievably relieved he is gone from Canada until I read the next part. He has been in France less than ten days and is planning to head to Bangkok. My stomach drops – I had to flee that place once already to get away from his psychotic death threats. I am so angry that he's deliberately going there to threaten me. I have to just let it all go, not think about it, just breathe. I hope he doesn't try to go to the prison to see Liam or Ivan or to harass my Iranian guys. I mustn't think about any of that – just live my own life with intention, gratitude, eyes wide open, heart not closed. Reading the email stirred up more grief and pain about lives lost and dreams crushed. Fuck, I wish I would never hear from him again.

I saw Morgan today. She convinced her boss to bring her to Victoria to come and see me, and we spent an all too-brief few minutes together. We cried when she left the dock – she told me that she misses me so much and regrets all the times when, as a teenager, she blew me off to go spend time with her friends and now realizes she can never get those lost moments back. I miss her so much too. She is my whole world and now I feel so adrift without her to protect, to cherish and take care of, to hang out and be silly and goofy with. No matter how brutally hard it was raising her on my own, I made sure that we laughed a lot every day. No matter the shitty choices I may have made, I hope that she always knew she was loved. She was the center of my world, my purpose. Now, I have no idea what comes next for me...

Tomorrow I will meet the new deckhand, Etienne, new skipper Cyrus, and we off-load our paltry 1300 Tuna, stock up again and head out. I am pretty nervous. I am going to miss Shasso a lot. Mak doesn't want him to leave either and keeps trying to bribe him to stay. He offers Shasso a portion of his expected pay, and of mine. Thanks for that.

Set out today at 1:30 pm after fuelling up on dock, doing final checks. Feeling odd about going out without Shasso, but a few things have mitigated my concerns. Firstly, George took me aside and stressed that he'd been really impressed with my work, and with me. That was a big surprise, and I know he wouldn't have said it if he didn't mean it. When I told Morgi of George's parting words to me, she said: "I'm not surprised, Mama, you're so hard-core and a super-hard worker." That may be, but that's still no guarantee that I can hold my own with 230-lbs fishermen built like brick shit-houses with 25 – 40 years' experience. I also had a great talk with the owner, who told me I'd get 10%, not 8%, another surprise. (Of course, 10% of nothing is still nothing).

I feel good in initial impressions of Cyrus and Etienne, both seem serious about fishing and infinitely more respectful than George in their style of communication. It would be hard to imagine getting worse than his abusive screaming and it's clear that at least neither of the two other guys will be using the N– word with regularity. This morning, I left my laptop in Victoria to be fixed. Kinda bummed to not have my music or journal. I gotta start writing on paper again. I hope this trip is productive, lucrative. I am the youngest on the crew at 40. Etienne is 41, Mak is somewhere in his late 40's, although one never knows, as he changes his story each time he tells it, and Cyrus is late fifties, all solid muscle. I'm feeling much more optimistic about our crew than I was yesterday when I hugged Shasso goodbye. I bought George a card with a picture of a Red Rooster on the front of it, and wrote a wee note thanking him for showing me the ropes on my first trip ever as a deckhand. It was a little challenging to find nice things to write in the card, but I wanted to do it even though Shasso shook his head and told me not to bother, that George deserves no kindness. Under the inappropriate asshole he presents to the world, George is still a human being and I wanted to reach out to that guy and thank him for what he taught me, and wish him well in the future. I left the card in the wheelhouse and forgot about it. Later, he approached me, eyes wet. He was genuinely touched by my card and we hugged goodbye.

I am happy, looking forward to big fish, big money on this next trip. Reassured Morgi over the phone that I'd be safe and back in a few weeks. I am sending out love and prayers to James for his safety and to Ivan for his release and happiness, and to Liam. I don't feel capable or willing to send out positive thoughts and prayers to David – maybe I feel they'd be wasted or that I am just depleted, nothing left to give to that sucking void. Years of offering loving kindness to a selfish vacuum of human energy. Don't feel bitter so much as just empty of any desire to waste any more energy.

I enjoy hearing Cyrus and Etienne grumbling about bodily aches and pains – makes me feel like less of a weakling knowing that this is punishing work for all of us.

TUESDAY, AUGUST 14, 2012

PORT ALBERNI, B.C.

Never would have believed this. More breakdowns. We're in Port Alberni, after limping in a few days ago, looking to replace our 32V alternator. Been in port two days – this season has been so unbelievable. No idea it was the middle of August – days and date all lost. In the shop today, waiting while the owner is on the phone to his suppliers, trying to rustle us up two alternators, Cyrus and I look at the wall calendar and eventually figure today is probably Tues. the 14th of August. Makes the most logical sense, although we could be off by a few days in either direction. These breakdowns have been non-stop – six weeks since I started this fishing stuff and we still haven't even really started. Endless hours and days of waiting on parts and ripping apart old wiring, hoping to fix problems on this boat. Mak's being pretty negative, and his mood is infectious. I stay pretty quiet, and just hope things will turn our way, but I am not stoked.

Talk to Morgi on the phone who's worried about me, but I'm fine, just wishing I could know whether you're ok, James. I wish David would stop emailing me abusive nasty emails from France or Bangkok, or wherever he is. Delete them and try to just forget about how much I hate him in moments. This is all starting to get to me. Staying positive and hanging on is getting quite challenging. Keep the mantra going. It's gonna be alright. I'm smiling, James!

AUGUST 16, 2012

Four am. Profound relief as we finally leave dock. It's hard to believe that we're actually getting underway. Again. All repairs done, systems checked, and we head out yet again. No one wants to jinx this, so there is uneasy silence as we leave port and we all seem to be holding our breath. It's been pretty hard to stay upbeat these past few days stuck in port, living on a boat with three guys in a small redneck town. Every moment we weren't on the boat, we were drinking at the nearest bar. So discouraging, frustrating. As we head down the narrow channel and out to sea, the ocean breeze feels so good, moving the stagnant, stale hot air we've been cooking in, and finally we exhale. YAY! Never felt so happy be on the ocean again.

Highlights: Stealing an hour in the middle of the baking hot day before leaving port today to jump in the clear water of a local lake. Met a guy last night at the bar, hooked up, and he drove me to the lake today. Wants me to look him up whenever I'm in Port Alberni. I dunno. I like that he cries when he talks about his grown kids, that being a dad is the most important part of his life. He's the same age as me and already has a couple of tiny grandkids. Crazy. More of just a one-night thing, though.

Dreaming of buying real estate near this end of the island, where the cost of living is so much lower than Salt Spring, but the trees, lakes and ocean are all still magnificent and I may find a wee cabin in trees affordable that I can call home, play around in, fix up, and have Morgi and friends come and visit me at. I try to visualize this so it doesn't feel like a lonely trap, instead seeing it as a blessing: I need to visualize safety, a nest, a place to heal a battered soul. And friends. And love. A real partnership. Craving things I dare not dream of anymore.

Earlier today, before we left, I invited a family with small children strolling along the docks up to see our fish in the hold to explain our whole fishing operation to them. Even the adults peppered me with questions about how exactly we catch the Tuna, as I showed them our gear, table set-up, tubes to slide the fish onto deck, and the freezer plates. It was cool to see myself through their eyes, an experienced fisher (little do they know!) doing work totally foreign to them, this land-lubbing family from Alberta. Remembering that what we do is pretty cool and that I've learned a whole new set of skills here.

Lay down on my bunk at 10 pm in the stuffy hot foc'sle. Even though exhausted, I have a very hard time falling asleep. I appreciate Cyrus' mellow temperament and easy-going manner. He is all about teamwork and abhors the bullying autocratic style that George and most other skippers employ. Etienne's tendency to talk non-stop is annoying, but he is friendly, so I am grateful – could be way worse. We are all pretty good at staying positive while nerves are frayed from endless repairs and breakdowns and lack of income, but I miss Shasso's goofiness and our constant giggling.

Glad I got my computer back – Etienne drove the four hours down island and picked it up from the Victoria repair shop, when it became clear that we'd be in port for a while and he took the opportunity to go home to Sidney to his girlfriend for a night. Cyrus and I went out and had a few drinks. Etienne's a raging alcoholic and reminded me why I don't want to continue down that road, but it's been hard in port, what with boredom and frustration to not head to the bar in the evenings. Been dreaming lots of getting a wee home in this area, as they are way more affordable, but it brought up sadness at having no one to share it with. What would I do way the hell out here in the middle of nowhere, alone? Must envision abundance of love in my life. Glad we're underway again. It's 4 am and the stars are incredible. Two more hours of watch and I can hopefully go back to my bunk for some shut-eye.

Talked to Johann briefly on Facebook today and heard his acute loneliness. Severe depression and survivor guilt sinking him since his repatriation from Bangkwang prison to Holland. Says he is still feeding off the short and amazing time we had together in Strasbourg in June, how it made him feel alive. It breaks my heart that he is doing so poorly after release from eleven years in that hell-hole of Bangkwang. I send healing love and prayers to him. I can't imagine how different my life would be if I had never met him years ago and felt called to return to Bangkwang to support so many.

Two days out on the latest leg of a never-ending trip that never really seems to get anywhere: pulled 50-odd fish yesterday in a group of 20 other fishing vessels piled practically on top of each other, crisscrossing each other's tack, desperately vying for the same few fish. Finally, Cyrus makes the decision to head off-shore, meaning 500 miles from here (we are already 200 miles out from land, considered 'on-shore'). One other boat from our group decides to join us. This entails 3 days and nights of non-stop running, crossing the no-fish area to get to the hopefully 'big fishing' grounds. I no longer believe the oft-repeated tales of big fish days where the guys work their asses off and fill the boat in 8 days straight. "90,000 pounds in mere days," "stopping work by 2pm each day," because they can no longer fit any more onto freezer plates and spend the rest of the day stacking all the bounty in the hold. I admit I clung to that vision a few weeks ago, when I first heard the stories of the Golden Days of Tuna Fishing, but now I have no expectations, except that I'll be here a long, long time. I'm starting to understand squirrelly. On this small boat, there is nowhere for me to escape to, away from Etienne's incessant nonsensical chattering. Already I've heard all his theories and partying stories in a loop. Loud growly voice and big grin repeating sound-bites of fishing, 4-day coke and booze benders and the shit his 'Old Lady' gives him when he crawls home. Fascinating stuff. Like George, he feels the need to speak at a volume far louder than necessary, although he doesn't hurl abusive language at people, just punctuates all his loud stories with "FUCKIN'" every second word. Even for me, this is a bit excessive and tiresome. It is so very loud already, between the roar of the engine, and the freezer compressor, the music we crank high up, and we're all talking at high volume over the noise. I don't need Etienne's shouting on top of it. I notice Cyrus has a strategy of walking away as soon as Etienne starts in on a pointless story about nothing. My ears are ringing so much that I crank loud music into my ears for some peace and quiet.

I appreciate people who can do silence. I have no need to be negative, but I can't do chit-chat and be chipper all the time. I prefer quiet to forced cheerfulness. Lots of time I just need to 'be,' to be lost in my thoughts and not to listen to boring stories that require nods and grunts and smiles. Etienne sucks a lot of energy, asking for my approval and advice on cooking, on everything. I try to smile and answer his incessant questions patiently, even as I cringe at his lack of hygiene, grubby fat hands covered in Tuna blood and dick germs swiping at his nose as he puts together our lunch. None of this bothers me if I can just have my solitude, but he is needy, demanding an audience, and constantly intrudes on my thoughts. I escaped early this morning to the stern with a book for a few hours, watching for fish, but within five minutes of waking, Etienne brought out his coffee and started talking at me, even as I kept my nose in my book, trying to give him the hint not to disturb me.

Four hours later: watching lines that don't jump, cleaning gear of seaweed, scrubbing grease off the deck and drinking six mugs of tea, cold wind pushing grey waves across grey sky, I finally decide to return to the warm galley. The guys look at me when I enter the crowded space. I have nothing to say to any of them. I grab the laptop, put in the ear-buds and sink blissfully into my solitary world, mere inches from 3 other guys trying to stave off boredom in our separate ways for the next few days of travel. Cyrus doesn't talk much, but when he does, his stories are ok, if only I hadn't heard all of them seven times already. He's made a few passes at me. That's going to be a problem. Etienne is looking at me, squaring his bulky frame and beach-ball belly towards me, trying to catch my eye. I studiously avoid his eye, pretending to be heavily engaged in writing this lap-top journal. Mak runs outside to escape this tiny room thick with boredom, unspent energy, and steals the solitary post I just vacated at the stern. Two minutes later, we hear the tell-tale slapping sounds of a fish fighting for its life. Etienne runs out and returns yelling at me that Mak's caught a Yellow Tail, that we'll clean and eat for dinner tonight. We fish Albacore, so any Salmon or Yellow Tail that jump on our line are for us to enjoy. Yesterday, Etienne pulled in a 'peanut,' meaning a 10-lbs. Tuna, too small to sell. He filleted him on the hatch and threw the meat onto the freezer plates, for us to enjoy later.

The shoulder I injured within the first week of this adventure sends constant aching pain across my neck and down nerve-endings in elbow, wrist and fingers. The pain exhausts me, but I am loathe to pop painkillers all day, each day, even if only handfuls of acetaminophen and ibuprofen. I cannot decide which I prefer to live with: the pill-popping or the pain. I decide that the pain makes me grumpier and shorter with the guys and that I need to put in the effort to stay positive and cheerful, so I grab for the industrial-size bottles of pills that live on the galley table to take the edge off the pain.

Two weeks ago, a little farther up Vancouver Island, near Port Hardy, the skipper of a small fishing boat held his crew hostage with a shotgun. Paranoid from an extensive coke binge, he lost it and was threatening to kill his three deckhands. One of them managed to climb onto the roof and used her cell phone to call the Campbell River RCMP, who used the GPS in her cell phone to try to locate them. Hours later, they finally stormed the boat, rescuing the crew, removing the captain and his stash of coke. When I learned of this in port two days ago, I had an odd feeling of recognition, remembering how I had had worries of a similar scenario emerging when George's hostility and paranoia exploded exponentially on the last trip to the point where Shass and I were questioning his sanity. Etienne just told me that a few of his buddies called him up when they heard the report on the news, asking if Etienne was the coked-up guy on the boat. *Great, that's reassuring*, I thought.

This morning, Cyrus tells me four times in a row that the endless boredom and monotony drives him buggy. *Really? I hadn't noticed,* I refrain from answering. After roughly sixty years of living on the planet, you'd think he'd have more than four stories to tell. Not so. Maybe repetition is comforting. I appreciate Mak's silence. We give each other quick looks and brief smiles full of meaning, neither needing to say much and both missing Shasso's ability to make us laugh. Giddy laughter used to release our tension, but forced chippery banter does not. And the tension builds palpably. We are all here for only one reason, and the frustration is high. I sit writing, ignoring Etienne's repeated attempts to catch my eye each time he passes by me to go for yet another cigarette. He doesn't seem to be very good at amusing himself and it's like having an overgrown ADHD kid on board, demanding attention and energy. I can do my time here, with relative calm, patience and positivity, but I'm not willing to do his. Although I don't usually listen to music while reading, I leave the headphones in as I return to my book, hoping it will discourage

Etienne from yammering at me. I am so grateful for books, my laptop and these headphones: they are saving my sanity. Each day of 'travel' crawls by so slowly with not even the pretense of fishing to occupy the seemingly infinite hours to fill, minute by slow minute.

Highlight: Evening brings 360 degrees of orange, pink and purple band rimming the horizon.

Went to lie down to get away from the guys and finished another book: *Winter's Bone*. I like the writing: bare, stark, and evocative, like the landscape. Good story. Woke up to the smell of burning rubber or plastic in the foc'sle. I ran out to the stern and told Mak. He sprung up and we investigated the engine room, poking, checking and sniffing everything until he was satisfied that it was the rubber on the new alternator that was rubbing after Etienne brushed up against it accidentally this morning, ripping the ass out of his sweat pants. I go to the wheelhouse where Cyrus bemoans the lack of old-school knowledge by the new generation of skippers. He relays for the third time since I met him how, when 9/11 happened, he was out fishing off-shore. The US Coast Guard came on all channels announcing that GPS would be shut down by the US military, and many fishers panicked, heading immediately for shore because they didn't know how to navigate or plot a course by charts and compass, to Cyrus' eternal disgust.

Etienne has now figured out to wave his hand in front of my face to get my attention, as I sit here, so I can't ignore him. "How long does this fuckin' rice cooker take? How will I know it's done? Is there enough rice?" As soon as I answer him, he rapid-fires more questions and stories at me, all with the seeming purpose of getting my approval or just to fill the silence that seems to oppress him. It is tiring, trying to respond in a friendly way that doesn't shut him down, but allows me a little space for myself.

We have so much time on our hands these travelling days that each simple task, like moving fish off the plates and loading them into the hold, usually done in silence in the pre-dawn in a highly efficient system by the three of us deckhands, today takes five times longer. We four discuss all the possible ways we could do it, and whether we should do it now or wait until morning, or whether we should take out half and do the rest later, etc. It is farcical. Cyrus is pacing between the wheelhouse and the deck, antsy. He hates doing nothing, even more than I do. I almost want to dig out the power-tools from under Etienne's bunk and ask Cyrus to build something. As his style is hands-on, he's already frustrated not to be out pulling fish with the rest of us. Given that he does way more than George ever did, I tend to agree with him and Etienne that this boat only needs three of us crew and not four. But we don't want to jinx this by saying someone could get seriously injured or fall overboard and we could still fill the boat with fish. Hopefully when we hit the big fish days, we'll be running smoothly together...if we ever see those 'big fish days,' which now occupy mythical status in my mind.

Etienne fries today's Yellow Tail in bread crumbs for dinner. Yummy. Mak's keeping the head for soup. Too gross. Turns out Cyrus is a huge sashimi fan, as am I, so we will fillet every peanut we catch and eat those raw while we're out here. That's pretty cool.

Sending love to Morgan, Ivan, James, Liam, and Johann. Doing nothing all day, every day in extremely close quarters with three guys has been exhausting. Can't imagine 800 guys or 800 days. Only 8 pm and I wish I could go to bed. Another watch tonight, but I'll sleep the rest of the time. Our water tank is dangerously low and our water-maker only works when we drift. We won't be drifting for a few days. None of these issues will matter if we can just get into the fish: I won't notice Etienne's juvenile growling chatter, the lack of water, Cyrus' repetitive stories, nor my lack of income, if only I were catching fish. Argh.

Sitting in the galley, half-listening to Cyrus' and Etienne's conversation, I have a unexpected pang of remembering the sober David. I imagine what he would think if he were here listening to these crazy characters. Not great philosophers, by any stretch of the imagination. I can see him being unable to look me in the eye, for fear of bursting out laughing. A few years ago, at the first and only yoga class I convinced David to try, we found a free class with a student teacher in Ganges, the town on Salt Spring Island. We spread out our mats beside the dozen or so other students and waited in silence for the teacher to arrive. A heavily bearded young man in soft hemp clothing entered the room slowly with a wide smile. Moving slowly with deliberate intention, trying to project serenity and inner peace, he sits slowly down facing us. Silence. We all stare back at him in silence. He smiles and smiles and smiles, breathing a deliberately peaceful yogic cleansing breath for what seems like an eternity. Probably only a few minutes. Finally, he exhales deeply, closes his eyes and says slowly: "Let... us... begin." I make the mistake of quickly glancing at David and we both erupt in giggles. For the next ten minutes as the class follows the painfully slow movements and instructions of the smiling Jesus, I am shaking from the effort of trying not to laugh, but the urge just gets worse. I grit my teeth, tears streaming, stuffing laughter into my yoga poses and chewing on my breath, not daring to look in David's direction, or I'll lose it. David abruptly gets up and walks past me. The door shuts and I hear him hooting and howling outside. He reappears at the window and signals to me that he's done with yoga and is heading to the gym for a work-out. I escape an hour later and catch up with him and we laugh for days about the ultra serene yoga guru. I miss that. Intimate knowledge of someone I can be myself with and share the goofiness of life with. But not him. Not any more. After years of the hell, I finally don't miss any part of David any more. I do miss waking up beside someone I love and feeling cared for and loved, wanting to watch them breathe and wanting to touch and kiss every inch of them, and inhale their scent. I crave someone to share ideas with, and emotional intimacy. It's been years since I had a glimpse of that with anyone. Let's be honest: I had that only a handful of moments with him in the years I spent with him. The romantic and sexual part of our relationship was only a brief 18 months that he was sober – the rest was just negotiations of me trying to help a very sick man address his disease and his psychotic obsessions with me. Blah! Classic case of me trying to 'fix' someone and determined that all the time I put in would not be wasted. Yuck. What a waste.

Hopefully I can have that intimate ease and connection with someone sweet and kind and emotionally healthy and with their shit together one day. Someone who is into self-knowledge, exploration, playfulness, challenging oneself to grow and supporting each other to fly. Or just someone I can lean my head on when I'm weary. So fucking tired of taking on the world alone.

Today, I couldn't keep my cool. First day of my period, and the physical pain of severe endometriosis and my mental fog was shitty. I lost it when our steering pilot broke again. Cyrus decides that it's been set up all wrong and needs to be totally reinstalled. "We seriously couldn't do this shit the four days we were on shore?" I ranted. "We had to wait until we're 72 hours away from land before checking that it was installed properly?" I am not at my best, I know this. I cannot take Etienne's non-stop mindless blabbing at me. I try as hard as I can to smile at him, but I know it is a hard frozen grimace stuck to my face. I need to get away from him but there is nowhere to go. We are all turning in circles, in each other's faces and space 24/7. There is not even enough room to pass each other without each sucking in our gut to shimmy past.

My period brings up other hard stuff, too, that I cannot talk about, in addition to the physical pain. Today I write Liam a long letter, asking him to help carry my pain of Olivier, my lost son, and thus make real the loss – that is invisible. He is real, and I carry pain. I need for this grief to be witnessed, for him to matter. To someone other than me. Only Liam knew about him. And David. But David is lost in an inner hell of active addiction that precludes any possibility of healthy interaction, let alone grieving together. I cannot send the letter. Liam is too messed up these days in his own shit for me to burden him with mine. My raw anguish will stay silent in me, ripping me apart.

New day: starts shitty with the water-maker issue with Mak. The water sight tube I misread isn't the real issue. It's how to do conflict well. I fucked up a couple of days ago and we've been operating under the false impression that we're almost out of fresh water. The mistake isn't a big one, and Cyrus laughs it off when I apologize to him. "Not to worry," he shrugs. Mak, however, won't let it go. He decides he needs to harp on it, incessantly. I had hoped we could let this roll over in a more gentle, easy-going way, with humour and grace. I guess nerves are too shot. Mak puts his face in mine, jeering and mocking me, over and over and over. I smile and move away to keep the peace. But he follows me the ten steps to the stern, jeering: "How many times did I tell you?" he repeats, goading me. Finally I snap and shriek at the top of my lungs: "Don't fucking patronize me! DON'T FUCKING PATRONIZE ME!" Stunned, this shuts Mak up for many hours, during which he won't look at or talk to me. Etienne stares wide-eyed at me. Not my finest moment. Later, in the wheelhouse, Cyrus says: "You ok?" "Yup," I smile calmly. Must remain chill on this wee boat.

113 fish today by 7 pm as I'm about to serve kick-ass spaghetti and salad. What's amazing is how much fun the actual fishing is. Pulling fish is so heady, so fun, so satisfying. I am antsy for really big fish days, 'cause the fishing when we're going at it crazy, is so so so so much fun and I am not worried at all about my skill...I am totally fine and getting

better and I see now in retrospect that the hard part of this job is dealing with an abusive captain or boredom. Having Cyrus as a skipper makes this very same job feel ten times easier. We're still frustrated and bored for weeks on end, searching a vast ocean for the big schools of Tuna on a tiny boat prone to constant breakdowns. But in the occasional moments that all my lines are jumping and I'm cranking in fish, no one yelling at me, and I'm just going for it, it's such a blast and the time whips by. I can honestly say I lose fewer and I'm faster at catching fish than is Etienne. And he's a beefy muscular guy who has been doing this 25 years. He has no hustle to him, whereas I am hungry, motivated, and put my all into it. It puts my mind at ease to realize that I am not actually horrible at what I'm doing. Mak now respectfully steps out of my way when a fish jumps on my line even if he's closer to it, rather than pulling it himself or watching me and shaking his head, as he used to in the beginning. He is now constantly thanking me and giving me thumbs up. I am finally kicking ass. My muscles are not even sore at all any more. I LOVE the exhilaration of fighting each body of thrashing muscle. And I don't mind asking for help with things I'm just not physically capable of. Yesterday, I caught our largest Tuna yet. As I pulled him hand over hand alongside the stern and stared down at him for that brief second before the big flip-up, I realized that there was no way in Hell I would be able to get this sucker onto the boat. Rather than struggle and then drop the biggest fish yet, I asked Etienne, who was hauling a fish beside me to gaff my Tuna. He paused, saw the size of mine, and let go of his own fish to grab the gaff and stab my fish in the head and haul him in. I was happy, and Mak was elsewhere, so I didn't have to weather any critical reaction.

Days rolling into nights rolling into days, endless rocking of the sea.

Highlights: Lost in the hypnotic swell, watching the following sea for hours on end.

Blissful silence when Etienne sleeps. His mouth wakes up only seconds after the rest of him and goes non-stop. He is the authority on all things obvious, trivial and mundane. Naptime now for Etienne, so Mak and I revel watching the following sea in silence, well, relative silence: only the pounding surf, whipping wind, the compressor directly behind us, the ship's engine under us, and speakers directly above us blasting Mak's Cowboy Christmas music. My reverie is broken as the repetitive lyrics start to enter my brain: *Jesus is coming/and boy is he pissed.* That's pretty funny. After hours of Rudolph, Baby Jesus, the Reason for the Season, White Christ-mas, and more, all Cowboy-style, I wanna jump overboard, but the surreal cacophony is still heaven compared to Etienne's tiresome blathering.

Heading further out still. We are running through the nights to get out to the 141-block, as these guys call it (Latitude: 141 00). Three other vessels are travelling with us; that is, about 5 miles apart, we comb the ocean, hoping to run into schools of Tuna, and radioing each other whenever we run in to a few. I am regaled with stories of big schools of Tuna measuring 12 miles x 12 miles, where you fill the whole boat in just a week of non-stop fishing before returning to shore to unload. Today, we pull in 12 peanuts and Etienne fillets them on deck and freezes them. At noon, we slice a few frozen fillets, and eat them with wasabi and soya sauce. Absolutely divine. If nothing else, we'll each be taking lots of free Tuna home. It's evening and I've done the dishes: we've caught a total of 24 plus 12 peanuts. Tomorrow will be a better day. It has to be. We need at least 300 – 500 daily. We're averaging 40. We need roughly 5000 fish before we head in, and at this rate, we'll be fishing until Christmas, 2015 to fill the boat.

The ocean still startles me with her magnificence, even though the other guys are blasé about the stunningly gorgeous seascape that is our world right now.

23 AUGUST, 2012

143 00 N X 46 00 W

We ran again through the night. The 'hotspot' we were heading for a few days ago never panned out, except a few peanuts that Etienne filleted and froze. So we're heading out further, based on a shaky microwave image downloaded of sea surface temperature charts that show a supposed small bubble of warm water. Sharp edges between warm and cold water is where plankton and other feed thrive, and theoretically Tuna hang out there too. We arrive at 10 this morning to the 'bubble,' but it doesn't exist. The water is 3 degrees colder than the satellite info told us it would be — too cold for Tuna. The wind and waves have picked up substantially, and we are being thrown around willy-nilly.

A few hours of being thrown all over the galley, hitting drawers of tools that slide open, spray constantly showering the deck and the non-stop rocking, and my head goes back to Zen mode. None of the other worries about life matter. I can't get stressed anymore about whether we find fish. Nature reminds me powerfully, immediately that life is ferocious, fierce, intense, magical, beautiful, and we need to enjoy every minute of the ride, and not worry about the details. This surging raw energy leaves no room for anything else but primal existence. Thank you, Nature, for reminding me of the beauty of life – the hairier the weather gets, the more stressed the guys are getting – and griping about the lack of fish. Me, I was grumpy yesterday about the seven weeks I've been on this boat, no fish, no pay. Today, I am grateful for the ocean, for the wind, for life, for beauty, for the churning, electrical energy that flows in all of us.

New day and there are clouds in my mind – I can't shake off the thoughts of what's going to happen if there are no fish this year. All up and down the Coast the reports come from the other vessels – no fish anywhere, except inside the American 200-mile zone. I keep trying to push the negative thoughts away, but as I stand on the stern, watching the churning massive swells following and crashing over us, they intrude again and again. I come in to the galley and grab my laptop to take a break and warm up my chilled fingers and body. How can I return to Morgan, three months gone, with nothing but 20 lbs. of extra fat on my body from all the excessive eating, no money, and bills piled up, waiting. How do I make my dreams come true? A wee home to rest my head and to continue the prison work? How do I make this happen? No matter what I do, no matter how hard I work, I get no closer. What if I get cancer tomorrow? What will I leave for Morgan? I have nothing. No savings, no security. Those are the negative thoughts. I must banish them. Worrying changes nothing, Heath. Smile and throw those thoughts into the wind. I pull on another layer of fleece to buffer against the biting cold, grab a warm bowl of stew, and wearily head out for another 12 hours of watching, waiting. The hours drag on for years. I daydream. Sometimes I dream that you are transferred back to the US, and I hitchhike across the country to visit you, James. And I imagine how awesome it would be to hug you!

Day forever: no fish. No morale. Even the skipper says he wishes he had stayed home. We're coming on two months out here. There's nothing new to report. Endless days, endless boredom, frustration. Yikes. Last night, Morgan was at the Metallica concert in Vancouver that I bought her for her birthday. She and I were supposed to go together, but instead I'm out here, steaming up and down the ocean, looking for fish that aren't there. The summer is almost at an end. This is crazy. I have to believe that we'll find fish soon. I have to keep faith. It really blew the wind out of my sails last night when Cyrus turned to me in the wheel-house and said: "It's really gonna screw you if we don't get any fish this year, isn't it?" It struck me then that we might not, in fact, get the elusive big haul. Until that moment, I was operating under the determinedly positive assumption that it was a matter of when, not if. I can't let this get to me. I can't. Old shameful feelings of failure creep up in me and I see myself facing Morgan like I have done thousands of times before, brave face forward: "Oh well, I gave it my best shot, and I gotta just keep trying. It will be OK. At least I tried my best." The humiliation bitter in my mouth of never getting a fucking break. Of yet another failed endeavour to make ends meet. Oh, this self-pity is bullshit. I gotta stop writing and change my tune. This is garbage. Shut Up, Heath. Tomorrow is a new day. All is ok. I have my health and either we'll get fish or not. Can't let this get me down. Just keep smiling. Right, James?

My project today is to make a cribbage board. Found some 2" x 12" planks, power drill, sandpaper, dug out the skill-saw and tools from under Etienne's bunk, and I'm sitting at the galley table measuring. Called Morgan, asking her to look up how many holes I need (120) and where the skunk line is (90). Took a few hours to find a satellite signal, but finally got to hear her voice. I told her that I am feeling pretty low and she asked me if I would just give up and come home. I can't. First of all, it's not up to me – I can't turn the boat around and demand to be brought to shore. Guys have done it in the past when they couldn't take it anymore, but that's not my style. I gotta stick this out, see it to the end. I have to believe that we'll get fish. Two months in and what would I return to? Bills piled up and not a penny in my pocket or anywhere else, for that matter. I don't even have a 'home' to return to. Where would I stay, how would I eat? I know I am welcome at Morgan's place on her couch, but that is something I will not do. Too humiliating to have to sleep on my grown daughter's couch. I am better than that. I have to believe that this will work out, or at least keep trying until it is futile. All is not lost. Cyrus is making grumblings of wishing he were back on shore mushroom-picking, and we got messages today from two of the fleet, who are packing it in and giving up for the season, heading for shore. It is almost 4 pm, and we've caught two fish today. The ship closest to us, about 40 miles away caught three. It's getting harder and harder to joke about this, to keep morale up.

This morning, I invented yet another project to occupy the endless hours of boredom. I scrounged the shop-vac out of its hiding place and vacuumed the carpets in the wheelhouse and foc'sle, probably the first time they've been that clean in 40 years. Cyrus stepped out to smoke on the bow in order to give me room to clean. Wiping down the surfaces with disinfectant, it suddenly hit me how absurd all this is. I should be pulling in fish, and a paycheque, but I'm here, stuck out in the middle of the ocean, driving around in circles, trying to find things to do to occupy my time as the days keep slipping by, and not getting anywhere. Cyrus poked his head back in to let me know that the four dolphins we saw earlier are still swimming beside us and saw me crying. Just so discouraged. Blah! I wish I had a bottle or ten of wine. Would make this futility less dreary. I guess I'm supposed to feel guilty for saying that: *Red Flag! Red Flag!* An addict out-of-control, wishing she could have some good red French wine, but it's true. It's incredibly fucking boring here. Spiritual and intellectual poverty is not unrelated. If I just wanted booze, there are fifteen cans of beer sitting in the hold, leftover from Etienne's last shore-binge, but I don't have the slightest interest. I don't want to be drunk, I don't crave alcohol. I've never been someone who likes getting shit-faced or just drinking any booze. I want to be less fucking bored. Wine makes the inane drivel seem slightly less moronic, takes the edge off the mind-numbingly pathetic utterances that pass for conversation here. I've burned through all the books on board and my brain is itching for something, anything to latch on to. These guys aren't intellectual giants, sorry to say. I'm not even sure Etienne is capable of talking about anything that is not directly in front of him, in his immediate gaze, let alone contemplate abstract thought or discuss ideas.

I run to the galley and pop the kettle on to make another mug of tea. Etienne sees me:

> *"You're drinking tea, eh? Eh? Just boil up that fuckin' water and slap in that there green tea bag. Good shit, eh? Warms you up and gives you something hot to drink in yer mug. Warms you up out there, eh? Not doing*

the Orange Pekoe this time, eh? Yer sticking with the green tea? Ya? It's
good fuckin' shit. Good for ya, too. I drink it sometimes after me and the
Ol' Lady are hung over, eh? Out all night, doing blow and drinking beer.
Fuckin' holy hangover, man. Wake up and BOOM! My fucking head, eh?
FFUUUUCCCKK! Gotta make up a mug of that green tea and it helps, eh?
Fuck, tho', my Old Lady won't touch that shit, though, she and the Kid like
their fuckin' Doctor Pepper. Can't come home unless I make sure I got a
case of Doctor Pepper in the car or she'll fuckin' FREAK. Can never run
out of that stuff. Might as well not come home. Don't go home if there's
no Doctor Pepper. She and the Kid drink a 2-4 of that shit every day. We
fuckin' buy that shit by the caseload for the Kid. Kids, eh? Hey,.that kettle's
pretty fast, eh? Just put the water in and push the button and it boils it
up, eh? Ya, good kettle. The kettle we had on the Star 64 was bigger and
it took fuckin' forever to boil water. Remember Cyrus? We'd wake up, push
the button on the kettle, take a crap and still the water wouldn't be boiled.
Fuckin' thing, eh? Remember, Cyrus? The kettle on the Star 64, Cyrus? One
time I was boiling some fuckin' water ..." [ad nauseum]

I am nodding and inching away with my tea, but he'll go on for hours and hours and hours and days and days like that. It's painful. Sometimes I see myself grabbing a needle and fishing nylon and sewing his mouth shut.

And I'm messed up, because I want to tune this out with a glass of wine? Yup, James, I'm an addict. I don't care. Spiritual poverty. I don't have Jesus or God to hold my hand or talk to. Much as I'd like an invisible buddy who's always on my side, and I envy people who get comfort from that, I just can't do it – it makes no sense to me. I understand the need, the longing, and why humans invent myths and all-powerful entities to alleviate loneliness or fear of death. We are meaning-making creatures and we are very good at constructing coherent narrative out of random events. We all have our methods to get by. Mine is daydreaming and wine. Not my first choice. A real human to laugh and cry with and share moments with, to snuggle, discuss ideas, share our hearts and fears and to stimulate my brain is first choice. Wine to me is preferable to humans that can't stimulate or comfort me. Most people bore me so much I want to scream. I prefer to amuse myself than to be around morons. Sure, I overdo it sometimes. I don't like it when I am sabotaging myself with endless months of non-stop wine. That is totally not cool. But in small doses, it fills the void, bridges the gap. Self-medication for holes in the soul and intellectual boredom. Sorry, but it's true. That's the latest rationale, anyway, and I notice it, write it down, and turn it around in my mind, from various angles. Hmmm. Interesting how much my addiction throws so many different rationales my way. It's all theory anyway, as there is no wine here. Could erase the last paragraph so that I don't disappoint you James, but I prefer truth to trying to make myself look better by not expressing the strong wish that I had some wine right now. If it were here, I wouldn't hesitate. I'm sorry, I hope you don't think less of me. ☹

Just called Shasso on the satellite phone. To try to connect with anyone. He sounded genuinely concerned about me. It's so surprising to me that anyone cares about me, so hearing the concern in his voice floors me. Letters from the prison have arrived for me, Shass said. I have such longing to have them in my hand and to read them. Are they from James, or Liam, or Ivan? Maybe one from each, I dare hope. Pretty crazy that my best buddies are in prison? So what?

I wonder if I seriously screwed up by sending a copy of my fishing letter to James via the American Embassy in Bangkok, what with joking references to Al-Qaeda, Guantanamo Bay and water-boarding. Hopefully they have a sense of humour. Hopefully he does too. I cannot help but worry that I may have made a serious tactical error in doing so. Americans can get pretty huffy about stuff like that. I didn't really think it through – I only had one hour left on shore and really wanted to get the letter to him, to let him know that I was thinking of him and that he's not alone in his shitty new situation. I mean, not alone in thought, anyway. I hope I haven't inadvertently caused him more problems. What's done is done. Yikes.

We four sit and eat another repulsively massive meal in silence. I eat only the salad greens, avoiding the pork ribs dripping in grease and thick bbq sauce, rice and potato side dish. We all have hit a low point today – each is having a hard time keeping morale up. I am dying to scream and get off this f**king boat, but there's nowhere to go. I sit watching the guys inhale their ribs, mere inches from me, fighting the claustrophobia. I breathe in, I breathe out. 8 pm. Two more hours to kill before we can put away the gear and slip into the oblivion of sleep. Hope tomorrow is a better day. Sending positive thoughts to you, James.

Day eternity: Finishing up my cribbage board all day occupies my time and I feel somewhat relieved of the tedium of this endless fishless voyage. 5 pm. Cyrus announces yet another change of direction. We'll turn and head North now, as the owner has told us to come way up to the top of the Haida Gwaii, where he today caught 70 big fish. A month ago, even a week ago, we were leaving places that had only 70 fish, because they were woefully inadequate, but now, after days of only a handful each day, we are going to steam for four days and nights straight to get to where we too, might have a chance of catching 70 fish. I can't describe how I feel. Morale is so low here. Frustration so high. Driving around this massive ocean, counting on one hand the number of fish we catch in a day, and paying attention to every report from each other vessel, so that each time a guy reports catching more than 50, we turn and head in his direction, even if he's hundreds of miles away. Our maximum speed is six knots (6.6 miles/hr). We have been driving in massive circles for weeks. No fish. I can't find anything to say to anyone, because I have nothing positive to say and I don't want to be negative. My shoulder is shooting pain down my arm into my wrist just from the sanding I did today and all I can think of is jumping off this boat as soon as I see land. I'll swim for it. Deep breath, this will pass. Deep breath, don't talk, just smile. All will be ok.

I do love my massive cribbage board, 11" X 24" X 2". It's pretty cool, and I look forward to finishing it with a little black and red paint, a handle to hang it up, and some varnish, when I get to shore. It's funky, and I'm proud of making it, even if I had to ward off Cyrus and Etienne with steely glares whenever they tried to take over my project. Cyrus wouldn't let me use the skill saw and so he cut the board for me. I accepted his paternalistic help with grace and a "Thank You," having learned over decades that making an issue of it will get me nowhere, except accused of being a 'man-hating bitch.' So I grit my teeth and let him use the 'boy' tools for me. Argh. And it's pretty clear that he likes me and uses every excuse to say that he wants to jump in the shower with me or to share a bunk. Yuck. I just laugh it off and say firmly: "No thanks." Meanwhile Etienne kept trying to interfere while I was measuring, drilling, carving, and sanding, but I kept my earphones in and ignored him, until he got the point that this is my project, not his. Now that it's finally ready to use, I have no interest in playing a game.

Neither Mak nor Cyrus play cards, and when I am on edge like this, I don't trust myself to engage with Etienne, 'cause I end up wanting to strangle him. I'm not good at hiding my irritation, so I keep the uneasy fragile peace by avoiding unnecessary interaction.

Reports up and down the coast. No fish in any Canadian or International waters. We are all facing the almost certainty that there will be no Tuna this year. Mak sits slumped in the galley not talking. His eyes are wet. He has three kids and a wife to support. He has been away from home for six months. I say nothing. There is nothing to say.

Walk out to the bow and stare at the infinite sea in front of us. Light a cigarette I took from Cyrus' pack. It tastes horrible. The smoke smoothes out the knot in my stomach. Reminds me of my first cigarette at age 12, behind the high-school I had started earlier that year. Our house had just been arsoned the day after Christmas and I was put alone in a small dorm room in university student residence while the rest of my family lived at friends' houses during the months our rental home was being rebuilt. There was no insurance to replace our belongings. Nothing ever brought back a sense of safety. Not sure I had one by then, anyway. The cigarette tasted awful, but somehow mellowed out the large knot of fear that lurked ever-present in my gut. I smoked a pack a day for about six years, 'til my first pregnancy and first abortion at 17. Today I smoke half of this one and throw it away. Feel sick from it. I want off this fucking ship! I notice the thought, and send it drifting off on the next wave. Warm wind, endless blue water, sky full of billowing clouds. I throw up my arms to the sky. What am I supposed to be learning here? I ask the wind. *What am I supposed to be learning? What am I supposed to be learning? What am I supposed to be learning? What am I supposed to be learning?*

Patience, tenacity, survival in adverse situations? Please... those lessons I am an expert in. I have survived many horrendous situations and have fiercely fought for my survival and for my sanity. Put so much work into healing the tremendous damage done, crawling through violence and mental illness and raised my daughter alone by virtue of sheer will, determination, perseverance and tremendous inner strength. I have been trying to learn how to do much more than just survive life. I crave abundance instead of marginal living. I am ready and wanting to thrive. So what is the point of this futile trip? *What am I supposed to be learning? What am I supposed to be learning? What am I supposed to be learning?*

I look up into the clouds. Am I here to discover God? I ask the sky. I try to talk to God, but it just doesn't work for me. I just can't believe there's an entity sitting up there, looking down, controlling the situation, listening to me. I lean over the rail and imagine jumping into the warm ocean water. What am I supposed to be learning here? I scan the horizon, each cloud, looking for a sign. What am I supposed to be learning here? I hear James's voice: "Keep smiling, Heath." I smile. This is just another beautiful day on earth. I must source from within me the strength, the patience, the grace. Life is beautiful. Breathe. Keep smiling, Heath. I walk back inside the galley to finish cooking dinner.

Another day: more of the same, the same, the same. I find myself not wanting to call Morgan. Too ashamed to tell her that in a few days I will start my third month of this futile exercise and that I am even poorer than I was when I left, now maxxed out on my credit card, with phone bills piled up and two months' rent owing when I return to Shasso for storing my few possessions in a room in his house. No idea how I will make any money come in to eat. I don't want to face anyone when I return, but that's all a moot point as I don't even have the ferry fare to get to Salt Spring if I got off the boat right now. Wow. I cannot let these thoughts get to me. Smile and appreciate the waves and sky. That is all I can do. I can do nothing about anything else. I can't even search for jobs from where I am or do anything to improve my situation. This is so incredibly frustrating, I feel so powerless. Breathe, breathe, breathe.

Looking at pictures on my computer from the past few years: the stolen pictures of me and Liam at the Rama VI hospital in Bangkok when the guards weren't looking. We hung out for two whole days during his stay for surgery for skin cancer. I never let go of his hand. What an amazing time together I will cherish forever. He will always be my little brother. Frog and Toad, we are. I can only hope he is finding some peace from his inner turmoil these days.

We are now within several hundred miles of Vancouver Island. Seas are calmer, much less choppy than in the past week. Blue sky and warm sun reminds me that it is the end of summer. We are all sleeping late every day. I lie in my bunk until nine, not wanting to face another endless day of tedium. When I do drag myself up, I busy myself with cleaning the galley, disinfecting surfaces, the head, laundry, more sanding of my cribbage board. I could use it as a weapon, thwack Etienne across the face with it. Hee hee, I am getting giddy. Deliberately drag out each task as long as humanly possible in order to fill the hours. Make a veggie and cheese omelet one at a time for each of us. Mak takes his out to the stern to eat. Seconds later I hear the sounds of a Tuna slapping out its life and blood. I go out to check, as each fish caught is now a big event, demanding all of our attention and even the occasional cheering and clapping. Mak is pissed off. He has flipped the bloody Tuna onto his omelet and toast and disgustingly throws the whole plate overboard. This will probably be the main event of the whole day, I realize. Any break from the monotony is newsworthy.

A few days ago, a stormy wind and swell had us bumping up and down, untangling criss-crossing lines all day. I stood for hours monitoring the gear and noticed that my dildo line had blown over the top of the boat and was caught on the stern light mounted on the roof. Boat rocking and swaying precariously, I climbed up the narrow ladder to the roof and made my way to the back where the wind lifted my baseball cap off my head and tossed it into the churning surf below. I freed the nylon line and carefully lowered myself down to the relative safety of the deck. A minute later, the dildo line jumped, and I pulled it in to discover that I had caught not a fish, but my baseball cap. Cyrus and Mak cheered the recovery of my hat, and we rehashed the unlikely event the rest of the day.

I reread some of my dialogues with my thesis advisor from a decade ago. I envy the intellectual engagement I had with him, and I am chagrined to notice the same themes weaving through my life then as now: having a hard time navigating a social world epistemologically incompatible with mine. I read Daniel's total support and struggle to really get me, as well as his impatience at my self-doubt. He repeats his underlying message in all his comments to me: "Accept that you're fierce, intelligent, astute, principled, and unwilling to play the same games others do. You are sensitive, deep-thinking and deep-feeling about injustice, wear your heart on your sleeve and also switch abruptly into harshness that people react to. So what? Use your voice, your critique! You have things to say – an unique perspective and insight from which to do it – get out there and say them." I think his advice is still very salient.

You Rock, Heath! I cheerlead myself, to ward off the self-loathing that's been creeping in. *Keep being Me!* So most people don't 'get' me. So what? Just go out and be! See, I'm human, I respond to positive affirmations too.

Highlights: Last two nights of August, perfect sunsets and full moon rising on opposite horizon, absolutely magical pinks, purples, oranges, periwinkle, and shimmery globe of the moon bathing the sea in silvery light.

Caught a few fish these past two days – over 120 big fish each day, which brought morale creeping up a little. Today, we tack in a muddle of 70 fishing boats all within a three – mile radius, zigzagging, crowding each other, all frantic for fish. Radio crackles non-stop with their inane chatter and gossip, reporting every fish caught. Deep sea container vessels charge through the middle of this at a break-neck 25 knots, scattering the fleet like marbles on cement. Weather reports forecast a 35 mph gale tonight, and our anchor winch is broken (figures!) so we'll head for the nearest tiny spot for a day or two. We're all looking forward to some time on land, and to drink (let's be honest!) and to fill up our fresh water tank. I might steal a shower today in anticipation, a luxury we haven't had in over a week. Last night, as the dark overtook the day, I sat at the stern catching the final fish of the night while Mak pumped out the bilge and Etienne washed the dinner dishes. As I reached down to grab the big fella, I lost my footing in the bouncing of the ship and somehow my left kneecap twisted or torqued and popped right out of alignment, twisted around to the side of my leg. I had the fish on the table and suddenly couldn't stand on my left leg anymore, excruciating fiery pain. Mak and Etienne sauntered back and I yelled at them to grab the last fish on the line, as I couldn't move. Mak grabbed me and helped me to sit. I leaned on him, ripped off my gloves, raincoat and hoodie constricting me, while Etienne pulled the remaining fish on the long line. After some time, some ice on it to reduce the swelling, and a sleep, the knee ended up ok, but fragile, like it could pop out again at any moment, so I wrapped both knees today in bandages to give them support, and more handfuls of the weak painkillers. I can't afford an injury out here.

Talked to Morgan this morning and found out that while I'm out here making no money, I'm wracking up hundreds of dollars in phone bills for our brief phone calls. What an irony, a piss-off. I have to pay for her to receive my calls that I'm already paying for. Serious racket, cell-phone companies in Canada.

I pop painkillers all day. I love catching the big fish, and these past few days of really big fish prove to me that I am a capable fisher. I am totally rocking the fishing! And proud of myself. My hands are starting to get pretty wrecked after just a couple of days of heavier fishing, despite the many layers of gloves and rubber protection. Tiny cuts that the nylon line slip into and slice deeper with each fish. It's hard to keep them from infection, with fish guts, blood and slime and constant wet. It's critical to not get infections, though, as bacteria from the anchovies I throw as bait cause major blood infections that have cost guys hands and arms in previous years, and necessitated a chopper rescue to nearest hospital. My cooking days are when my body gets to heal a little. Today is another slow start and I don't have much enthusiasm or positivity. Just trying to kill time. I'm pissed off at myself for having gained so much weight and find it hard to cut down on the excessive eating. I am grossed out, after having worked so hard to be in good shape this past year. Another piss off on this trip. I wish I had the letters that are sitting on Salt Spring so I could know what's going on with the guys. Chicken souvlaki for lunch and pork ribs for dinner. Yuck. The food is repulsing me now, but I still eat it. I'm bummed because it is now September and I have nothing to show for having left Thailand broke, in debt and motivated to return as soon as possible to support the prisoners. That was April. It is September and I am farther away even from being able to follow my dreams. So what? In the big picture, this is nothing.

The adventure continues...more breakdowns, fuck-ups, and nothing matters. I choose to focus today on the wonderful moments: pulling fish, draining over a hundred big frozen carcasses then loading them into the freezer, back and shoulders aching, loving the aching, knowing I am so much stronger than just a month ago. Gorgeous sunset licks the waves, sharks circle, Mak and I laugh and I LOVE pulling fish! Cozy afternoon nap, and I feel protected in the warm cocoon of the rocking berth. Lysol wipes taking blood stains off my face and arms before bed, as there is no water to wash with. I love ALL of it; stringing up coffee containers to catch hydraulic oil dripping from the solenoid in the engine room; Mak jerry-rigging saltwater deck hoses directly into our water-maker, bypassing the faulty intake hose under the ship, thus hopefully solving our fresh water problems.

Leaking another cry about money worries today. Cyrus hugged me and I dried my tears after three seconds, not wanting to be crying in front of him, nor wanting his arms around me. I am stressed about what to do with no money, no home, no income, no prospects, and Fall coming in quickly. Let it go, Heath, let the wind carry it away. How will I make a home for me and Morgan? How will I get to the prison to support the guys? How will I feed myself? The last part should be fine – I'll live off my new fat stores all winter. Worrying does nothing.

We are heading for shore, as we have caught nothing in the beginnings of this projected four-day gale. We'll head down Esperanza inlet to Tahsis, arriving tonight. Hopefully the break will lift our spirits and we can return to the ocean with renewed hope and enthusiasm. That's the plan. We are all acutely aware that the season end is just around the corner, when the cooler waters return and there are no more chances for Tuna. I wonder how long I can stave off Cyrus's increasingly intense passes at me. He makes every excuse to touch me and to offer me massages, cuddles and spankings. I need to be careful, as I don't want to piss him off, and mess up any future work. Been here a thousand times in work situations, where I get black-listed for not wanting to fuck the boss. Mostly I don't mind his lighthearted flirting, as he is not aggressive or pushy, just insistent that he finds me attractive. I tell him that I can't sleep with co-workers or bosses – it's never a good idea. I hate that I have to strategically save his ego in order to not get fucked over for rejecting him. He's an ok guy – a prince to work with compared to George, a team player, just don't have <u>any</u> interest in him. And even if I did like him, as the one single woman out here on these hundreds of boats of all-male crews, why would I sleep with the boss, just as all the guys expect, thereby undermining any respect they have for me for being a decent worker? There is only one other woman out here – a husband and wife team, Al and Angie, been fishing their boat together for 30 years – Cyrus keeps telling me that it's a great setup and he'd like him and I to be like them. Yuck. Just what I need.

TAHSIS, BC

We've been in Tahsis for 30 hours now, and it feels like a fantastic break. Coming down the narrow channel into this tiny town, I marvel at how beautiful BC is, and how lucky I am to be able to see it like this, from the water.

Etienne is quitting, jumping ship today and heading home to Sidney to ask for his construction job back. He's had enough of the no fish and needs to make a living. Mak and I do too, but we have nothing to leave for, no alternate sources of income, so we'll stick it out to the end of the season. The crappy weather that forced us in here is supposed to last another few days, so we'll be sitting here, bored out of our tree for a few more days. I wish I could get my letters from the prison and read them. Oh well, it is a beautiful spot. I wonder what the dynamics will be like without Etienne as a foil. I should try to find a grocery store here and see if we can pick up more fresh fruit and veg – we are out of them.

I walk to the main part of town – about two km. from the dock, and find the only store – a cornerstore/liquor/hardware/restaurant with about three small aisles and an East Indian owner who is thrilled that I want to empty his shelves. We place an order for fruit, veg and blue cheese that his son will drive in from Campbell River for us on Friday. This commits us to another two or three days here. Two other commercial vessels from the fleet pull along side us and tie up to us. The whole fleet is hiding in various wee harbours, waiting out the bad weather. A few more people to break the monotony, but it will be a piss-up and I am not good at not drinking when there's nothing else to do. Although wanting sobriety, sobriety is more of a challenge when I'm bored and there's absolutely nothing else to do. No bookstore, no people, no movie theatre, nothing. So I am careful. But not careful enough. I drink. Heavily. Sick as a dog the next day, I hide in my bunk for hours. Mad at myself.

Another day sitting around this 'town.' Cyrus and I have walked to the end of the only two hiking trails – we've also worn out the path between the dock and town – I know that road like the back of my hand. The other fishers were nice enough, but I became quickly bored of their endless nattering about the minutae of boats, fishing, etc. And they're heavy, heavy drinkers. 24/7 non-stop redneck drinking, endless. One guy comes over to our boat at 7 am, to start the day, breakfast beer in hand, not realizing that his stinky bloody fishing sweats are soaked in his own urine. He and Cyrus shoot the shit on deck, drinking beer. Need to get away from that. From them and their non-stop boozing. Some of the other hung-over guys start emerging from their boats and as the day progresses, I start hearing from them what I did the previous night (apparently in a blackout, as it's all news to me) after I thought retired for the night to my bunk. It's a hellava shock having one of the fishers pull me aside to tell me that I have a drinking problem.

Etienne's been gone over 24 hours and we haven't heard from him whether he made it back home. He was supposed to pick up Cyrus' truck in Port Alberni and drive it down to Sidney, but his love of alcohol and partying may have messed up that plan. He also left with a bit of a FU to us, as he scooped all the cash in the jar that was supposed to be for the four of us to share for the fillets he sold off the boat. We've had a steady stream of locals asking us to sell them Tuna, but Cyrus is turning them down. Etienne had no such qualms, though, and made himself some pocket money by selling directly off the dock, even though the fish belongs to all of us, as well as the owner. Then he took the money and ran. Nice.

TAHSIS, BC TO TAHSIS INLET TO NOOTKA SOUND TO OPEN WATER.

Going bananas in Tahsis, we finally left this morning, after loading up with a bunch of extremely overpriced produce. Glad to be back on 'dry' water, so to speak, away from the alcohol-fuelled dock life. Mak and I untie the ropes and we pull out, drop the poles, put out the gear and we all take in the breathtaking view down through the narrow Tahsis inlet. Sea otters basking in the sun and splashing around, sea lions bobbing, and a black bear climbing up the far hill. Mak is so excited to see a bear, and reminds us that he was right not to leave the boat and go for a hike, unlike Cyrus and myself, who walked as much as we could on land. Desperate to move my body after being cooped up on the boat, I explored the only two hiking trails near town and followed logging roads into the mountains, to the consternation of truck drivers hauling massive trees, not used to seeing other people in the middle of nowhere. Mak tried to venture down the gravel road leaving the gov't dock once, but only got 200 metres before turning around, afraid to run into a bear.

Now, as we head down the channel towards open ocean, Mak tells us of a movie he saw in Fiji about a bear attacking a man, and the man's only recourse was to jerk off the bear. The story, repeated many times over the past few hours comes with pantomime and graphic depictions of the bear's dick and the guy's masturbatory actions to save his life, punctuated by his bellowing laugh. Mak is a strange man. Is highly obsessed with stories of his dick and others'. Major theme for him. But I appreciate his laughter.

An hour ago, I was standing in the doorway to the wheelhouse when Cyrus suddenly moved in to me and put his arms around me, face approaching. I backed up, startled, "What are you doing?" My hat blew off in the wind as I backed out the door to escape his grip, and he retreated as I went to fetch it, blowing along the deck. I returned to say: "Cyrus, do not do that," which I hope he took seriously. He carried on as if nothing had happened, but now I'm not feeling so good about this situation. I woke up this morning to him stroking my cheek, saying: "Wake, up, Beautiful" and it creeped me out. He had better get the message loud and clear that I don't want him touching me. At all.

We're hoping to catch some Salmon before we get out to Tuna waters, just for the fun of it, and also to have fresh dinner.

Mak and I sit on the metal hatch covers, looking out to the stern. Behind us, the shoreline is getting farther and farther away and I watch the surf pound and crash on the rocks and beach. Ahead of us is open ocean and I have anxiety for the first time about my personal safety, out here with just two guys, alone. I just paused in my writing to go up to the wheelhouse and ask Cyrus if I have to worry or stress out about him trying to touch me. He shook his head.

"You're clear that I'm a deckhand and not your girlfriend?" I repeated.

"Yup," he said, "no need to worry."

"Good," I said, "I don't want to be stressed out here about that shit."

Hopefully all will be cool between us. I miss Morgi and wish I could call her. I will try tonight when she's at home, if the satellite phone works.

Reread a journal from Fall 2007 just before David came to Salt Spring after three months of rehab in France. My fears, my letting go of uncertainty, my feeling 'lost.' Themes for me of always trying to embrace 'lost'. What would it look like for me to not feel lost? What would it look like to be 'found'? Writing that last sentence brings tears to my eyes. I don't know what it would look like.

Hard in reading the journal not to regret all the years I gave to David, trying to support him, trying to heal him, trying to give him support to fight his ugly disease. I knew from early on that any possibility of a 'healthy' romantic relationship was impossible, but still I stayed on for years as a social worker to a lost soul. Am I supposed to feel that was all wasted, just because the outcome is shit, and his future is bleak, his disease raging more strongly than ever? Is reflecting to someone their inherent value wrong when they don't end up seeing it themselves? Are we supposed to only cheer the success stories? It's always easy to judge from the outside. Why would a strong intelligent woman be with an alcoholic loser? Because I believe in people, in not giving up on lost causes. I can easily compartmentalize and understand perfectly well that a healthy, adult loving relationship is not possible with that man, but that he is still a suffering human being in need of support with his shitty illness. If his illness had been cancer, no one would judge me for my determination to offer him support, no matter the impact on me. But no one can take on another's disease of addiction, and beyond that, I absolutely cannot be on the receiving end of what has become a wholly intolerable way of relating to me. Parts of me have grieved deeply the lost of a good person, someone I used to love deeply, now stuck in a shitty ever-downward spiral, and all that his addiction has robbed us of in our shared dreams of future. Another part of me sees a suffering individual and prays from a distance that he will find his way to recovery, but is clear I will not have any more contact with him, ever; and a third part hates the fucking hell and damage he has done to me and must strive to release it, not wanting to hold on to any lingering bitterness.

Night sky finally on the ocean and I will sink into sleep. Talked to Morgi tonight and Shasso too. I realize that I really love Shass — truly one of the friends I'm closest to. But still he is not so good at being emotionally present: guys rarely are. Too bad I find it so hard to relate to straight woman culture – I'd like some women friends, more emotionally open, but they mostly act so fucking shallow and pathetic. Gee, I'm not being at all judgmental! Yikes! Shasso has a raging headache and is stressed from school. Worried about me, he's asking me to please, please jump ship and end this nightmare trip. I tell him I won't. I will see this through to the end. I am not a quitter.

New day. An endless day scratching out only 57 fish. The hours took years to trickle by and morale was very low – there is little patience for more of this bull-shit non-fishing. Also, things are now a wee bit strained between Cyrus and I. Years ago I would have raged at the injustice that women constantly have to deal with harassment, then get blamed or vilified because we are only seen as sexual beings instead of co-workers on the job. But I am so used to this, it just is another example for the thousandth time. Who knows now what he'll say about me to all the other fishers, just because his stupid ego is bruised that I rejected his advances, and what impact that will have on my future employment prospects in this tight-knit fishing world. Gee, never been here before!

Our music is on the fritz, so sitting for hours at the stern staring at lines that don't jump, and constantly cleaning gear in the chilly wind and fog is way less tolerable when there's no tunes to get lost in. This sucks. Not a single distraction from how much this sucks. I am ready to be done this. Grumpiness everywhere, including on the radio and phone all day long from all the rest of the fleet, fed up and stressed from a season that will leave us all broke, away from families, and further behind.

Days in, Days out. Days in, Days out.

Day 77: Hit a big wall today. Dark, bitter thoughts. Cried and cried. Feeling so shitty. So demoralized. So bitter at everyone who has money given to them, without working for it, who knows nothing of the shame I feel always working so hard my whole life, in the full-time workforce since age 12 and never getting a fucking break. Ever. I have NEVER been given a break EVER without some guy expecting me to fuck him for it. Finally get a supposedly lucrative job and it's the one year it all goes to shit. Snapped at the skipper: "Stop fucking telling me about the theories of fishing, and how it's 'supposed' to be. I've been doing this two and a half months, hearing hourly of the theory of fishing, hearing every five seconds that it isn't 'supposed' to be like this. Hearing every five minutes of the huge money each of you made last year and the year before last, and the year before that. How you've bought so many houses outright with cash from fishing. I don't want to hear it anymore. It's not supposed to be like this? Well, it is like this, and it sucks." I am so fucking resentful of people with money. So unbelievably bitter about working so hard unsupported, only scraping by barely and being shit upon constantly for being a 'morally degenerate' poor single mother, the scourge of humanity, as if I didn't want better for my daughter, but 'chose' instead to struggle in poverty. All the constant hard work at being a compassionate present loving parent eclipsed by the daily struggles to just stay sane and feed us. And going crazy in my isolation. I hate their homes that these fishers bought with their fishing money. I am so envious, so resentful.

I call Morgan feeling so low. She is so great, believes in me when I can hardly believe in myself anymore. So tired of always just trying to 'keep going, it will get better!' And it never gets better. And feeling a tiny glimpse of what the guys in prison must feel like. How do they stay positive each day? Blah. Blah. Yeah right, like it's even comparable. Just lay down to rest my weary aching body and sore neck and to try to shift my thinking to positivity, as all I can feel is bitterness and despair right now. Wake up and Mak and Cyrus are sitting looking out at the unmoving lines. I don't need to ask, their resigned faces tell me that we haven't caught a fish in the time I've been lying down, not since about nine this morning, in fact. My body is wracked with chills. Look outside and it's pouring icy rain. I can't make my body put on my heavy rubber suit and go out to face the endless empty sea.

Another day. Cyrus gets me out of bed at six, and it's a relief from the smashing. The ship is poorly designed, according to all who have been on it, and tips constantly, smashing us in our bunks. It is impossible to sleep, and bruised limbs, aching shoulders and neck get a relief from constantly bracing against the smashing. I shift position a million times a night, trying to wedge myself into as tight a ball as possible, to stop from banging my head, but nothing seems to work. I end up just shifting in order to change the body part that gets the brunt of each successive assault. My neck is so stiff, I can't move it, and Cyrus and Mak are creaky and exhausted too, from endless sleepless nights being thrown around our respective wooden boxes. We throw out the gear, and I cheer mentally: "Ok, big fish day today!" as usual, laughing at myself for continuing the mantra. Yesterday, I resorted to writing a note to the fish asking them to please come and bite our lines at their earliest possible convenience, signed sincerely, with Warm Regards, the Crew of the *Gaffe*. Cyrus and Mak watch me solemnly as I roll the note around a dead anchovy, kiss the package for good luck, and toss it out to the churning ocean. Then we wait. And wait. Speculating occasionally about whether the Tuna can read English and might it be better to write in Japanese or Spanish?

This morning, as we make our weary bodies to the stern to put out the gear in the cold dark pre-dawn, Mak discovers that the lazarette is full of water – full. The alarm which would normally go off, warning us in the night of this dangerous situation did not go off. Now we are using our one inadequate pump to empty the room, and Cyrus and Mak are cursing the highly dangerous inadequate equipment, faulty set-ups, unknown leaks and mysterious malfunctionings, which are now routine on this boat.

No one is catching fish anywhere, except the Americans. I wonder how long we will continue this charade, before we admit that the new policy has totally decimated the Canadian Tuna fishing industry. There simply are no fish in International waters. That's why we had the fifty-year long treaty in the first place, because the Tuna are all within 200 miles of American soil.

I am astounded and impatient with Cyrus' non-logical reasoning and constant changing of direction and plan, every time he gets a radio call of another boat having picked up two fish. 49 years of fishing experience aside, he has absolutely no grasp of basic principles of math, logic or probabilities. All the fishers seem to be operating on the same faulty logic. Let's say a group of 50 boats, all in a four mile radius each has between 0 and 12 fish for the day. One guy has seven fish and another guy has three fish, the fishers actually praise the guy with seven fish as if he is somehow a 'better' fisherman, as if there were a significant difference between 3 and 7 fish on a large ocean. There is NO DIFFERENCE, I want to scream at them, as they blast away on the radio for hours, trying to figure out how James over there managed to get double what Bobby did. And all arrogance aside, there is a lot I see in how they make their decisions that would greatly benefit from some basic understanding of sampling distributions and logic.

Last night, we were at 45 fish for the day. Mak goes for a rest, and I sit out there and suddenly take in 20 fish in the space of thirty minutes. Brings us up to 65, quickly. Boom! a heady, exhilarating patch of really large fish, and we need to turn around and back-tack to keep catching in that patch. That's the largest patch we've crossed in weeks. I tell Cyrus, and he, inexplicably, decides to continue in the same direction, away from our patch of fish. This from a guy who will turn around and back-tack endlessly crossing the same spot on the ocean for hours, if we catch two fish in a row. "I don't understand," I say: "20 fish. Why aren't we going back?" His answer: "If you go back for an hour, you lose four hours." *Did I just hear him right?* "How do you figure that?" I ask, trying to sound neutral, and not incredulous. "Well, it's just known fact," says Cyrus, "that if you go back for an hour, you lose four." Oh. He leaves me at the stern, scratching my head, trying to figure out how that could possibly make any sense. He is the expert fisher, so there must be something in there about tides or currents or something that I cannot see. Try as I do, I cannot fathom his reasoning. So I wander back to the galley, where he is pouring himself a coffee. "Uh, Cyrus, can you explain the whole, uh, losing four hours thing to me?" I ask, again, trying to sound casual, nonchalant. (In my reasoning, if we back-tack over a patch of fish for an hour, then we return for an hour, that's two hours we've used, catching fish. We'll be back in the same spot two hours from now, with more fish than we had, probably in days. I don't see how that's a problem.)

"Well," he explains slowly, as if speaking to an idiot, "we're heading South. If we return North for an hour, then we head South again for an hour, we used two hours." "Yup." I concur. "So we're two hours behind," he continues. "Then, on the other end, when we get to where we're going, we're two hours behind, so that's another two hours." "What?" I am incredulous. "It's the same two hours," I say, "if we head North from any point for an hour, then return South, we use two hours. Just two, not four." But he is adamant, digs his heels in, and refuses to believe me, even when I go get a piece of paper and map out two boats leaving a spot in one direction, and one heads back for an hour, then returns, I show him how that boat is then only two hours behind the other boat.

"Nope, he insists, it's four hours you lose. You're not counting the other two hours when you get there."

OMG I want to scream! His faulty math doesn't even address the larger logic issue: How can you LOSE hours, when there is no destination? What is it exactly that we're supposedly four hours 'behind' in getting to? We are here to fish, and we are leaving the only patch of fish we've seen in weeks because the skipper has an irrational notion that he will somehow LOSE four hours of his life if he stays and fishes. Did you have an urgent appointment to get to on the open ocean that you will be two or four hours late for if you stop to catch fish? OMG. I can't do this anymore! OMG. He doesn't want to talk about it anymore, he is pissed off that I have questioned his reasoning. I think he's just pissed off that I refuse to let him grope me.

So we ran through the night again last night, burning more fuel to get nowhere. I was on edge all day, but really practicing in each moment to be positive, despite not feeling it. I can only control my attitude, not others' decisions or the situation. No one needs a grumpy, pessimistic asshole on a trip in very close space, and I don't want to be that person. So I remain smiley, although with great effort. We keep leaving places where we scratch out 70 or so fish to travel fifteen hours overnight to grounds where we then, sleep-deprived, eke out 40 or 50 fish for the entire day, along with 25 other boats, all fighting for the small catch. Head-on collision we almost had with one guy crossing our path either asleep, drunk or simply absent from the wheel. Cyrus veered sharply just in time. Called the guy on the radio but he didn't respond. So last night we leave again, even though as night was falling, we suddenly got 30 fish in the final hour. Along with ten other boats, we race up to where we are now. We were here three days ago and left it in a hurry, not wanting to stay and catch more large fish, 'cause one hour of fishing is actually a four-hour delay, apparently (!).

Today, we've caught three fish so far, and I can see 20 boats around us. I'm going fucking bananas.

More days in and out: At the night bite, we were having a blast, loving the feel of a sudden burst of fish jumping on our lines at once, adrenaline pumping, grinning at each other, cheering on each fish, we pull and pull and pull. The sky is magnificent and I snap a dozen pictures of the gorgeous ocean sunset silhouetting other fishing vessels. It's moments like that where I know that this job could be AMAZING, IS AMAZING, when there are fish.

Last night, I got totally triggered. Here's how it goes down: I think that Mak has lied to me. I see him catch two fish, and me, four. He goes to put them away, and returns to tell me there were 13. I look at him, confused. How could there be 13, I think? Is he including the 9 I already put away 15 minutes ago? I check our whiteboard in the afthouse, where we record each body, as we stack them on freezer plates. I casually ask him about 13 – you sure about that? I had 4 and you had... 9? "Yes," he grins. "Maybe you didn't see me catch all the ones right here on the side?" He points to his side-line. I shake my head. I know this guy is lying to me. I know he's competitive and it kills him when there's a bite on and I catch more than him. My mind whirls on this for hours. Do I tell Cyrus that Mak is padding the numbers to make himself look better? He routinely cheats at cards with Shasso, and lies constantly about his age and money in all of his stories. We have a running tease going on because I refuse to play Rock, Paper, Scissors with Mak. Two days ago I offered to settle a small matter, such as who would do first night watch, or some such matter. He cheated, waiting until my hand was shown to then throw his. First time, I assumed he didn't understand the rules and explained again. Then, I realized he simply plays that way. I refused to play again. He has been begging me to replay ever since.

"Please Heather. I cheated before, I won't cheat again."

Any idea how much those exact words trigger me? He doesn't understand. I fucking hate deception. I am not into giving lying deceivers another chance, as if it was ok for them to lie in the past, but now that they promise not to do it again, it's only required of me to let them redeem themselves. No thanks. I don't give second chances on deception. I'm all out. I have no time for liars. He thinks it's funny. I don't. I take it all in good humour, and we laugh as he begs me every day, every hour to play Rock, Paper, Scissors again, but I am firm and resolute. No. Here, now, I am pissed off that he has lied about the fish count.

Later I call Morgi and we talk. She is low, missing me, hating herself and binging and purging. I am fearful for her. She cries and tells me she is worried about me out here making no money. She wails: "Mom, how can someone like you with such a good heart get handed shit on a plate by life at every turn?" My heart breaks as she cries. I try to stay upbeat and I reassure her. Life's just like that sometimes and I need to stay positive and not become the bitter alcoholic that lurks within me, wanting to succumb to self-pity or despair at times. So it's yet another example of shit not working for me. So what? I am better than that – I just need to keep putting one foot in front of the other and stay positive – that's all anyone can do. You win some, you lose some, you just gotta keep getting up and trying again and staying positive. I tell her about Mak, about being triggered by his pathological lying, about how I know he quit drinking in 1994 and carries only a bible as reading material. Another fucked up addict who may have stopped his substance abuse, but hasn't addressed the self-deception, the lying manipulations that often go with the territory. In that moment I am so not happy to be on the open ocean with the groping dim-witted skipper and his lying, retarded sidekick, driving endlessly in circles, making pointless smalltalk. I want out.

This morning, I wake up from the first relatively restful sleep in a while, neck not as sore, ready to jump up and be cheerful. "Let's slay some fish," I announce. Mak and I drink our first tea in silence, then move the fish from the freezer plates down to the freezer hold. I decide to confirm my suspicions with cold hard fact, and I count the fish as we move them. There are two days' worth, and I know the supposed numbers for each day. I count and when we have stacked them all, I realize that I was wrong. We have exactly the number of fish Mak claimed we have. Hours later, as my mind is still sifting and sorting through this new information, that I was wrong about him lying, I nonetheless see how powerful the confirmation bias is in me. Even though I now have proof that I was wrong and he did not lie to me, I refuse to give up all my other stories about him. *Well, this time he maybe didn't lie, but that doesn't mean that he's not basically a liar,* I say to myself. I have mounted a case against him, gathered supporting evidence, and even when I realize that a key piece of my evidence is false, I still maintain my case. I KNOW that we humans do this. I have studied these cognitive biases we all have, I have seen it in practice and STILL as I sit here writing, I hold on to my story that Mak is basically a liar. Pretty messed up, eh? I will make it my project today to release that old story and to construct a new one, to not let the shadows and contours of David's and others' actions, and of my fear and loathing of deception to cloud my picture of Mak. But deception IS pretty messed up, I maintain. I HATE deception, and I shouldn't have to take it. AND, if you lie, you don't have the right to expect people to trust you. Ever. So self-righteous I sound, eh?

This afternoon, the big fat fish start rolling in! Big bites, where all the lines jump and Mak and I are pulling with all our might and speed, Cyrus running from the wheelhouse, blood flying everywhere, the sounds of huge fish slapping onto the deck and fighting us desperately; tangled lines, quickly dealt with; hook stuck half way down a fish, cut it out, toss him down the tube, throw out the jig; Cyrus stands ready with my knife to slit their throats so that I can concentrate just on pulling, getting the jig out, pulling, getting the jig out. Bang, grab another one; hose the blood; Mak yelling: and laughing: "Go Heathiss, pull pull!" all of us grim and determined and laughing and whooping all at the same time, and it is so exhilarating. I love this!

The Tuna in these waters are huge, really heavy and it is not a pretty sight sometimes to see me heave and grunt and swear and slip and regain purchase and get the fat fucker up and over, but I do it, and I don't lose any anymore. Watching Mak and Cyrus do it, awkwardly, and lose some, I realize that I am not a bad fisher. Mak keeps grinning and giving me the thumbs up. We are all so stoked! U-turn, back for another round! 29 fish in five minutes. Huge fish. Gorgeous bastards, with huge glistening bulbous bellies. Man, I love slaying Tuna. I talk to each one. Whether it's nicely, or swearing at him, or easing him to his death, or screaming at him, I deal with each fish I kill individually.

"Hey buddy, here we go!"

"Fuck you, you're coming with me."

"Not a good day for you," as I slit his jaw.

"Where you going buddy?"

"Oh I don't think so, mister" as I jam my knife into his eye to keep him from taking my tag-line down the tube with him.

I like this part. It isn't a mass slaughter, it's a one-on-one individual struggle between me and each fish, and I have to work to get him on the boat and kill him to be eaten. Occasionally he wins and gets away. But not often. I don't feel badly about killing them, I appreciate that I look at each one in the eye that I kill. I see each face and notice its features. I love the look of Tuna – they are the coolest looking fish, not ugly or lopsided, like Carp or Halibut. Tuna are elegant and classical and cartoonish, all at once. I don't hear Cyrus or Mak ever talking to their fish, and I wonder what they think of my non-stop monologue as I pull fish, but I don't care. It's so amazing.

Mak has told me at least half a dozen times today how much he appreciates me: that I am strong, fast, good at everything I do, and that I pull fish really well. He is generally critical, so I am very pleased. I feel that I am good too, and I am really proud of myself. I wish there was an abundance of fish, because I LOVE this! I could see myself doing many seasons Tuna-fishing, if it were actually like The Golden Days of Tuna I heard so much about these past months, where you work 10 – 15 days at a time to load up a boat (not three months to get only a quarter full!). I love how my muscles feel right now – I feel strong, powerful, and happy.

It's amazing how a little positive feedback and positive outcome can go such a long way – today I felt such a joy at just working hard, getting the job done. So much satisfaction, that I started to think of all the other accomplishments I have. What set me off was unloading Mak's tube full of big fish after a particularly awesome bite, in which we each had snagged 7 or 8 fish in five minutes. One fish had its tail stuck and was blocking the exit of all the rest of the fish and I reached my gloved hand up into the tube full of struggling, thrashing bodies, salty seawater and blood splashing all over my face and arms, and groped the slimy tail, trying get it free. It felt like reaching into a large vagina and trying to get the breach babies out. I told Mak this, after finally birthing his litter of half-dead Tuna from the plastic Mama, and he recoiled in horror. I explained that I have helped animals give birth, like when I lived in the Fulford Valley with Morgi and one of our landlord's elderly ewes was dying giving birth to triplets, her uterus and bladder pro-lapsing out onto the earth and trailing guts behind her as she struggled to walk. I have reached into sheep, to yank babies out. One orphan lamb, Kaos, I subsequently bottle-fed every two hours over weeks and cared for him in the basement of our place in a makeshift crib of hay bales. He imprinted on me and he'd follow me like a puppy as I walked down the hill in our valley to meet Morgan at the bus stop, coming home from school each day, much to the amusement of the other kids. I was pretty good at flipping adult sheep over and cutting foot-rot out of their hooves, injecting them subcutaneously with antibiotics or holding them down as the 'vet' castrated them. Huge balls, sheep have. In this case, though, I remember calling the neighbour to bring a rifle and shoot the suffering ewe in the head. As the 'vet' ripped and raggedly sawed her body with a shitty knife to free the unborn lambs, she struggled again to get up and we realized in horror that she was not dead from the bullet to the head. I'll never forget the look we exchanged as we realized how much torturous pain we were subjecting the poor animal to and that the only way to stop this horror was to continue to saw through her flesh, muscle, fat and tissue with knives to reach those babies, before the 'vet' could finally administer the drug that would put her into oblivion but that would harm the babies if we administered it before ripping them out. The long heartbreaking morning included swinging lifeless baby lambs around in circles in order to expel mucus from their lungs, massaging their chests to try to get them to breathe on their own. Coaxing, pleading, rocking, willing them to live, finally each sputtered and slowly succumbed in turn. In total disbelief, I couldn't bear to think of all the senseless pain – that despite our hard work and determination, not one life had even been saved, and many beasts had suffered such agonizing, pointless deaths. We placed the lambs alongside the mutilated mass of guts and flesh that was the remains of their mother to be buried together later. I washed away the total craziness of the previous bloody hours with me in Blackburn Lake. I jumped into the water naked for the second time in only twelve hours and allowed the nurturing embrace of the peaceful water to carry away the memory of the carnage.

Mere hours earlier, in the wee hours of the morning, I was also naked in that lake with a friend and a shadowy figure I had picked up hitchhiking on my way home after a night of drinking. It was a pitch black sky, and the lake a murky pool of black ink. Bats swooped low around us as we splashed in the dark warm lake water. Driving drunk, following the yellow middle line, I had just killed a deer with my car, was a few hours away from discovering a massacre in my hen-house, and the staggering, dying pregnant ewe. First though, a stop at the lake on the way home, I informed the hitchhiker. After the swim, we piled back into my car. Dropping off the shadowy figure whose face I never saw miles from the turnoff to my road, because I had a sudden gut feeling that this 'person' should not know where I live, I left him at the side of the rural road with the eeriest sensation that I had just given Death a ride in my car. The rest of that story should be told another time, but suffice to say that the eerie spectre of death was clearly all around that evening, and into the morning.

Remembering that day today, I allowed myself to see how many things I have tried, including sheep-farming, and how I excel at many things I try and I love learning anything new that challenges me. I am one to jump in to the deep end of any experience and just GO for it and take joy from the smallest experiences. I'm not trying to impress you, James, but I am so demoralized these days, and trying to keep my spirits up by remembering that I am not always a failure. Self pep talk. I need to continue to just go for it! "Keep teaching your transformative, somatic, sensory, sexual healing workshops," screams my inner voice. Just DO it, Heath! I know I have a strong gift to bring huge transformation to people through simple exercises in negotiating power, intimacy, humanity in intentional, present engagement. A decade has past since I put those explorations aside, not wanting my daughter to suffer the fallout from having small-minded people in our small community vilify and try to shame her or me for my sexual politics and expression.

SEPT. 13, 2012

10 am. No fish. Again. Can we please go home? I am disgusted with my weight gain, and I just want to be at the gym, running this fat off. I feel gross. It's not going to help my momentum to be packing around these extra pounds when I get back. Gotta stay positive and work hard to get back into super-fit shape. I felt so good when I was moving, doing. Got to be at my best, to stave off depression and to give me momentum for the next projects.

Out of books, rereading some of my writing I see, a dozen years later, the same themes and struggles in me. How to just learn to be loved, to be present in loveliness with someone? This is what I am here to learn. I can give it. Can I receive it? Can I learn to allow myself to be loved? My heart breaks for my mom, as I see that she never has. I will not be her. This, I must learn.

Can I learn to break this cycle? Can I use the wisdom from my knowledge of ethical, healthy, present engagement to re-grow this ability for myself, even as I teach it to others? Wounded healer, indeed, I laugh at the irony of trying to be present with men who are behind bars. I don't want to think about how much my past has turned me into a bitter, hurt person who is afraid to trust anyone. Oh well. I refuse to regret any part of my past: it all helps to teach and to allow me to grow.

Days just run into each other. Yesterday was one of the worst days, in so many ways, at many levels, and it feels great not to bother to relive it or recant it to you, just let it wash away and be grateful it's over. So brutal yesterday. We were all at our worst. I'm realizing that

Cyrus is starting to really lose his shit out here. Today is a new day, better, maybe deadly boring, frustrating, but I will seek out the pockets of beauty and gratitude.

Highlight of yesterday: after two serious dangerous near-misses, remembering that each moment is precious and that all that matters is being grateful for the miracle that is this life. And just wanting to get home safely to Morgi.

Dear James: I remember in a recent letter you wrote: "I can't take it anymore." Hitting that wall and then pushing through. I don't comment on your situation when we talk or write, because I feel that it would sound shallow, but I realize today that, I want to tell you that, in addition to sending you positive happy thoughts and smiles at many points during each day, I want you to know that I am here offering you my shoulder, my strength. I want you to know that I am sending love and light towards you and that you can draw on that anytime, knowing that I am on your side. I hope I can offer something in your low moments.

Today, a thousand times, I want to scream, to leave. But cannot. I draw strength from you James, from Ivan in moments, too. I don't know how you do it. How many times did people say that to me in my life? "I don't know how you keep going, Heath." Good to remember that I am not enduring any hardship right now. I have lived real hardship in my life. This fishing trip, this is just a frustrating, pointless exercise in futility. It is not a hardship by any stretch of the imagination. I will put this computer away, find a crappy condensed book to start in the volumes of Reader's Digest that Etienne left here, and I will drift off to sleep and start all of this again tomorrow. It is September 15. There is no hope left of fish. I just want this stupidity over with.

We got word today from the owner, to pull the plug on this season in one more week, if nothing changes. No one anticipates anything changing. Last year, all the fish in Sept and October were on shore, i.e. American waters. After decades, this year suddenly, after a unilateral decision by the Americans, there is now no more Canadian Tuna Fishing Industry. We've already talked to other boat owners who are retiring or planning to sell their boats to Americans for next year, as we have been effectively removed from this industry in one fell swoop. So goes the grumbling, anyway.

As for me, I have to keep doing what I've done for forty years – keep putting one foot in front of the other.

We are all precious beings, and so is Life precious, but we're also insignificant in the Universe, like grains of sand, like drops of ocean, and there is nothing 'against' or 'for' any of us – it's just the luck of the draw – not Karma, not a Deity granting some favours and others piles of shit. It just is. And that's why we must be grateful for every precious second, source beauty from within and breathe it deeply, work to be kind and fair to everyone, to show compassion for suffering, work against injustice, and not take it personally when life bashes us about. Let us dance and laugh and celebrate as much as we can. I gave this fishing a try, it didn't work out. And I will sing and find a new way to make my dreams come true.

And now we've limped into Winter Harbour as yet more bad weather approaches and I just got your letter via Yvonne. And I got a message that my father was just in a serious car accident a month ago but they had no way to contact me. I will head to Vancouver when we finish this nightmare of a non-fishing trip and see how I can support him.

I am rereading your letter. About detachment: I absolutely agree with your observations about being detached when others are losing it. I became conscious of developing my detachment and acute awareness when I was five. It was when I realized that there was a big game being played by adults in how and what they said and what they expected out of interactions, that were ostensibly about communication: How was your day? or What did you learn? but are actually about power dynamics, more specifically epistemological power struggles. I remember that vividly and it has informed me ever since. I developed an observer status and a deep interest in how and why people do what they do. I have always felt like an alien on this planet (and in some moments a persecuted freak, but still always observing why people react the way they do to me and to the 'other'). I am intuitive, always engaged, my dear, even if I make many mistakes and am awkward and imperfectly human, as we all are.

We are here, as far as I am concerned, to live fully engaged, to be present, aware, and not just sleepwalk through life. We are also here to learn how to love and to be loved. To leave the world better than we found it. To extend compassion to ourselves and to others.

About you saying your actions (recording on an illegal smartphone inside the prison) was a bad idea: I have heard from many people who condemn what you did. I will say to you what I said to them: I support your actions. It is so easy in retrospect, especially given the sanctions you are receiving because of the video to say "How could he do that?" and I admit, I was quite astounded when you first directed me to the video last year. I was amazed at your boldness. This gradually shifted to great admiration for your courage, for your willingness to flout the conventions and to dare to claim space and voice for yourself in a lost world. I wrote about this in a recent academic paper about mapping social space. About the human need to define our lives, to be witnessed and to show our lives. You stood claiming space and showing the wall that separates you from the outside world, and also your 'house.' In doing so you dared to claim a life for yourself in a place that would deny it of you, that supports only 'bare' life. Too rarely do people have the courage to speak and proclaim their truth in the face of persecution and I maintain that this was important and I am glad you did it. It's like you were saying: "I am here, I still exist!" And that matters. You matter. (I know, that wasn't necessarily your intention, but that's the celebratory post-modernist in me coming out right now to choose that significance of your courageous action). So I say *Thank you* for the video.

It is easy for anyone to say that you should have seen the consequences coming. Yeah, so what? And there are clearly issues of consent from people you show in the video, etc. but despite that, you did something profoundly important, the ripple effects of which will change down the road many peoples' lives for the better. Please remember that. That's what I think anyway, and I stand by it. Regardless of what I or anyone thinks, though, (since no one has the right to judge unless they are in your shoes) I just want to say I do hear your regret about it and I hope for you that you are extending compassion to yourself and being gentle on yourself. ☺

Can I ask you a few questions? I'll just fire a few off, and see if you feel like responding to any of them. When we talked about 'dignity' in January, you prefaced our conversation by saying that you thought of the concept as a masculine attribute. Something that applies to men only? Something like that. Could you tell me a bit more about what you mean by that? And why you think that might be? Other things: I am curious about other aspects of your life: who was the first person you fell in love with? What are you the most proud of in your life? I had a million questions and they all just fell away. I gotta rush to get this letter off.

Well, looks like one more trip out to the big water to look for fish, then I'll be shore-bound again. Will smile, keep my chin up and figure out how to make all this happen. Got an email from a Burmese friend in Bangkok yesterday, asking me if I could send him money, he's in a really tight situation. I have two Burmese migrant worker friends I try to squeeze a few hundred dollars to on occasion, but I had to tell him that I can't. That felt shitty. Oh well. Looking forward to what comes next, new ideas, new endeavours. Hoping to find my way to really shining big, and to actually tap into my unused talents and passion instead of always just 'getting by.'

I really hope this transfer stuff to the US gets cleared up quickly for you. Sending positivity. Hang in there, friend!

Oh, hey! I wanted to tell you that in Tahsis, BC ten days (?) or so ago, when I got internet briefly, I received an email from a British guy finishing up his M.Div., working as a pastor in an Anglican church. He has several Karen Burmese constituents in his congregation, and they have a connection to the Umpiem refugee camp up near Mae Sot, which I visit regularly when I take breaks from the prison. He was googling through the etherverse and came across my blog about visiting the Umpiem camp, a story about talking with the refugees and me struggling to answer their question of what democracy feels like. The minister wrote me to tell me that he was using my story in his sermon that Sunday and to thank me for the work I do. I thought it was pretty cool. Just wanted to share that with you.

Well, James. I need to get this off to Yvonne asap and hope that she can get it to you. Ok, my friend. Be well, Stay safe, and know that I am sending a million happy thoughts, strength, courage and hope in every day to you. YAY YAY YAY YAY YAY

Big hugs,
xo Heather

FISHING III

Dear James:

I hope this letter finds you getting ready to head home to the US!

Here is the final leg of my fishing trip journal, I thought you might want to know how it ends. Thanks for letting me share this with you:

OPEN OCEAN AGAIN

We leave Winter Harbour after two days on the dock, after a massive piss-up by dozens of fishers all around us, including me, all waiting out crappy weather. The end is in sight, and I am no longer grumpy. We will give it four to five more days of fishing, up at Haida Gwaii, Cyrus has decided, then we'll head back to dock and call it a season. Cyrus is sleeping, unusual for him to nap during the day, and I am in the wheelhouse.

The foc'sle smells unbearable, after Cyrus left the water hose running into the fresh water tank yesterday and flooded the ship. I awoke to water pouring into the foc'sle and I ran outside, certain that we were sinking, only to see that we were tied properly to the dock, no sign of the boat listing or going under. I yelled for Cyrus, who came running and he took one look at the water pouring under my bunk and turned off the water hose, which had overflowed the tank, seeped through the engine room and soaked the foc'sle. The 40-year old carpets have released their treasures and the mildewy, nasty smell where I sleep is horrendous. Can't describe the particularly toxic combination of odours and I wouldn't want to imagine exactly what they all consist of.

I woke up from a deep sleep at 4 am to the awareness of Cyrus standing next to me, inches from my face. He's vibrating and babbling about checking in on me, and he's not making sense and I am totally groggy, wondering if he's sleepwalking, horny, drunk, or all three. I tell him to go back to bed and he leaves. He says nothing to me in the morning about the incident.

What a relief and joy to receive the letter from you, James from Kao Bin Prison, and I'm glad I was able to send another fat letter back to you, via Yvonne today. I think I've read your letter 10 times already. Really glad to hear that your Embassy came to you, finally. What a relief that there might be movement there. Very soon, I hope.

I also learned via Facebook that two of Morgan's friends were in a drunk driving accident on Salt Spring. One is dead, the other in a coma in Victoria hospital. Both are 18. What a horrible, horrible tragedy. I am so looking forward to seeing Morgan. I can't wait.

Today Mak is happy, he knows he will leave soon for Fiji and rejoin his family. I hope Paul and Diana drop some money on me, and not just the expected 10% of our Tuna that won't even cover my bills while I was gone.

We're only half a day into our latest trip, and I am awakened at 10 pm by the engine shutting down, diesel stench overpowering the fo'csle, sleeping as I do mere feet from the engine. For the next hour, I lie bouncing around the hard box of my bunk, listening to each attempt to turn over the main engine. I step out a few times onto the pitch dark deck, to rid my head of the heavy fumes which have given me a headache. Finally the main engine kicks in and a few hours later, when Cyrus wakes me for my turn to watch, I learn that we have changed course and are headed for Port Hardy, where we will take on more fuel, as we cannot seem to draw fuel properly from our back tanks. I doubt Paul will want to spend more money on fuel this season, as he is losing money while we drive his boat empty, so I imagine that this is probably our final limp home. We will end this season on the *Gaffe* with more breakdowns and mechanical failures and take her in to port, mostly empty of the bounty we were supposed to fill her up with. Such is life.

It is mid-morning as we head down the channel to Port Hardy. Thick grey fog surrounds us and the visibility is nil. It is so penetrating, this cold wet air, and Cyrus tells me that this fog here means that it is hot and sunny on shore. Well, at least somebody's got warm sun. He has tried calling the owner a few times this morning to see if we continue this voyage or if it's time to end it, but no answer. I am thankful I get to see Port Hardy, as it is one of the places I've always wanted to check out in BC.

We all see the end in sight very soon, so as Mak and I go pull up the poles, fetch the Scotchmen and ropes, readying ourselves to tie up in port, I start to reflect on all the positive things I've learned, the wonderful parts of this non-fishing, fishing experience. I love that Mak and I are a smooth team, executing all the necessary tasks seamlessly and easily. I know he appreciates me and my work ethic and I do him and his.

I am proud at having mastered fish-pulling and also now the gaff. On one of the few days where all the fish we were catching were massive, I grabbed the gaff and decided to just learn how to use it, struck two or three times before getting the metal spike into the fish's head, and pulled the huge beast up effortlessly. Exhilarated, I repeated that several more times that day, realizing that the gaff is a cool tool, way easier to use than it looks. So proud of the huge beast I'd brought onto the boat by myself, I ran to show Mak, and he laughed at my child-like enthusiasm. 5 am the next morning, as we stacked the fish in back-breaking silence, Mak pulls the same massive frozen fish out and inspects it: "Who pulled this one?" he says for my benefit, eyes twinkling. *I did!* Thank you Mak, for your gentle good humour.

I appreciate Cyrus too, even though it's still strained between us. He made a few snarky comments about me not wanting to sleep with him in the few days after the wheelhouse incident, and some inappropriate ones about how I'd probably fuck the other guys on shore in Winter Harbour, but then he lightened up a little and mostly let it go. Mostly. Except in bizarre moments it resurfaces.

NOON, THURSDAY, SEPTEMBER 20, 2012

FIFTY FEET OFF PORT HARDY FUEL DOCK

Mak, Cyrus and I are standing on the bow, staring at a small vessel on the Port Hardy fuel dock, filling her tanks. We are waiting our turn. After 24 hours in Hardy, where I checked out the used bookstore and local coffee shop, Cyrus has decided that, against all of our wishes, against all logic and sense, we will fill this boat with fuel, and head out one last time to the big water and look for fish. None of us wants to go. Reports from the other vessels in the fleet from up in the Charlottes to down in Estevan to out in the open water trickle in by email: One fish caught today; three fish; zero fish. I ask him one more time: "Are you sure we have to do this?" Why don't we just call it a season, point the boat down the East Coast of the Island and head back to Salt Spring or Victoria or Vancouver, and unload? We are almost there. We are so close, and all any of us wants is just to go home. But Cyrus wants to try one last time, knowing we won't find fish, knowing the water is rapidly cooling off and the few fish are disappearing, even inside American waters. One final trip. Sounds so ominous. If this were a movie, you know this is the trip where we all die. Every cell in my body is screaming NO! and try as I may, I cannot wrap my head around doing this. In fact, I sit here writing when I should be out tying Scotchmen and ropes, preparing ourselves to tie up to the fuel dock. I can't make myself do it. I can't. Even the other fishers Cyrus has talked to are incredulous. "Why are you guys coming out again? Why don't you pack it in?" Because Cyrus doesn't want to give up, he feels responsible, a failure. We haven't been able to get ahold of the owner for the past 48 hours. He has apparently gone on holiday, sports-fishing off Port Renfrew with his girlfriend and neither is answering their cell phone. We apparently need his ok to pull the plug on this mess, five days after he already gave us the ok to stop within the week. I point out this last bit to Cyrus, that the owner has told Cyrus to pull the plug on this at any time, but Cyrus doesn't have the balls to make the call himself. "That's your JOB!" I want to scream at him. I stare at the satellite phone, willing it to ring, welcoming the shrill piercing shriek that may bring us a last minute reprieve from the owner. But it doesn't look like it's going to come.

I should go. Cyrus just walked into the galley, took a look at my face and said jokingly: "I've confiscated all the knives and sharp implements for this next trip, so you guys don't kill me. We'll just eat soup." I replied: "Hot soup can scald you, Cyrus." He turned to the wheelhouse, muttering nervously.

Last night, I slept with all my clothes on. As I went to turn in for the night, Mak took advantage of Cyrus being out drinking at a bar somewhere, to tell me that he's decided that I can be his Canadian wife: he's going to have sex with me. He grabbed my arm and pulled me to him. "NO, Mak, I'm not going to have sex with you." "C'mon, Heathiss, we gonna have sex." For the next ten minutes we argued, meaning he kept insisting and grabbing for me and I kept hitting his hands away, pushing him back and saying: "No Mak, I don't want to have sex with you." The tiny space in the fo'csle suddenly filled by this large guy and his insistent demands. I pulled away repeatedly and kept reminding him that he has a wife and he'll soon be home with her. "I will not have sex with you. No. No. No." "C'mon Heathiss." Finally I retreated the 18 inches to my bunk, and said sharply: "Goodnight, go to sleep, Mak." Climbed up and pulled the blankets over my fully clothed body, pissed off that he is in the way of the only exit from this cramped space. When I got up this morning, he was gone to town. Now he's making small-talk, acting like nothing happened. Between that and Cyrus' dark-hour visits to my bunk, I don't want to go back out on the ocean with these two guys. Last night, I called Cyrus on his 4 am excursion to my bunk a few nights ago, saying: "What the fuck was that about?" but he claims not to remember waking me, all amped up for sex. Great. I just want to go home.

Fuel is filling. It's our last chance to head down the East Side of Vancouver Island towards home. Please phone, ring. Please let the owner call and tell Cyrus to take us home. I am typing. The engine is still off. Any minute now, Mak will close the valves to the spare tank. I will hear the roar as Cyrus turns the ignition on the great beast, and we deck-hands will spring to life, untie the ropes and turn West again, out to open water and out to look for Tuna. NOOOO!!!!!! Out the grimy streaked galley windows I see Cyrus pacing at the top of the ramp. Is he stalling the inevitable, too? This is pure stupidity. There is absolutely no chance we'll find fish. This is not pessimism, this is the reality of the situation. It's time to head home, cut our losses, and put our energy towards our next respective projects, goals, work, whatever. Hug our kids. Not another pointless mind-numbing, useless trip around the ocean. And I'm sure, knowing Cyrus, we'll run through the night, each night, just to burn additional fuel pointlessly, and to keep us all sleep-deprived as we race to the next empty patch of ocean. I want to be at home with Morgi. *Heath, you can do this.* Just one more week or so, I have to wrap my head around. The guy at the fuel dock is staring at us, scratching his head, wondering why we're not leaving. All of us stalling. Cyrus pacing. He just tried the owners' cell phones again. No answer. C'mon Cyrus, make the right choice. Don't make us go through this pointless exercise that none of us wants. Mak is ready to fly home. He has called his family in Fiji and told them he's coming soon. It's time to stop this.

I need to stand on land and face my life, hug my kid tightly, and move on to the next project. Open my heart and life to abundance, ask the Universe to send some good things my way, and work hard towards it. Here I sit writing in my civilian clothes – not wanting to put any energy towards heading out fishing again. My dirty fishing clothes are hanging up and I am wearing jeans and a t-shirt. Last night I dreamt that I went through my duffel bag and threw overboard all the fishing clothes, blood-stained as they are, useless for anything else.

NOOO! I can hear them shouting that the fueling is done. I go out and say to Cyrus: "You know, it's never too late to make the right decision!" half-jokingly. He scowls at me. Mak is putting away the tools in the drawer. "No," I say. "We're not going." He shakes his head slowly, eyes heavy. We have to. ARGH!

I am against this. Totally opposed to heading out. Mak is beside himself. Cannot understand Cyrus' decision. Mak and I sit on the hatch talking, while Cyrus pays for the fuel. Neither wants to go, but we have to respect the captain's decision. We have been loyal to a fault, committing to the full season, rather than jumping ship for better prospects as did Shasso and George and Etienne, and we need to see this through to the end, even though I know our loyalty to this flailing vessel and this horrible season will neither be recognized, nor rewarded. Argh! OK. We must go through with this. We have to go out one more time.

I have to try to keep a sense of humour about this last trip that we are all dreading. Cyrus jokingly tells me that he's afraid to give me the first watch tonight, as he'll probably wake up to me having turned the boat around and headed on a new course: East towards home. Mak and I are keeping coils of Tuna cord within arm's reach so we can ambush Cyrus and tie him up when next he sets foot out here. We'll toss him to the sharks and steer the boat ourselves to Salt Spring, we joke. I just can't believe we're doing this.

I was thinking about what you wrote, James, about concentrating on the preventative side of things, working with youth. I did that for many years in several ways: started a support group for single queer moms in Vancouver to give each other support, to reduce our isolation, and to provide a place for our kids to be able to get together. Facilitated workshops for 'at risk youth' up on Cortes Island, using arts- and creativity-based tools (art, writing, music, dance, nature walks, sports, random cool stuff) to give youth opportunities to transform hardships and histories of violence into self-empowerment and to shine as leaders, as motivated people making positive changes. Researched feminist violence prevention curriculum in Salt Spring middle and high schools, evaluating the results and impacts of these in a longitudinal study, following kids for years. Lots of focus on preventing dating violence, too. I've done positive self-esteem and healthy boundary work with many groups, in many contexts. Just wanted to let you know I've got some background and experiences in some of that work, if you want to bounce ideas around together.

A few days ago, we got word from someone in the fleet that an American Tuna vessel tried to off-load and sell its fish in Vancouver, something they were allowed to do in previous years (all part of the treaty). Within an hour of unloading the fish, the DFO (Canada's Department of Fisheries and Oceans) was all over them, threatening to arrest them and confiscate the boat if they didn't pack up and get the f**k out right now. Our guys cheered when they heard the story, but I didn't. This tiff between the two governments is no good for anyone. That American fisher has only foreign crew, who are not allowed on American soil (they used to pick up and drop off their foreign crew in Canada or Mexico) but now, he's barred from Canadian ports, in retaliation for the Americans barring us from their waters. Well, not exactly retaliation. The Americans tore up the treaty, which gave free access to commercial fishers on both sides to all ports and waters. Now that they ripped it up, the Canadian officials are no longer required to accept Americans in our ports. This guy has a boatload of fish he can't off-load anywhere – he can't set foot in American ports, because of his country's stance on 'foreign' crew. How is screwing him and his livelihood good for anyone? It's not his fault his government and mine decided to escalate this shittiness. Ah well. We shall see where this all leaves us. Right now none of it looks good.

Engine springs into life. I untie the ropes, wrap them up and start to climb the ladder to the roof where we stow them in a large blue plastic tote. Mak stops me: "Wait, Heathiss, wait. This is wrong. We must talk to him." He is totally opposed to going out again. But we've already made our case, and it has been rejected. A few seconds pass, staring at each other in silence, frozen, unwilling to move our bodies in the direction we have been ordered. Finally, resigned, we move to secure the Scotchmen on the roof; store the shore ropes; pull up the ladder; lower the poles. I'd better go change my clothes. I got fishing to do.

A few more days or weeks, hopefully, and then I'll be able to start figuring out how to get back to the prisons.

So my thoughts are no longer on this fishing, they must start again to move further ahead. I think I will make a direct solicitation to my lengthy email list of contacts from off my website – ask them to please dig deeply, to donate cold hard cash to support my work in Bangkok prisons. I hate asking for help, I hate asking people for money. But I have to learn to do this. That's step #1. Hopefully that will get me somewhere.

Next, I think of all the places I want to go and ways I want to travel...train, walking, biking. I crave movement, momentum, I am not good at being stagnant, sitting still. I'd like to go visit family in Ontario: aunts, uncles and cousins I've neglected to stay in touch with for too many years. And get to Baltimore, MD, too, to see my brother. I'd also like to bike across parts of Europe. South America. And walk the El Camino from Spain to France over the Pyrenees. This time of year, as the air gets crisper and cooler, I crave road-trips. Tunes, car and open highway call out to me. Tacky little diners in North American hick towns and wacky characters dotting the gorgeous varied landscape are immensely enjoyable for me. I sure can't see myself trying to stay on Salt Spring for very long, what with poor employment prospects and very high cost of living. Just long enough to regroup and hopefully get some awesome time with Morgan. She knows I'll go batty if I stay there with no stimulation or engagement, so we'll have to make a plan to backpack together somewhere in the world, as soon as possible.

One of my oldest friends from high school has contacted me. He lives in South Hampton, England – his wife of almost twenty years is leaving him and he is devastated. He's been leaving messages on Facebook, urgently asking me to call him. I haven't managed to get a hold of him. Maybe he'll be up for an adventure somewhere in the world with me. Might be what he needs. Also there's Nathan, hankering for an adventure too. And Raoul, calling me from Panama, begging me to go down and visit him there. Lots of straight male friends, I guess, who all appreciate how I bring out the 'alive and intense' in them, but in return, we always have to deal with the sexuality issue. I end up feeling like a performing monkey: "Be the crazy Heather who makes me laugh all the time." They LOVE me as long as I am crazy, hard-core, and we talk about eating pussy and how we want to find some sexy women and make them come like freight trains, but they have no time for the other parts of me that need to read a book or discuss ideas or explore deeper things. I often just 'represent' the parts of themselves they are not exploring or that they feel they've given up by marrying and doing a boring 9 – 5 job until retirement. That's the down-side. Actually, I have great moments and connections with these guys too. (I am acutely aware that in my stressed state right now, I am only focusing on the negative of EVERYTHING). I will contact Jason and find out how he is. I know he's prone to severe bouts of depression and I hope he's doing ok. Maybe Jason can take a leave from his job in England and come to Thailand this year. I am not a big fan of Asia, in general, let's be honest. But I return each year because of my commitment to not give up on the guys. They deserve more.

I really miss teaching. I love educating about things I'm passionate about and transforming lives through experiential learning. Real teaching, not the bureaucratic administrative function at universities or schools. Real learning, that engages more than just the mind: body, spirit, creativity. I gotta find a way to incorporate that into my next plans.

I reacted a bit to your sentence "those poor kids forced to grow up without dads" as if all kids are automatically deprived and deficient if they grow up in households without fathers. Granted, most kids would benefit from having more adult, loving, mentoring support in their lives, and support for their mothers, too, but I bet a few of them are far better off for not having had their father in their life. Just my two cents. I hear what you're saying, though. Taking these men and locking them away from their families and society for a lifetime is absolutely horrific and devastating to many people's lives, especially to their children.

I am sending you so much hope about a transfer and so glad to hear in your letter that your spirits are bouncing back. Really glad you got an Embassy visit finally and that they're (hopefully) working for your transfer.

I got a good kick in the head the other day, when we were tied up in Winter Harbour. A young deckhand on a boat next to us developed an instant crush on me and followed me around like a puppy. While all the other fishers were getting shit-faced and obnoxious, this guy and I sat and drank tea in the galley of his vessel and talked for hours. Of course, I talked about what I always do – how my daughter is the love of my life and the importance of the prison work to me, as well as my frustrations at not being able to have income from this shitty Tuna season and really craving a home of my own. He instantly called 'Bullshit' on me and my self-pity. Smart guy. He said everything to me that I know already, but forgot in my recently developed fear and obsession of dying poor and alone – that this fear of lack of security or money is garbage and is fed by the media. I don't have a house or car or big-screen tv in part because I chose to use my meager earnings to raise my daughter travelling and having adventures and not taking more lucrative 9 – 5 jobs that would have squished my independent, adventurous spirit but may have offered me financial 'security.' No, I've never had any leg-up from anybody, and I have worked very hard my whole life for very little income, which sucks, but any income I did have I used to live in a way that was consistent with my values, like putting myself through university and helping others. I followed my own path, even though it meant not following the money. Never easy, but always true to myself, to not just do what is expected of we sheep in the world. I know he's right and I felt foolish complaining that I have no savings or security. I am white, Canadian, live in one of the most peaceful and privileged parts of the world. I will not fall hard, if I fall down. I will never be without some kind of roof over my head. I will always have friends or someone's place I can crash at. It was good to get a reality check. I needed it. I thanked him for reflecting back to me that truth that I had momentarily forgotten. Not everything he said was as well received. For one, he kept asking why someone with my education and intelligence would be 'slumming' as a Tuna deckhand. I resented the shitty and disrespectful implications of his question. To fishers and to me. He'd never ask a guy that. He couldn't accept the fact that I went for this job for the same reason that all the other guys out here did – I need to support myself, my daughter, and this work is a cool opportunity to work hard and bring in a big paycheck and I jumped at the chance to try it. Nope, not good enough for this guy who obviously took two psychology courses once and thought that qualified him to dissect me. He was a little too "Psych 101 babble" and it was annoying, as well as calling me a Femi-Nazi and telling me I <u>need</u> to be less angry when I speak. (I prefer to call it 'passionate'). He told me that I am 'all over the place.' *Actually, you just don't like that I don't fit into any of your little boxes.* He grabbed my hand at one point and said: "You bite your nails, you need to stop that too." (See previous letters about men always assuming that it's ok upon meeting me to tell me what I need to do differently.) "No," I responded, "I <u>don't</u> need to change anything about myself for you. If you don't like how I am, walk away. Don't tell me that I need to speak calmly or change my behaviour." ARGH! Then, he gives me his email and invites me to come and <u>live</u> at his house in Qualicum Beach when I'm finished the season?!

He also invited me to stay the night with him. I declined both. Early the next morning, I woke up to him standing next to my bunk, face next to mine, telling me they were leaving port and he wanted to sneak over to say goodbye. [Insert really ugly language here]. Do I have to build a metal cage and padlock around my bunk? I can't stand waking up to guys standing over me, watching me sleep. It's creepy. The jerk then stole my gaff as he left. It's an $80 gaff, the only one I have. I sent an email to their ship demanding the return of the tool, but so far no response.

In the bookstore in Port Hardy yesterday, I bought on my credit card (!) two books and am so looking forward to sinking into them. What a treat! I am holding on to them like precious treasures, stalling opening the first, wanting to draw out the pleasure. The first is written by a psychologist, called: *Party of One: The Loner's Manifesto* about the psychology of loners and that being a loner, rather than being a deviant or dangerous socio-pathological condition, is a valid choice for many people so inclined. That wanting to share experiences with others isn't necessary for all humans, especially those creatively or intellectually inclined. That's pretty obvious, but I want to see if there's anything else interesting in there. The second book is all about rats, the history and science of those loveable rodents. YAY books! ☺

As predicted, we are running through the night and I am on first watch tonight, the best shift, normally reserved for the skipper, but I think Cyrus is a little afraid of me today, not wanting to piss me off. At 9 pm he offered me this shift (9 – 12), whereas normally, as the lowliest crew member, I would get the worst shift (12 – 3 or 1 – 4) type of thing. This way, I can get uninterrupted sleep from midnight until six am, maybe even later, depending on the water temperature. We don't put out the gear unless the water is over 59 degrees Fahrenheit, because Tuna don't hang in water colder than that. So we might not start fishing until later in the morning, when we get to a bubble of warm water he's found on the satellite chart 70 miles from shore. I sit here, monitoring the radar for ships and occasionally changing our course a few degrees so we don't get off-track on our run out to Big Tuna Waters. Have to smile. I wish you could come and experience the thrill of pulling Tuna, James. Hey, you're American! Maybe we could hire ourselves out one season to a US skipper. It's really super fun when you're actually pulling fish. And lucrative, I hear! ☺ Seriously, though, what a cool experience I'll never forget.

Oh James. Your low moments must be very low. Lots of dark thoughts, dark places. So glad you are strong enough to turn them around. It is truly in the hardest, darkest places in which we really discover our inner strength, what we are made of. Doesn't make it any more fun, though, does it? Glad to hear you have found your 'people' at your new prison, your southern Thai folk.

Sending prayers that the Embassy is making headway on your transfer, that movement to wonderful new situations is in your imminent future.

FALL EQUINOX, 11 AM

49 59 N X 129 53 W

Mak is MISERABLE! He just went back to bed after grumping around for a few hours, so pissed off that we're out here. Me, I'm working at being into it, I know there's only a few days left. Again that detached observer, watching his shitty mood and striving for the opposite affect. We have seven fish so far today, and I am listening to music, feeling incredibly blessed to be alive and to have had this adventure, even including the days I wanted to scream and kill someone. I have just exacted a promise from Cyrus that we will stop this charade and just fish down the West side of Vancouver Island, making our way South to port over the next two days. I can do this. Hang on.

Reading the 'loner' book: it's alright, not fantastic, a bit of a stretch at times, and clearly a decade old, not much new information, probably would have worked better as an article. Some of it resonates with me, like I'm not really into many people. I have no trouble meeting people, it's just that I am very picky – I prefer my own company to that of most people, and I prefer getting lost in the world of ideas, thoughts, experiences, than in the world of things or social activities. If I spend time in a group, I need to retreat and rejuvenate, as I often find people draining. Not always. I belonged to an Ultimate Frisbee team for a few years and we all played and hung out together all the time, a rag-tag mix of very different characters and it was absolutely fantastic. Some of those people are still very good friends. Only on the rarest of occasions do I crave being around lots of people and feeding off that energy (two to three times per year, max). Mostly, I prefer to have one or two very close friends and intimate relationships and share conversation, laughter and adventures with them one-on-one, rather than a million superficial, shallow acquaintances.

Not particularly illuminating, but some interesting analysis of the 'loner' stereotype in pop-culture, film, advertising, crime news, and in different religious texts and traditions. People often act as if people who prefer to be alone are somehow deficient in their ability to love or to interact with others. Not so. On the contrary, I am a good friend and lover to people I choose to let in, I just don't let a lot of people in and also need to have lots of space. I have lost many 'friends' in my life who push and push and push, always whining that I don't want to spend more time with them. The casual friends who 'get' me know that I'll see them when I see them, and we'll pick up where we left off, even if it means that we haven't communicated in months or years. Quality over quantity of interaction. I like those friends. I don't need to call or write, just look them up next time I'm in their part of the world, and it's no biggie. I'm a big fan of personal space, and I need lots. I assume that others do too, and I often feel way too crowded when people want to do too many things with me all the time. Whoa, take a break, back off. It just feels like they're sucking my energy. Real friends know how to take their own space and how to inhabit silence and to give space. I definitely don't understand people who can't be alone or who always need others around. The only pitfall I see of putting all your proverbial eggs in one relationship basket is that when you lose your one very close relationship, it is quite devastating and there are no buffers around.

Like my last girlfriend, Josée. She and I were together for three years in my mid-twenties, very much in love and yet we chose to not live together. We each rented out separate places on Salt Spring, and often slept at each other's, spent much of our free time together, but it was wonderful to be able to NOT sleep over and to stay home or to have a dinner with just me and Morgan, without always having Josée around. And to know she was enjoying her life, her separate friends and interests, and we only saw each other when we chose to, not 'cause we were stuck together. Space in relationships is important. I like missing people. The feeling of wishing you can see them again and appreciating, from a distance, all the loveliness and aspects of them that make you want to spend more time together, but would drive you bananas if you felt obligated to spend ALL your time together. Related issue: one thing I HATE doing is explaining to someone why I won't spend time with them. My time is my own, I don't owe it to anyone. How I use it is no one's business and I owe no one an explanation. Just a pet peeve of mine. Similarly, I want people to hang out with me because they choose to and want to, not because they feel obligated or expected to. Of course, I do have a rejection default position, always assuming that people don't want to spend time with me. Except guys in prison, 'cause they're desperate for anyone.

You strike me as more of a social butterfly. Is that the case, James? Or am I misreading, just because you are so smiley?

Anyway. I'm rambling because I am extremely bored. WAY too much time on my hands with nothing to do. This 'journal' is now just self-indulgent narcissistic drivel. Bad mental masturbation. Wish I had more books. I'll finish this one and move on to the rats. ☺

Did you like teaching when you were in S. Korea? I do remember you saying you weren't a huge fan of Asia. What age-group did you teach? What other jobs have you done? Mak asked me that question a few days ago and I astounded him and myself by listing off all the many varied jobs I have done over the years – lots and lots. My least favourite: bank teller at Bank of Montreal in Vancouver in '89 & '90. I've had many much more grueling or physically draining, but that job was just deadly boring and pointless, and I hated how people were about their money. I doubt they realized that I was 17 and not legally bondable nor legally supposed to be handling thousands of dollars in cash and millions in transactions per day. My only wish working that stupid job was that I'd get robbed, just for the thrill of it, but that never happened. We got robbed twice in the time I was there, both times just after I'd left my shift to go to my night college courses (where I was discovering how sexy and desirable women are – had a crush on every woman in my class!). I got paranoid that management would think I was in on the robberies. The shy blonde teller next to me was embezzling the whole time I worked there and we only found out after he quit and I got interrogated by cops and fraud specialists, just to see if I knew what he'd been doing. Nope, I was oblivious. Your least favourite job? Hey – wait a sec. I keep asking you questions in letters that you don't answer. Am I annoying you with my questions? Maybe they're the wrong questions. Just trying to get to know you a little. Or maybe your daily focus is more immediate, concrete, just the next step to getting transferred? I really hope that this is the last stretch for you.

Remembering more moments on this fishing adventure and noticing how much I've learned. In the early stages, mere months ago, every time I would do something unthinkingly, as the novice, like walk towards the stern on the wrong side of the boat, not having checked which way the waves were crashing over, only to get a full-face wall of ocean crash over me, soaking me and filling my boots with icy wet, Shasso would shake his head and say: "Greenhorn move, Heath, greenhorn move." We'd laugh and he'd repeat his mantra throughout the day at every little thing I did wrong. Appreciating now all the millions of little things I've learned since – attuned to subtle variations in how a jig dances that signals a piece of seaweed an inch square caught on it that I could never have noticed two months ago. Small things like that. Like the sixth sense of how not to let the bight catch you, even when the wind is blowing hard and tangling the tag-lines all over your head, face, arms, and the fighting fish is jumping all over the table, I throw out the jig and maneouvre deftly out of the bight in split-seconds without thought. How to bleed a fish efficiently so there's no ruining of the meat. How to change the oil in that massive engine. How to cook meals in heavy swells. 'Tis cool, this learning, this fishing.

Another moment I'll never forget: during the three days in a row we were catching only peanuts and Etienne was filleting them on deck, we got to the point where we started wondering if we should just throw them back, rather than fill our boat with fish that we can't sell. I mentioned this as Mak pulled in yet another peanut. Instead of flipping him onto the boat, in one fluid motion, Mak released the hook from the fish's mouth and punched the poor dude in the gut, yelling: "This is for you, George!" The sight of the poor slippery fish being punched in mid-air, then falling back into the ocean because of this large Fijian man's displaced anger against the abusive skipper he worked with for six years was too much. I grabbed the camera, and took a video as Mak punched the next hapless fish and the next, each time calling him 'George.' I guess getting punched back to the sea is better than getting your throat slit and eyeball stabbed, but it was a sorry, pathetic sight. Too funny.

Two hours ago, after a deadly slow day with our tally still at seven fish, I went to the wheelhouse and saw that Cyrus had changed course and was heading back North. "What are we doing?" I asked, incredulous. ("We" meaning "You.") This, after his assurance that his momentary loss of reason had ended and that we are headed home, albeit checking for fish along the way. Cyrus says he got a call that someone found 20 fish 40 miles from here and we're headed there. I stare at him, unable to speak, and he holds my gaze until I finally manage to croak: "I hope you're fucking kidding me." "Nope," he says defensively, daring me to question him. I run out of the wheelhouse, stopping myself from launching myself into the water and head instead to where Mak stands, sleeping upright as he monitors the unmoving lines. I yell, I babble incoherently, I shake my fist at the sky, I curse. Mak shakes his head slowly as he hears of the new course. Unbelievable. I gaze mutely at the vast empty ocean all around us. Breathe, Heath, Breathe, Breathe. This will be over soon. I avoid Cyrus for a few hours on this thimble-sized boat, because I don't trust what I will do if I try to speak to him or even meet his eyes. I am very bad at hiding my feelings, and right now, they are evil.

Later, Mak and I see a large blue shark circling the boat and I yell at him: "Hey shark, I have a small snack for you!" and I pat Cyrus' shoulder, who has come up behind me. Mak laughs and Cyrus gives me a dirty look.

As I write this in the galley now, I hear Mak screaming at the stern: "WHY WHY WHY WHY WHY WHY?" The frustrated wailing continues, it sounds like keening: "OOOHHHH, WHY WHY WHY WHY WHY WHY?"

Is Cyrus just messing with us? Does he not realize how close we are to the edge? I know he's not the brightest light, but he keeps coming down to report to us each new email from a member of our fleet that has packed it in for the season and has said their goodbyes today, all leaving for shore. Meanwhile, we steam on a never-ending mission to nowhere, for nothing. Does he want us to do him grievous bodily harm? Deep breath, Heath, it's ok. I have to keep my cool. He walks by me as I write this, and I smile at him. He looks relieved. Mak just keeps shaking his head.

Dinnertime. More pork ribs drowned in bbq sauce and salad and rice. After dinner, Cyrus retreats to the wheelhouse and Mak beckons me. "You know, Heathiss, I can do something in the engine room, and he won't know." Seriously? We're at this point? Contemplating mechanical sabotage to get off this ship, to stop this guy from holding us on the empty ocean, when all rational argument, logic, pleading, cajoling and sulking has failed to produce results? "I dunno, Mak." This has got to end soon. Then I see Cyrus plotting another course to the middle of nowhere, further out, based on the flimsiest whisp of rumour. What's with this guy? Is he afraid to go home? Has he lost his mind? I asked him point-blank earlier today: "Are you afraid of failure? Is that why you're not pulling the plug?" He denied it angrily and I regretted saying anything. Oh man, I could just start screaming and screaming and screaming. He'd turn around and take us back. Or would he? I wonder if he'd just club me and throw me overboard. Now who's going batty? Patience, deep breath.

Another breathtaking sunset and I take another few pictures. Cyrus handed me an empty wine bottle a few hours ago and told me that if I wanted to write a note saying I was being held hostage, to go ahead. Where did this wine bottle come from? Suddenly I better understand the late-night bold visit to my corner of the dungeon. I write out on a piece of paper: HELP! I'M STUCK ON THIS TUNA BOAT! GET ME OFF HERE! and sign my email address. Fold the note into the bottle and chuck it into the ocean. We'll see if I ever get a response. It's not that I can't stick it out another day or three or twelve or thirty. It's that there's no reason for this. He knows it is futile. He knows Mak and I are totally opposed to being here. I am not consenting to continuing this. I want to get home and to the possibility of continuing my life. I fear that he's lost his marbles and that feels precarious in the middle of the Pacific Ocean, on a rickety vessel with many problems and many, many opportunities for people who go ape-shit to do considerable harm to their crewmates with impunity. This is not a place you want to be with someone who's not operating with all fuses lit. Cyrus' jittery appearance at my bunk and all his behaviour since is making me a little nervous. This guy definitely seems a few clowns short of a circus. What's the best course of action here? He is adamantly refusing against all reason to consider heading for shore.

How many more bottles of wine does he have hidden in his state room? Do I have to worry about more night-time visits? I hear the shrill ring of the satellite phone. I hope it's the owner telling Cyrus to head to shore. Dare I go ask? Cyrus tells me to pull up the gear, so I go out and secure the gear for the night. I can't bring myself to ask him if we are running through the night again. Mak is washing up at the galley sink. He goes wearily to his bunk without a word to anyone. I will wash my face and crawl into my bunk and hide. Hopefully tomorrow will bring some movement towards land.

New morning, cobwebs gone from my brain. We get up in the cold and dark and make tea, head out to the stern and put out the gear as the engine roars to life and we start our big tack for the day. Sunrise is stunning and Mak and I stare at its magnificence, light peeking here and there through clouds, cracking open our new day with mottled spots of purply blue on the grey water. Pinks and orange streaks breathtaking. Cat Stevens and me singing "Morning has Broken" at top volume and I feel blessed to experience this moment.

I take a few photos, including one of Mak waving his makeshift "Black Power" flag (a stick with black garbage bag attached) as another boat crosses our wake, Fijian crew all waving frantically at him. He waves his flag anytime a boat with Fijian crew passes anywhere within the vicinity, even if it's just a speck six miles away. He tells me his body is here, but his mind is at home. I imagine you can relate.

I have renewed perspective: there is nothing dangerous or ominous about being here a while longer – only the dark places my mind goes to when my body and brain are forced to be stagnant for far too long. I have tried over the months to do exercises, like squats as I stand at the stern, but that is the extent my lower body moves all day long, except the occasional trip from stern to galley, about 35 feet of walkway, too treacherous a space on the rolling ship to use as a track to pace.

I walk to the wheelhouse and try some friendly chit-chat with Cyrus. I must keep a lid on the simmering tension. We joke about nothing and I act interested and amused as he trots out a few stories I've heard a thousand times before. Are you brain-dead? How can you not possibly know you've told me this countless times? Deep breath, Heath. How long must we continue to be here, subject to one man's poor judgment (and poor boundaries, to boot)?

I jump up when I see my boat line has snagged some kelp, and when I pull in the line and remove the piece from the hook, I see a face staring at me. The bulbous face of the kelp has eyes, a nose, a big smile and long locks of flowing seaweed hair. Mak carved this piece as an effigy of George, then stabbed it and tossed it into the ocean. That was hours ago. And now I've re-caught it. Here, on an ever-moving, flowing gigantic body of water that covers 70% of the planet, I've snagged the same piece of seaweed Mak threw over hours ago. How is that possible? Just adds to the crazy-making sensation that this is a big cosmic joke. Totally surreal. I turn this over in my head, unable to comprehend.

The few remaining boats report scratching away the smallest numbers of fish: two, ten, eight. It's noon, and we have four. Cyrus refuses to give us an exit strategy. I'm starting to like Mak's suggestion of the hammer in the engine room more and more. Don't get me wrong, if the fish suddenly turned on, I'd happily stay another few weeks, picking up 300 fish per day. But that's not happening. And it won't. The season is over.

More hours roll by. We tack up and down, catching nothing. Mak and I scrub parts of the equipment out of boredom, in preparation for the big cleaning we will give the boat when we finally dock and unload the fish. Again to the wheelhouse, I ask Cyrus if I can use the phone. He grabs a smoke on the way out to give me privacy. I think I will dial Morgan and see how she's doing, but I suddenly feel panicky and frantically dial Shasso: his cell, his house, no answer. Morgan's cell, Morgan's cabin. No answer anywhere. I'm almost relieved no one answers because I feel a sudden heavy rock in my gut, a lump in my throat and I'm afraid I'll start crying if I hear someone on the other end. *Get me outta here!* But I don't want to scare Morgan or Shasso with my panic. I return to deck and tell Cyrus that I wasn't able to reach anyone. He moves sideways away from me. I realize that he stopped speaking to us, hours ago. I look at Mak and ask him: "Did Cyrus say anything to you?" No. He moved away from Mak, too, when Mak approached him. This is not good. This is a guy who reports every detail of every email and radio call at least 5 times an hour to us. Reports each change of mind and direction – both very frequent. Plus his stories, anecdotes, joking comments, and inane babble. Not anymore. Cyrus is now pacing in the wheelhouse, avoiding us and not talking. I hear him on the radio going through the motions of reporting water temperatures, locations and fish caught with other vessels?! It is now eight days since the owner gave him the orders to give it maximum another week then return to shore. He is not pulling the plug. Something is compelling him to keep us out here. Pride, ego, fear of failure, stubbornness, insanity, lost marbles, psychosis? Who knows? What do we do? I'm trying to keep my cool, but this really doesn't feel ok.

Cyrus sits in the wheelhouse engrossed in a murder mystery that I borrowed from the young deckhand on a neighbouring boat on shore, mere days ago, when we thought we were finally heading on our last trek home. On deck, Mak and I discuss the situation for the umpteenth time.

"He is the captain, Mak says, he must make the decision to turn this boat around." Shakes his head in disgust. I tell Mak that I am this close (fingers an inch apart) to overpowering Cyrus, tying him up and steering the ship myself to land. Mak, not prone to fits of hysteria, nods in agreement. Not a good sign. Should we? How long do we humour this guy? What are his intentions? Is he totally insane? All the hundreds of stories I've heard of skippers or deckhands going totally bonkers out here flit through my brain.

Each time I run in to write a few more words in this journal, the hairs on the back of my neck tingle, and I turn sharply, afraid that he's going to club me across the head when my back is turned. Something is very wrong here. If this were a novel, one would have to wonder whether it is the narrator or the skipper who was paranoid and losing it. I guess the same holds true for this journal, but I feel pretty sane. Just excessively stressed at being held here, against all reason and all expressed wishes, because of this man's unfathomable whim. Wailing starts again at the stern: "OOOOHHH WHY WHY WHY WHY WHY WHY WHY?" and makes it's way back to me in the galley. I wonder if Cyrus can hear it in the wheelhouse. I wonder if he can hear anything.

Put away this journal. Go back outside and sit in the sun, Heath. Listen to music and watch your lines for fish. You've done that for days, weeks, months, you can do it again. The day will pass and tomorrow something will change. Never mind that I woke a dozen times last night, acutely aware of every additional sound, brushing away phantoms of men standing too close to my bed, staring at me.

Hours more of standing on the stern. Cyrus comes out and tells us that the owner has called again and told us to pack it in, when we want to. So Cyrus decides we'll stay and fish these grounds some more. "Then, we'll head home." I am suddenly so angry I cannot breathe. "I'll believe that when I see it," I say. He shakes his head at me. Bitch that I am. I am seething with rage that this man is taking my time and Mak's, keeping us here against our will. I grab the 50-lbs. box of bait and heave the whole thing into the ocean. Mak starts laughing: "Heathiss, I gonna tell my family about you." Mak is happy we're heading home. Mak didn't catch the part where Cyrus added: "When we want to." We are exactly in the same position we were in before the owner's call: We are opposed to being here; the owner has told us to leave; and Cyrus still makes new plans to run up and down the ocean to look for non-existent fish. It is

3 pm. We have caught four fish today. And his plan is to stay and fish some more, indefinitely. I am filled with a burning rage.

Mak slices Tuna sashimi for dinner, and I make a plan to calmly and firmly tell Cyrus tonight that it's over. I will ask that he bring the boat to shore. Plain and simple. I am nervous about it, but resolute. Mak and I are in agreement. At the stern, Mak slowly repeats the words: "Brutal. Bullshit. Horrible. Horrendous. Ridiculous. Brutal. Bullshit. Horrible. Horrendous. Ridiculous." I laugh. New fishing adjectives I inadvertently taught him these past months.

Cyrus makes another u-turn to start yet another back-tack and says to me: "I can't believe we didn't catch any fish right now, there was a pile of them." I just stare at him. I imagine my expression isn't exactly friendly. I don't trust myself to speak. I retreat to the stern and continue to look out at the ocean with Mak, stamping my feet to block out the cold wind biting my bones. Mak is singing: "I just wanna go home. I just wanna go home."

I will put on Bob Marley and forget about all this. Just breathe and hang in there. The alarm goes off. Engine room flooded. YOU HAVE GOT TO BE F**KING KIDDING ME! Mak spends the next hour pumping it out, as I wearily watch the lines that don't jump. I call Morgan and I rant about a psychotic, moronic skipper holding me hostage. She laughs. I feel WAY better. Time to go back and watch the lines.

Wow. So many emotions in the past two hours. Best not to relive it. I've raged and ranted enough inside my skull. I'm just kind of numb now. It's 9 pm. I'm going to bed. Cyrus has decided we'll run three days out to another far-flung region of the ocean on the off-chance that we load up there. He asks for our input. Mak stays silent. I say my piece, calmly: "What value do you place on my time (here and away from my family); Mak's time (here and away from family); your time; and, Paul's' fuel and expenses? What number of fish would make it worth it for us to continue this? And what are the chances that you'll get that number if we go to your new spot? Include in your calculations each and every day that we travel and get no fish." I remind him that we've averaged fewer than 40 fish per day in the eighty or so days I've been fishing, despite hearing on numerous occasions exactly the same circumstances that he's proposing rushing towards again. He ponders my words for a millisecond and his eyes glitter, from the false light of the gambler's fallacy. He decides to fish. It is clear that he wants me to force him to stop, so that he can blame me for this failed season. I'm not willing to be his scapegoat. So I repeat that this is pointless and not worth it to us in what it takes us from in time, lost earnings and separation from family to chase non-existent Tuna. "However, this is your decision, this is what you get paid to do, as skipper. If you decide that we will continue this farce, we'll do whatever you decide." I think I am being reasonable, but it is obviously not what he wants to hear: he storms off and now we are running somewhere, who knows where, on this endless trip for elusive fish. I can't get worked up anymore.

Good part of the past few hours was me pulling 50 huge fish in the space of an hour and a half on a late evening bite. Cyrus got three and Mak got twelve for the day. It was fun and super-satisfying, but still nowhere enough fish to make this worth my while, let alone all of ours, in my estimation. It's past time to go home and hug my kid. Mak needs to be with his three kids and wife. This needs to end.

New day. Only dark thoughts. I have to change my head-space from one of being held unjustly without my consent in the illogical shittiness of one man's neurotic world, to just going with the flow. Look at the ocean, Heath, it is always churning, moving, flowing. This is just a part of fishing. Let it go, wash away, be cleansed. All religions of all types use water in symbolic rituals of purification, renewal, rebirth, cleansing for good reason. It shall pass, Heath, this, too, shall pass. Hours and hours of standing in one spot, staring out at the empty grey sea, renewing, washing away my negativity. All will be ok. Cyrus and I are not speaking to each other. I can't muster a smile and light banter. I can't. I won't. Mak is touching my hair right now as I sit typing, and he suddenly bends in and kisses my hair. He mutters something about me being his "Canadian wife." WTF? Let it all pass, Heath, let it all flow. I tell him to go away. My anger is useful, powerful, strong, but also serves no purpose if it just eats away at me. Just let things flow.

A massive Tuna I thought was a shark suddenly snapped the nylon line to my bird (I have three mice, one bird, one boat, two dildos as my current configuration on port side – identical to Mak's on his side of the stern). About an hour ago. Scared me to death, as the remaining Tuna cord tightened so much that my first instinct was to protect my face. Having been whipped in the face badly about a week ago by a line snapping back after a Tuna broke it, I was afraid of the bird or hook as projectile taking out my eye. Mak got the fish for me anyway, and I pulled a few more who were on my other lines and then we set to work repairing the bird line. Ship is rolling so much we are taking on water on each side over the deck with each roll. Reminder not to worry about small stuff. Just want to get home safely, in one piece.

While Mak snoozes at noon, I watch all the lines. A fish grabs Mak's mouse, pops off and sends the mouse hurtling over all the other tag lines and I spend frantic long minutes trying to untangle the messy snarl, willing other fish to not bite right now. It's not an uncommon occurrence, I just don't want Cyrus running out and sneering at me as I try to undo the mess. We have to ignore the fish if there are knots, tangles, snarls – cannot throw tangled lines back into the sea, even if fish await. Too dangerous (a knot is a weak point and will snap the line) and foolish, as you risk greater snarls. Few days back, I noticed a tiny knot on my long nylon dildo line and pulled it in, ready to cut and replace it with new hardware and line. Cyrus is standing there and tells me not to worry about it, just keep fishing. *What?* I look at Mak. This goes against everything everyone has been telling me. But I don't have over forty years' fishing experience. He's the boss, the experienced fisher, so against my better judgment, I throw it back out. A few hours later, a large Tuna grabs that jig, and the line breaks at the knot, whipping back into my face and slashing across my cheek and right eye. I shriek and grab my face and all Mak sees is my bloody glove covering my eye (Tuna blood, not mine) and thinks my eye's been taken by the hook. The shock of the whipping of my face has stunned me momentarily, but, thankfully, face stinging, I can tell right away it's not a bad injury. It takes me several hours before I can trust myself to speak to Cyrus again, furious as I am that he would so callously put me at risk by making such an obvious and stupid call. He apologized to me a few days later for all the shitty stuff he had done that day, including that poor call on his part. (Cyrus had been in a hissy-fit ALL day, so much so that I asked Mak if he had pissed in Cyrus' coffee that morning. Mak looked horrified and said: "No! Who said I did?" I laughed and explained that it was just an expression meaning that Cyrus was in a really grumpy mood). Anyway, all just pressure-cooker dynamics in spaces where small mistakes can have serious consequences.

I'm actually hugely relieved Cyrus isn't talking to me today. It is far less crazy-making not being subjected to his every change of direction, nonsensical rationale and pea-brained reasoning three or four times an hour as he drives us around and around. I refuse to feel like I'm being kidnapped by a crazy person: I can just listen to the heavy steady roar of the engine, look to the heavy grey sky raining upon us that doesn't betray which direction we're headed, and pretend we are pointed homeward. That comforts me, that land is somewhere.

The head is plugged so we are using buckets on the deck as a toilet. YAY. Staring out to sea, scenarios flit through my brain that involve major injuries or trauma to one or more of us and desperate phone calls to the Coast Guard to get us OFF THIS SHIP. These are not comforting thoughts.

Trivia I've learned these past months fishing: A Tuna heart is the exact same size, shape and colour as my sunburnt nose. You could attach a pair of glasses and moustache to it and it would be a Hallowe'en disguise. Mak was the first one to point out the similarities. When pulling a fish hand over hand in the following sea, it's important to keep the tension constant, especially on the long lines that are 20 fathoms long (60 feet), as each time the fish pops out of a wave, he risks grabbing enough slack to pop off his hook. You can use the sea to your advantage when you have him against the ship, though. When you lean over and down to grab him from the high stern, you can be as much as 2 fathoms from the struggling creature, but if you wait until the next wave either brings him up or you down, you can get better purchase and fling him way more easily into the air and over your shoulder onto the table behind you. That half-second of waiting for the next wave, as long as you keep the tension constant is a make-or-break move. What else? Oh yeah. I remember in an earlier letter to you, I mentioned that I felt a bit like a fish out of water when I met you, James, because it was a situation unusual for me (You being American and with some support and intelligent and easy-going). Now, having spent a lot of time around fish out of water, I need to revise that statement. I didn't mean slapping around with all my might, whacking the shit out of my body on every surface available, splattering blood and life force everywhere to a crazily fast rhythm. I simply meant awkward. ☺

I imagine if you were to write a journal of some of the crazy, stupid, pointless, funny and insane moments in each day, it would fill volumes. It is hard for me to justify putting these moments to paper, as it gives them far more import than they deserve. Daily life is packed full to the brim of the mundane, the bizarre. Best just to smile and let it all wash over, right James? But it also helps me to pass the time to observe and note it. I just don't have enough distractions. I'm kicking myself that I didn't stock up with 100 books for this trip (Having initially been told it was just three weeks of non-stop work, no time for reading!). I have been craving reading material.

Well, I will drag myself up and cook us another meal. ☺

Wow. I just lost it. Blew it. Big time. And have totally fucked things up. Just now, I go to the back to say hi to Mak at the stern. Grey fog is closing in around us. We sit on overturned buckets in a space six feet by four, engine rumbling under us, staring out to sea, the fog so heavy that I can see only twenty feet around the boat. A perimeter we can't even touch, walk on or exchange for the small fiberglass vessel that is our cage. This tiny moving world we inhabit is so, so small. Mak looks at me with sad eyes, and says softly: "I think he's going to keep going until we run out of fuel." Anxiety overtakes me. I have to release this panic, this intensity of being stuck, not knowing how or why we are being taken... nowhere. Hundreds of miles of ocean between us and land. I laugh, I cry, I shout, just to release the tension to the wind. Mak starts laughing too, until I throw my mug into the ocean and scream: "I can't take this anymore." He looks at me, scared, and says: "Let's go tell Cyrus that it's time to go home. No fish are biting, let's go home." I agree (big mistake), instead of taking a deep breath and realizing that all I really need is to release some pent up energy. So we walk to the wheelhouse and I say calmly to Cyrus: "I would like to respectfully request that we go home now."

Suffice to say he freaked out, swearing up and down about damn crew members who don't have the fucking right to tell him what to do. Mak stayed silent. Cyrus and I argued; it ended with me calling him a "fucking idiot." Twice. Mistake number two. Or three or seven, I'm not sure.

We had an insane few hours of an afternoon bite and Mak and I pulled 130 big fish in three hours (figures!). Then dinner, and I went up to the wheelhouse and asked if I could talk to Cyrus. He grunted. I said: "I'd like to think we can disagree about stuff and do it respectfully, without a difference of opinion being seen as a challenge to your authority. However, without revisiting the issues, I know I was really disrespectful in how I talked to you and I should never have sworn at you and I apologize for that." Silence. I left. Ball is in his court.

Revisiting the whole encounter, the rising tension in me the past few days, I realized that I was completely triggered by his non-stop shifting of rationale, so that we couldn't count on anything he said as truth. I was trying to get at a firm rationale to stand on instead of the shifting sand of his crazy ever-changing decisions. I know I was triggered, feeling quite scared, actually: We're going home now, but now we're not actually and heading out far away instead? Crazy-making to me.

Never mind, all that's over now. I've been kicked off, I've just been informed. Not five minutes ago.

He's just informed me that we're steaming for Port Hardy and he'll put me on a bus. Mak is really sad. He is shaking his head: "We are so close to the end, Heathiss, why is he doing this? We started the season together, we should end it together. This is wrong, what he's doing." I agree, but it's my fault for losing it instead of keeping my cool. I guess I bruised his ego too much, and challenged his intellect and authority and now I need to be punished and shown my place. Sent home like a bad egg. Hmmm. I guess I get to be heaped in the pile of all the other deckhands and crew who went squirrelly and 'lost it.' Yeah, I feel pretty crappy. Not how I wanted it to end, but I have only myself to blame. So much for smiling and staying positive, James. I just couldn't do it. Blah. And I feel slightly guilty for writing this, because I know that if you suddenly started screaming that you couldn't take it anymore, no one would drop you off at the nearest town and tell you to go home. Not that we're supposed to be comparing situations.

I'm feeling pretty down on myself right now. Mak's gone to bed and Cyrus is motoring us faster than he's ever gone anywhere to drop me like an asshole in Port Hardy. Without groveling or begging or even wanting him to reconsider his decision at all, I still want to try to mend some damage and repair a little of the relationship – to honour a little of what we've been through together. We did have some great walks and talks on shore and I did enjoy a lot of his stories and experience as a fisher. And he was a stellar captain, aside from inappropriate groping and temporary loss of sanity and reason. I don't want this working relationship to end on such a shitty note. How do I try to do this in the next few hours before he goes to bed, without it sounding like I'm trying to suck up to him? I guess I need to start by expressing my regret that it is ending like this. I don't know.

Well, I just went and tried my best. His response: "I got nothing to say to you. And that's it." OK, fair enough. I guess I will go try to get some sleep. Well, there goes my short-lived career as a Tuna fisher. Not exactly something to be proud of, how I handled it. I'll pack my things, leave when we get to shore tomorrow and hitchhike down the island – I think it's about 500 km to Salt Spring. I guess I'll throw my fishing clothes overboard tomorrow, try to leave with the smallest amount to carry. Wow, I'm feeling low. It's ok. I'll bounce back and start singing when I'm on land. Off to the new adventure, right? Who knows what comes next? I'll keep you posted.

Hey, hoping you are dreaming big dreams and getting excited about new adventures for yourself.

Hi, I'm back on my last overnight 12 – 3 am shift. Mak is acting very strange and his body language is intense – getting very close to me, touching me a lot, my shoulder, my hair, brushing by me. That's not something he used to do – always made a point to never touch me until this past crazy week. He says he's deeply disturbed that I'm leaving, and asked me to wake him at midnight so he could do my final wheelhouse shift with me. I got really uncomfortable and a strong feeling he wanted a last chance to try to grope me, so I said I preferred to be alone. He's being weird – telling me that there must be a greater reason why we spent the past three months together. He keeps telling me he loves me. I really hoped that he felt like we had bonded what with all the crazy adventures we've shared, and that he meant he loved me in a friendly way, but I'm getting the feeling he's just trying to score before I leave. That feels shitty, like everything we've shared over these months is meaningless, reduced to whether he gets laid or not in the end.

Maybe it's a good thing I forced the issue and am getting dumped like all the other refuse. Did I mention that fishers are not the world's environmentalists? Man, I have seen used oil filters, broken engine parts, cooking utensils, boxes, books, clothing, fuel, used oil, pop cans, shoes, garbage, you name it, go overboard. I'll admit after the initial shock, it became a guilty pleasure for me to just chuck anything overboard. Except plastic. The only thing we're diligent about collecting is recyclable plastic – we keep that in bags and drop it on shore. And now me.

Ah well. My mind is turning to the next phase of things. I see from Cyrus' notepad that we caught 1785 fish in the time I've been with him.

Now it's late morning. Could cut tension with a knife. We are a few hours from Port Hardy. Mak and I put away the fish into the hold and I am drinking tea. I am looking forward to new beginnings but still very disappointed in myself. Endings are very important to me. It is a learned skill to do endings well. Relationship break-ups, leaving a job, any kind of ending is a very important transition and it takes work to do it well, with integrity. I messed this one up. I'm mad at myself. Burned a bridge, again.

Talked to Morgi on the phone. She knew already that I was being dumped off as she saw the owner's wife at the gym today. Diana told Morgan that she offered to drive up island to pick me up and bring me to Salt Spring, but that Cyrus had refused her, saying I didn't want a ride back and he'd stick me on a bus. Nice. Well, a few more hours and I will be gone. I'm all packed, dumped all my bloodstained fishing clothes overboard as well as all the books I finished. Sacrilegious to throw away books, but I'm feeling petty and don't want to leave any of my things here. Mak has agreed to care-take my massive heavy cribbage board, 'cause I have enough to carry, what with bedding and clothing, everything. Cut up a cardboard box I found holding our last few fresh veggies, and I'm looking for a Jiffy marker, so that I can make a sign saying: "SOUTH" and get outta Dodge as soon as we land. Trouble is, we won't be there until evening, so that doesn't put me in a good position to get to Salt Spring. Final ferry leaves at 9 pm and the terminal is 550 km down island. I'll figure something out for tonight. Mak tells me a storm is coming and Cyrus has told them they'll stay in Port Hardy and wait it out. Then back to fishing. I sincerely wish them good fishing when I leave – maybe I just wasn't patient enough and the big payoff is still to come. Or maybe Cyrus found his scapegoat and can blame the whole rotten season on me. Or maybe we all just snapped. Talking to Morgi made me ache to see her.

Lying in my bunk last night I couldn't sleep and I reflected back on this weird and whacky three-month trip. It was a break from the usual, a removal from all normal context, and also a crucible, a micro-cosm of all the larger issues of my life and it sure taught me a lot. Put into the spotlight some of what I need to let go of (and did on the trip), what I am grateful for, and that attitude really IS EVERYTHING! You were right all along! ☺

Thanks for sharing this trip with me, James. I know you weren't really here, but I have written this journal partly to myself to relieve my boredom, partly to you, hoping it would relieve yours. Writing to you, sending you good wishes and prayers and retelling you events and thoughts of my day has been a really huge blessing on this trip. I haven't shared any of this journey with anyone else, and the whole time I was on the boat, I felt like you were there, in part, with me. Thank you, dear friend!

Hope prison will soon be a distant memory. Hope you will be watching a basketball game with your brothers soon.

Looking forward to sharing ideas and laughs with you!

xo Heath.

1PM SEPTEMBER 25, 2012

JAMES!

I HAVE to share this final bit with you! We docked in Port Hardy yesterday at 3 pm. I left within minutes of tying up, carrying three large bags of bedding, clothes, toiletries, laptop. I said goodbye to Cyrus, wishing him well and the luck to find a zillion fish. Mak walked me to town. I hugged him goodbye, walked to the highway, and stuck out my thumb. Total calm and serenity overtook me as I waited for a ride. Surreal being on land, surrounded by dense forest, bisected by a concrete road. First car, the guy stops. Very large, slurring, body odour of an ageing incontinent hippo stuffed into a sports' car. He drove like a maniac, tailgating and passing people at 150km/hr, to the next town, where I was grateful to jump out alive.

As he drove and babbled at me, I nodded at appropriate moments. I looked out the window and a wave of complete clarity and happiness washed over me. All the sights, sounds and colours were vivid, sharp, magnified. I was filled with total joy. I couldn't stop grinning. I know now what I was supposed to be learning out there, and I needed to be removed from everything else in my life to really see it. Choose positivity. Choose sobriety. That's it. It's that simple. I feel incredibly lucky and incredibly joyful for every aspect of my life. Calm and peacefulness, even as this maniac swerves around. I know that I released a lot of my old stuff on the boat. All that time on the ocean to feel old feelings I was hanging on to, and let wash away. And all the whining and worrying and 'woe is me-ing' I did in this journal feels so silly now. I am totally happy and grateful and excited about my life and not worried in the slightest about anything.

He dropped me off, the next guy picked me up and brought me the next 200 km. This guy reminded me so much of you, I kept sneaking peeks at him, amazed that he could be so much like you, even his laugh was exactly the same as yours and his energy easy-going (although could never be as lovely as you). I smiled at the Universe who put this guy in my path: "I get it, I really do. Thank You." Choose positivity. And sobriety. That simple. Larger feelings of grace and tingly connection to the beauty of Life were there too, and I was giddy with happiness. This young guy just came out of camp where he works falling trees 25 days on, ten days off. I invited him for dinner and we spent the night in a motel. This morning, we headed in our separate directions (definite spring in my step and grin on my face). I stuck my thumb out and got a series of small rides. Punctuated by long hours at the side of the road watching cars zoom by, giddy with the wonder of Life.

Then, the home stretch.

I stood on the highway, marveling at the beauty of this incredible province resplendent in her Fall colours, and I reflected back on all the fear and stuff I was going through on the fishing trip. And the ranting in my journal about "why don't I get a break?" in life. I laughed and laughed. What exactly do I think the Universe owes me? I have all that I need, blessed far more than most and an abundance of energy for more happiness! Life offers me gifts at every turn – I just need to be open to seeing them and to accepting them, even when they are challenges. Choose positivity, Heath.

A small old beat-up Toyota caught my eye and instantly, I knew he was going to stop, even though there was no sign he'd even seen me or made eye contact. He swerved two lanes over, stopped. Friendly, positive guy, we spent the final two hours of my trip talking about nothing and everything. He mentioned Thailand, I said: "Oh yeah? I go there." Pause. He says: "I know you." He realized that he had met me on the riverboat heading up the Chao Praya to Bangkwang five years ago and we had talked then for ten minutes about my prison work. He says he has remembered me since then because of the impact on him of me talking about the prisoners, and about my daughter. I brought he and his then girlfriend to visit Johann that day. I filled him in on what's happened to Johann since, and about seeing him recently in France. Silence. Out of the blue this guy continues: "I didn't know when I met you back then what I know now. That I am blessed and that life will always provide for me what I need. I feel I am walking a life path in a valley where I will encounter all the people and experiences that I need, as they all will roll down towards me and be placed in my path." My tears started pouring as he talked, and I replied: "I didn't know it when I met you back then, either, but I do now: I have within me all I need. I simply need to choose positivity. Every moment is precious and every experience that comes around each corner is exactly the gift I will need. I have been reminded of this since starting this trip down this island with some new-found clarity." We both got shivers as we marveled at our random encounter five years ago on the riverboat in Bangkok and then now on a highway on Vancouver Island. He dropped me at the ferry terminal for Salt Spring, we hugged, and he said he and his wife will keep in touch, as they are opening an art gallery in Victoria and would like to feature some of Ivan's work!

What an absolutely amazing journey, in so many ways! Life is AWESOME!

I am minutes away from hugging my daughter as hard as I can. I AM SMILING, JAMES! I AM SENDING YOU LOVE!

Thank you for being so totally, absolutely wonderful and for reminding me what is important.

xo Heather.

SEPTEMBER 25, 2012

I have been home just five hours and spent wonderful time with Morgan. I picked up your letter from early July (one I didn't get a chance to read before, as I was out on the ocean.) I shared with Morgan my amazing journey home and revelation and then met with Paul and Diana, the owners of the *Gaffe*, who were worried that I would hate them, that I'd had a horrible experience. I reassured them that the non-fishing trip was fantastic, an amazing, mostly positive experience and I would do it again in a sec if there were fish – that Cyrus and Mak were both great to work with generally and that I had snapped inappropriately at Cyrus and therefore he ditched me in a fit of pique. They were relieved and wrote me a cheque for a bit more than I was owed but still vastly less than I was hoping to make. All is well.

When I was hanging with Morgan, I brought up the words she had uttered to me a few weeks ago, crying on the phone: "Mom, why is someone with such a big heart like you always handed shit on a plate by Life?" Today, I said: "How could I EVER say I've been handed 'shit on a plate?' I have been blessed with the most incredible daughter in the whole world, and I have so much to be thankful for everyday: my health, my wonderful daughter, and to live in a peaceful, privileged part of the world with clean water. Look around us at all this beauty." She didn't seem convinced, but she'll get it one day. She's doing really well compared to a year ago, and just signed up for night courses at the high school to finish up her last few credits. Doing therapy in Vancouver and making plans for her future – maybe college next Fall or travelling with friends to Europe. YAY! Does NOT want me talking about returning to Thailand yet. We've planned a wee road-trip for two weekends from now up Vancouver Island to Tofino, where I'll drive her to a yoga/surfing retreat, then drive her back after the weekend. I gotta find something to do to amuse myself for the two days there. Sober. And cheap or free. I'll figure something out. Wish you could come – truly one of the most magical places in Canada – surfing, tiny community surrounded by whales, bears, salmon, massive trees, temperate rainforest and the beauty of the Wild West Coast. Ocean straight out to Japan.

Your letter was AWESOME! Beyond awesome. Thank you. You are wonderful! And very sweet. I reread your other letters too, and felt so very warmed by your generous spirit and the love shining through in your supportive and kind words. Letters are vastly different than talking, aren't they? We spiral and touch upon other areas and ways of being that enrich our understanding of each other, and also feel like a whole other type of relationship than the hanging out, talking one. I miss your big smile!

Responses: You are so absolutely right about my crappy email to that woman I discouraged from visiting a prisoner. A visit is better than no visit. Should never have dissuaded her. I should have identified in myself that I was run-down, burnt out from exhaustion, instead of bristling at her list of criteria for inmates (innocent, good-looking, White, blah blah). In my defense, there are some serious whackos, especially women, who have 'fetishes' for inmates and while that not's necessarily my problem to deal with, or necessarily something you guys mind getting, I feel overly protective of the prisoners sometimes and don't like how weirdos with poor boundaries have done damage to some of the guys. This, however, was more about me feeling exhausted, overextended. I put a lot of energy towards all that is entailed in supporting inmates but can't always muster the energy to help more people get to the prison, as it invariably involves WAY more energy for hand-holding than I have (for obvious reasons, it's not so easy for someone to go there and they always have a million questions and concerns and stuff and they need often a lot of care-taking to go the first time), depleted and run-down as I was this past spring. So I should have directed her to someone else to help her get to the prison, realizing that sometimes I just can't do it all. Oh well. Live and learn. Thanks for giving my head a shake via pen and paper. ☺

I guess sending books is a moot point, now, as I am unsure even how to get that to you in Cowbin (Khao Bin Prison), but we can revisit that as we see how things move in the next while for you. And please don't ever hesitate to ask me for anything. I am more than happy to do anything I can to help make your world a bit easier. Or happier. Or sillier. Or just 'cause. Ever read *In the Realm of Hungry Ghosts* by Gabor Maté? He is a MD turned addiction specialist who has worked in the infamous Downtown Eastside of Vancouver (poorest area and highest concentration of addicts in Canada) for the past 30 years in Canada's first safe injection site. He writes brilliantly, wisely and compassionately about addiction and about other topics he is sought out for on speaking engagements. I would love to have more conversations with you about recovery.

Congratulations, by the way, on the early successes with your guys in your recovery group in Bangkwang you wrote about. What a wonderful accomplishment! That must be hard, knowing you cannot support them from Cowbin, but maybe your work and support has laid the foundation for continued positive developments. So sorry that you lost that connection when they transferred you. ☹

I really, really appreciate your support in my drinking issues. More than I can say. What an incredibly kind and loving letter you wrote and I appreciate that you're more emotionally open with me and talking about some of your history. And to know you're on my side is, well... very important to me, to say the least.

I am an asshole when I drink. 100%. Used lots of drugs in my youth, went very hard for several years, then decided early on that I'm not into that – quit when I was 16 – but alcohol remains more than vicious enough a foe.

These moments of clarity about choosing positivity and knowing that all I need is already within me have come repeatedly to me over my life and then I forget and have to remind myself and relearn them. It takes practice. So will sobriety. But I have the rest of my life to practice, so I expect to get really good at both! ☺ Not drinking will accentuate the mood swings for a bit (several more months) while my brain learns to deal without numbing, so I know there will be challenges. No, it is not easy standing on sober ground. But I am one for challenges – they make me grow. I am learning and strive to make this my way of being in the world. I have become a much lighter and happier being over recent years, after a tremendous amount of work put in on self-exploration, healing, therapy, and have a lot of insight into my issues. AND the beast of addiction is the one that I still have to conquer. I have known for years that sobriety is the only way. But chose to ignore that knowledge. Addiction grabbed hold of me and whispered its sweet, seductive lies in my ear, telling me that I can handle 'just a little' or 'now and then' or that wine 'helps.' That's not the case. I know there is nothing positive about alcohol in my life. Maybe I will have to find a 'higher power' to vanquish it. I do know that we are part of something much bigger, Life itself, and I draw on that in my own spiritual beliefs, but probably not how you mean.

I have been to AA meetings: three or four a few years ago. Too much of it turned me off – the literature, the philosophy, the endless sob-stories of how everyone's lost their wife, children, job(s), self-respect, money, house, car, bladder control, all to the demon alcohol (all while they compulsively chain-smoke and gulp down a thousand cups of coffee or caffeine beverages). Sorry, I'm just saying how I experienced it. It's not that I wasn't feeling for them, I just didn't latch on. It seemed like a few people just replaced one addiction (alcohol) with another (compulsive meeting-attending) without actually engaging in any serious self-reflection or taking any responsibility for their lives or behaviour. I do want help and support with my sobriety. I DO know that addiction is the issue with me. I know that my mental and physical health is much better without alcohol and I KNOW that life without alcohol is a far more rewarding, enriching one. I am not in denial about any of that. I WANT AA to help me – but try as I may, their philosophy doesn't resonate with me. It's just not for me. I refuse to believe that that's the ONLY way for 100% of people in the world to conquer addiction issues. It has been shown repeatedly that AA is wonderful and highly successful with a certain segment of people. As medical and other professionals I've discussed this with for years agree, there are other models that work for other types of people too. For me, for now, I need to stay positive, learning, growing, reflecting, and sober. I know it won't be an easy road, and I may stumble, but I am sure of my commitment to invest in myself to really shine as the best me possible, and that is a sober me. Just to show myself that I am not being intransigent, I will go to an AA meeting this week. Maybe even tonight. It can't hurt. I will try to glean any support from it or something to latch on to that will make sense to me. All that aside, again, James, I am deeply grateful for your wonderful encouragement and support! ☺

I need intellectual, spiritual, and physical stimulation, movement, growth, learning, and I will seek ways to feed the parts of me too long neglected, instead of feeding the addiction. And remind myself daily to be gentle with myself. That is where I am right now.

In case you were concerned from my fishing story that I am replacing booze with pill-popping,

a) they weren't narcotics or heavy drugs, and
b) now that I am not required to work my stiff joints and torn muscles, I am letting my body heal, pill-free. My shoulders and joints, wrists and hands are aching and sore, I am covered in deep black bruises from the boat/fishing. My hands seize up a dozen times a day. All will mend. I feel fantastic and I am going to the gym to run. I love running. Like you, I find it harder NOT to run than to run. It's so powerful, meditative, healing, and grounding!

I am happy. And I am smiling. I send you big, big LOVE! ☺

What about you? What do you write? You said you wanted to do a Phd in creative writing. What do you write where you are? Is any of it something you would share with me?

Something very deep has switched in me, James. For the first time ever I am clear that I can do this sobriety thing. And that I WANT this. Other times I quit, I would mentally give myself permission to start again after a month, two weeks, three days, or two hours. I would convince myself I could go back to 'just' drinking 'a little' wine, because I could not envision myself sober for life. And didn't want that. That's not the case anymore. Obviously I cannot claim success when my sobriety is in its early stages right now, and this requires a life-long commitment, but something feels profoundly different in me.

I am giving myself the best gift possible and reminding myself that I deserve to accept this wonderful gift. The abundance I asked the Universe for exists already within me, I just need to let her shine! ☺

Too much theory with no follow-through or results is pointless, so I'll stop the rambling here. Got to go live soberly.

Like when my ex- David told me he found God in rehab and AA last year and went on and on and on about it. Listening, all I could think was: *Great! If that works for you. I don't care who you found – Buddha, Allah, Jesus or just dust bunnies under the coffee-stained couch. The real question is: are you going to stay sober?* He didn't, and when he would contact me from the dark hell his brain was in, I was regaled not only with his usual threats against me and entreaties to help end his suffering, but also an additional bonus package of newly learned bible quotes. Nice. I'm being flippant because it's better right now than thinking of him suffering, which I know he is, or dead, which I imagine he will soon be. Apparently, God doesn't save new converts. Even ones who go to church and bible-study three times a week and AA meetings twice a day, which David was doing, trying so hard to get support from God to fight his demons. Sorry, I shouldn't criticize. That's the part of me that hates that another human being is living in such agonizing torment and wishing that something, anything, he was reaching out to in desperation could have helped him. I don't want to end this letter with that negativity, but I wrote this past paragraph last night, and something cracked in me and I imagined myself screaming at you, James: "WHY WHY WHY did your stupid God not save him?" Isn't He supposed to do the lifting when the human is too weak to do it on his own? Isn't that what you guys believe? David was struggling so hard against his demons, reaching out with all his might to God and God just kicked him to the gutter. I cried myself to sleep, grief stuck in my throat.

I don't need you to answer that question. It's not a theological question, it's an age-old human one. Life just isn't fair or just and human suffering is part of the deal. Heart-breaking as it is. Must choose positivity.

Maybe this gives me something to bring to church to chat about. They'll probably just say that the demons were stronger than his faith, or something nonsensical like that. Or that his 'soul' is 'saved,' just not his life. Or that God works in mysterious ways. Gee, thanks for that one. I keep trying to stop this letter on a positive note, James, but I can't. I am so angry, so unbelievably furious that David wasn't able to pull out of his addiction hell and suffering and I am <u>unfairly</u> trying to take it out on you and your faith and that's <u>not right</u>. I will stop and go to the nearest church and go talk to them – see what they have to say.

I left the coffee shop where I had been sitting writing to you, and went to the local United Church, looking for someone to vent at. First time I'd darkened the door of a church in decades. No one was there. Returning to the coffee shop, I then saw a wise friend, Jamie, a toothless old, incredibly intelligent and astute man who used to be my neighbour ten years ago. We started a 'philosopher's grotto,' he and I, and two other dear souls, and we would gather in his shack on the property we both lived on. He and the others would chain-smoke, they'd smoke pot and often we'd drink wine, but we were all so poor, just trying to put food on our tables, so rarely had drugs or booze. Mostly, we'd discuss ideas and our lives for hours, days. Sometimes I would just show up and cry, just so depressed, stressed out from the intensity of being a working single mom putting myself through school, and many times we would debate, or ponder, or just be, supporting each other in our cravings for intellectual debates. He was a single dad, raising an extremely troubled boy whom he had adopted at the age of four from a very abusive environment. He lost career, wife, everything in order to stay focused on a boy that the rest of the world had given up on, practicing endless patience and compassion as a parent, when the rest of the world gave up on the kid. They lived in a tin-roof shack beside the place Morgan and I lived in and he lived on social assistance, unable to work, as his son required constant attention. One day I showed up only to jump on his son and hold him down, to stop him from putting every sharp knife in the house into either his own or his father's body. I heard the son is now in prison and Jamie ekes out a very marginal existence, busking. He builds beautiful guitars by hand, but he has never sold one. Plays steel guitar stunningly well, and has a million other skills that lie unseen, invisible. No one pays attention to this old toothless man, nor any of his incredible many varied talents and wisdom. He is 37 years sober. I see him today after heading back from the closed church, and, relieved, I say: "Jamie, I need a theological question answered." He replies: "That's all? That shouldn't take long." We both laugh, atheist humour. I tell him about my grief and rage about David's suffering, and tell him of my displaced anger, wanting to kick every Christian I see and scream at them: "What the hell good is your stupid God anyway?" We dispense with that part quickly, as we know it has nothing to do with 'God'.

Jamie reminds me that grief is a prayer, a holding of space, a meditation that acknowledges David's pain, even as he cannot hold all of his own, nor face it. Jamie knows me well enough that he doesn't think that my tears for David have anything to do with bad boundaries or co-dependence or not understanding that David's journey is his own and no one else's. All that I know and have understood very clearly for years. I'm not stupid. I still wish I would never see that guy again in my life. Jamie knows me though. He knows that I have a deep sensitivity to injustice and that I grieve deeply for people who are suffering. He reflects back to me that the holding of space I do for others is a valuable gift, something I have done since I was small. Compassion has this side of it too, he reminds me. He doesn't call me 'over-sensitive' as others do. He thanks me for my grief as I sob and we spend some time talking and grieving. I feel infinitely better just having spent a few moments witnessed by a deep-thinking and loving person who gets me and doesn't trot out quick, pat answers.

I go to the gym and run, after replenishing the litres of water I cried out. Then I go to an AA meeting. It was ok. Not great, not bad, just felt fairly neutral. People were welcoming, we meditated for ten minutes, then people spoke, and I did too. Everyone drank coffee. It was ok, I guess. I will try to force myself to do it a few more times just to prove to you I'm not close-minded.

Well, friend, I thank you again for being on my side in my journey. I am praying for you James, for your health, safety, and imminent return to your family. For your transfer, for your release, and for new exciting adventures. Don't forget I'm on your side, too. Sending love and light. Hugs and Kisses to you Smiley Guy!

XO Heather

At times our own light goes out and is rekindled by a spark from another person. Each of us has cause to think with deep gratitude of those who have lighted the flame within us.

~ ALBERT SCHWEITZER

PART III: THAILAND

BANGKOK JOURNAL

Wanting to know what to do about the effects on the guys I see retreating...the ones in here for over a decade...who are harder and harder to reach. And my pain and fear of watching men I care for disappear over time into the dark recesses of their minds.

A few years ago, Zaw specifically requested to be left to live in his tiny inner world and to be allowed to leave the world of outside interactions. I understood his rationale: he had been inside over 15 years, and whatever 'reality' the outside world had been for him through memories, hopes, dreams, and fantasies, no longer existed. The 'world' as he knows it is a tiny one, inhabited by 800 men, one building, one outside compound and four walls and barbed wire. There is nothing that exists beyond that and it pains him to try to talk to people belonging to a world that will never exist for him again. When he explained this to me, my heart broke, but I respected his wishes and I stopped visiting.

Now, others I have visited I see also retreating, falling into an inner world that becomes increasingly hard for me to reach. After ten years, Ivan's lived world and his inner world have shrunk. I see in the three years I've been visiting him, how his reference to the outside world has almost disappeared and he cannot talk about anything except the tiny, insignificant to me moments of prison life, like someone snoring loudly next to him, or a ten minute-long story about mailing a letter. These interactions dominate his exceptionally monotonous daily life.

Last week, when I visited him, a small child ran behind me in the visiting area, and I pointed him out to Ivan, saying: "It must be cool for you to see a child." Ivan looked at me blankly: "That child is just like seeing it on TV – not real." He laughed bitterly: "Even you, Heather, you are behind glass, it's like watching tv. More and more, I am not sure you are real. I don't even believe the world out there actually exists anymore."

I find myself exceptionally impatient with him these past visits. Each time he speaks, I find myself unable to listen, all too aware that his story about the minutae of prison life will eat away our precious minutes, so I interrupt: "Is it really important to use this whole visit telling me this?" and he gets frustrated at my interruption, at my insisting that he get to the point quickly. I want to talk about things outside his daily monotony. But I am torn. Should I listen to whatever he wants to talk about, whether it is deathly dull to me, or can I impose my agenda of getting him outside of this minuscule, unchanging world that he spins in 24/7 for over ten years? I decide to ask him to limit his talk about his prison world to five minutes max at the beginning, and for us to discuss larger topics for the rest of the time. Maybe this is just selfish, and only for my benefit, and doesn't help him at all. But I believe that his mind needs to stretch and grow and be challenged and have new vistas, perspectives, and stories or it will continue to atrophy, to crumble in upon itself. I see in him other horrible imploding quirks visible in every guy who has been inside longer than roughly eight years. Ivan agrees to try to talk about other topics, but he has lost the ability to engage in turn-taking and perspective-taking – normal conversational cues we take for granted when talking. This scares the shit out of me.

DECEMBER 1, 2555

A horrible week, where my brain felt under siege and I was fragile, on edge and felt like a basket-case. I was gritting my teeth through a painful medical condition without narcotics that I normally take in Canada (but cannot in Thailand) and without my normal second choice of copious amounts of wine. Dealing with the pain, my drug and alcohol-free brain was throwing a lot of crap my way and I felt intensely fragile. My irritable self didn't go well in my visits with Ivan and James, and I felt guilty about not being able to be very present for either of them. Thursday, I was angry at Liam, tired of the bullshit bravado and for blaming everyone else for his misery. I am especially scared by the radical change in his behavior this year. Dark moods, evasive responses, bitterness, and paranoia lead me to suspect heroin use. Our conversations felt off the past while and I was contemplating giving him an ultimatum – cut the bullshit or I'd 'take a break' from our visits. And feeling torn about whether I could or should do that. I showed up Thursday, caught up in my own whirling stress, and told him that a good friend of mine had just died, and that I'd been struggling in my new-found sobriety (65 days) with crazy shit my brain was throwing at me, hating my thoughts and sobriety at that moment, but determined to do this, and hanging in there. I prodded gently about how he was doing, and he said quietly: "I'm scared." We sat in silence for a long time. Tears starting pouring down his face. As he cried, he shared his fears of the damage the prison was doing to him, his fears of never making it out alive, never making it out 'ok' again after ten years in, and his struggles to keep going. We cried together and just sat with all of that, me not wanting to say anything that would dismiss or try to 'fix' or remove what he was feeling. I left crying, but relieved that we had shared a real moment, hard as it was.

I can't bear watching what that place does to those men.

DECEMBER 3, 2555

What is a 'successful' life? James asked me in a letter today. I think instead of how I judge my actions. My mental process invariably goes like this: If I were to die today, would I regret what I did? And it comes down to: have I done something positive for someone else, can I look myself in the mirror, have I strived to be a better, more loving person and not selfish, obnoxious, aggressive, fill in the blanks...? If so, then I think I have a 'successful' life. It never comes down to: what material possessions have I left for my descendants? It comes down to: have I left good memories, have I treated people around me with respect, love and compassion?

EXCERPT FROM A LETTER TO JAMES:

How do I measure success, you ask?

I am reading *The Better Angels of Our Nature: Why Violence has Declined* and I borrow from a paragraph I just read in which our 'greater angels' of moral reasoning are explained, because it echoes my own beliefs:

> "It is a forcible motive...reason, principle, conscience, the voice within, the great judge and arbiter of our conduct. It is she, who, whenever I am about to act so as to affect the happiness of others, calls to me, with a voice capable of astonishing the most presumptuous of my passions, that I am but one of the multitude, in no respect better than any other in it; and that when I prefer myself so shamefully and so blindly to others, I become the proper object of resentment, abhorrence and execration... It is this inner voice that reminds me of the propriety of generosity and deformity of injustice; the

propriety of resigning the greatest interests of our own, for the yet greater interests of others, and the deformity of doing the smallest injury to other, in order to obtain the greatest benefit to ourselves."

Think outside of your own experience meeting me, James, because it is not the usual scenario for inmates – you would have been perfectly fine never having met or known me. Yes, it's been awesome for me to have met you, shared visits and great conversations and writing to you. But you are unusual in the amount of support you have: your inner spiritual resources, external financial ones, and your Embassy and family support. Now put yourself in the shoes of the many men you know with no family or financial or Embassy support, and no hope of a transfer or eventual freedom. So many men you have shared cells with who don't have all the benefit and privilege you experience – I have visited dozens of these men and brought visitors, and connected them to pen-pals. Many of these men now have supportive relationships with people on the outside who help to sustain them, who care about their struggles and pain and fears, who share in their hopes and joys. How do we quantify the effects of that? The ripple effects inside the prison, from these visits and letters and efforts transform a dark corner of the world, as you put it yourself in your letters.

I don't believe in Karma or in Heaven, or that some great cosmic reward awaits me for doing this. I simply do this because I feel called to do it. As for lack financial security, of course I dream about getting a salary for this, about somehow the Universe recognizing this work and alleviating the personal and financial pressure on me which is a heavy burden – but I don't wait for it or expect it.

I am idealistic, I know this and I have been told this my whole life. I don't expect that others in the world will see things the way I do. Even the inmates I support, I harbour no illusions, would not sacrifice large parts of their lives to help others in need. I'm sure none of the men I have visited would walk into a women's shelter and volunteer helping battered women for years on end. Some are even ungrateful. Some try to con me or use me. But it doesn't make it the wrong thing to do. So yes, I AM occasionally bitter about a lack of financial security,

---

* *The Better Angels of Our Nature: Why Violence has Declined*, Steven Pinker. Random House, 2011.

about scrambling all the time in Canada with no savings or salary or home – but not bitter enough to change my convictions that I am doing what I truly believe to be right. And succeeding at it. I can look at myself in the mirror and know I have made a positive difference in a few people's lives. That some people now wake up less hopeless: that is huge for me. That is success.

My greatest success has not been visiting prisoners, bringing hope and joy these past years: it has been being blessed with being the mother of a most exceptional human being, and the incredibly powerful spiritual, emotional, magical experience of being her mother. I tried every day to make her feel respected, listened to, heard, loved, and cherished. We played non-stop, laughing, singing and imagining, no matter how hard our external reality was. Of course I made many mistakes as a parent and regret some very poor choices, and still feel much shame about not being able to provide many material comforts, but I attempted every day to bring undivided attention and love, and respectful loving communication. She was not dismissed, minimized or treated with contempt. To me, that is success.

Would I like to expand my vision of success to include financial stability for myself and my daughter? Yes, of course, and I am striving to learn how to do this. And there is much more I want to accomplish in the world too. I have drawn my goals, put them up on the wall and I uneasily wrote down a salary and a home, a sanctuary, a place to rest my head... Many of my goals involve my need to engage, laugh and play, live silliness instead of struggle...I have admitted to you that I don't know how to ask for help. Maybe this is something I would ask for help with...getting financial compensation so that life is not such a struggle for me. But meanwhile, I am at peace with the knowledge that if I die tomorrow, I have left some positive memories in how I treated people – people I have no vested interest in, except that they are just like me – human, precious, every one of us – and that is fundamentally more valuable and rewarding than anything else I could aspire to.

Love and Peace to You,
xo Heather.

Took a friend Charles again to the prison today – he has pledged to go once per month to visit Fatouk, and they talked again about meditation. I always feel guilty when I can't fit in more time in my crazy schedule with some of the guys, and it has been difficult to fit Fatouk in more than once a month. Today I am relieved, as I consider Fatouk now in good hands, with Charles able to see him more regularly. I left my visit with Tirgar feeling so peaceful today – I love my talks with this smiley young Iranian man. Our talks are always so real, yet uplifting, as we buoy each other's spirits in sharing about how to choose more loving and grateful responses to challenging moments in our days.

A weird encounter before going in with an Iranian visitor in the waiting area who asked to speak to me in private. We stood off to one side and he started telling me quickly about being sent by his government to Bangkok to get 'metals' for 'batteries' and that he doesn't want to do it. He is seeking asylum, a political refugee and can I please help him? As he's repeating his story about the batteries and stuff he's supposed to procure in Bangkok, all my alarm bells are screaming wildly and I'm thinking: *I don't want to fucking hear this, I don't want to know this*... Thankfully, he soon understood I was not an Embassy official and I suggested he go directly to an Embassy. I asked him not to tell me any more. We stood in awkward silence and then he was called to go into the prison. Was at least 24 hours before my paranoia left me that someone had seen this guy talking to me and that I was now on some terrorist watch-list somewhere.

Reminds me of last Valentine's day in Bangkok, when three Iranian guys were apparently making home-made bombs and something exploded unintentionally. They ran out of their rental house, down crowded streets, trying to escape. On guy, dripping blood from his face tried to hail a cab, threw a grenade at it, then threw a second grenade at an approaching cop car, but this second grenade bounced off a tree, back towards him and blew off the guy's own legs. Bystanders videoed the incident with their phones and posted it on Youtube. Just another whacky day in Bangkok.

WHITE FUNGUS BIRD'S NEST: GREASING THE WHEELS, THAILAND-STYLE

It has been a real trial trying to get to see James during the past seven weeks. He was transferred to a new prison a week after my arrival and I tracked him down there with great difficulty and frustration. I had begged my way in to see him late one Friday afternoon in early November after a long day of travel to Khao Bin, the new super-max prison 150 km south of Bangkok, and all the waiting, heat, stress and tension that entailed, only to be told he had been moved the day before. Motorcycle taxi then next bus back up to Bangkok, I am now at Klong Prem prison asking the head of the prison's Foreigner Services, Kuhn Fah, if I can please visit him. I don't know the prison rules for this institution, so when Kuhn Fah asks me what my relationship to the inmate is, I hesitate then blurt out: 'girlfriend,' because I know most prisons don't allow non-relatives to visit. I haven't had this issue for years at Bangkwang, where they know me, nor Bangkok Remand, where they don't care. She allows us a short visit and tells me I need to get a letter from his Embassy for future visits. Over the following weeks, the American Embassy, (like all Embassies here, staffed by locals rife with incompetence, stupidity or simple overwork), is singularly unhelpful. Seemingly indifferent to their incarcerated citizens, the US Consular staff reluctantly furnishes me with permission letters that often have the wrong date or are incomplete – so I end up in a position of begging my way into the prison each week with inadequate documents, pleading my case always to this same woman, Kuhn Fah. As Thais are very oriented towards status and face, I dress at the prisons in business clothing: skirts, heels and blouses, which count here for a lot. In various conversations over the past weeks with this same prison official, I tell her various stories that are mostly true: that I have been sent by the Embassy; that I am a 'friend'; that I don't exactly work for the Embassy; but that they want me to visit James. Last Friday, I was beside myself with frustration and fury, because the US Embassy had yet again fucked up the documents and I was unable to see

James on the week before Christmas, a particularly lonely time of the year for all inmates. Each of these mistakes costs me hours and hours of emails, travel time between Embassies and to prisons, where I am turned away and miss visits with other inmates as well. In desperation, I went again to the prison to plead my case, although the previous week I was denied entry and told in no uncertain terms not to come back without correct documentation. Today I must try again, even though I know I am very close to using up Kuhn Fah's little remaining tolerance. I am sick with fear. I risk being banned from visiting James altogether.

I go to Bangkwang in the morning, visit Ivan, and we discuss arranging an 'inside' visit with his Russian Embassy and all the hassles that entails, then I jump in a taxi to Klong Prem and Bangkok Remand prisons, where I am each afternoon. Outside, I encounter a distraught Turkish man who is trying to visit a relative. He has just learned that his cousin has been sentenced to 44 years for credit card fraud. He doesn't know how to break the news to the man's elderly mother, who has been waiting for two years for her son to return to Turkey, having been told continuously since his arrest that it will be "just a few more months." I sit and listen to a story which I've heard a thousand times before, with different characters: the devastated and heartbroken family; the shock and outrage at the draconian sentences; the dawning realization of total and complete powerlessness; and, the vanishing of any hope of being able to buy the person's way out of prison (a common misperception). I witness the overwhelming immensity of what 'life' or 50 years in prison means for the inmate, and for the family. Nothing will ever be the same again. I sit with this man and we share some cigarettes as he cries – he is only in Thailand for three days and the Foreign Services prison guard will not let him bring food or books to his cousin, nor visit him more than this once, for the allotted half an hour. As I listen to him rage, I realize there is no point in telling him that if he had dressed in a suit, instead of a tank top and casual pants, he might have been able to negotiate more visits. That crying, raging and arguing your case gets you nowhere in Thailand – in fact, it will put you much further back in accomplishing your goals. Here, people do not appreciate outbursts of emotion, particularly anger. Now is not the time to offer a cultural lesson in how to save people's face or grease the wheels in Thailand, so I listen and my heart feels heavy for what lies ahead for his family.

Outside the prison there are crowds of such people standing about shell-shocked, grief writ large on their faces, each confronted with their own familial devastation.

I take a deep breath and go to see Kuhn Fah in her office. A diminutive Thai woman, maybe 4'7" and 80 lbs. with full military dress and heels on, she holds the power to admit or deny access to foreigner inmates. Next to her I feel like a massive oaf so I try to make my 5'7" Western body smaller as I crumple myself demurely onto a tiny chair in front of her desk, uncomfortable and awkward in my tight skirt and blouse that covers my tattoos, feeling like a giant drag queen. My head is lowered and I sit in silence in this dingy office for long minutes until she finally looks up and acknowledges me. I ask her for permission to see James. She tells me that she got a call from the US Embassy that morning, attempting to correct the discrepancies in my paperwork, but she still has one issue to resolve: What exactly is my relationship to James? "Here, it says: 'friend', she explains, pointing to a Thai word on some papers, but friends cannot visit inmates."

Smiling, I try to convince her that the English word 'friend' encompasses the Thai equivalent of 'family representative,' a relationship of special importance in Thailand that we have no word for. She nods and writes a few things down. She asks me to follow her to photocopy the paperwork. As we head down a dark hallway, she suddenly stops, turns, and asks: "What do you do when you are in Thailand?" Tense, mind whirling, I understand that her question is anything but casual: I cannot tell her that I bring support to many inmates, or she might think I don't represent his family. I won't lie and give the most common occupation for ex-pats, teaching English, because she's seen my passport that doesn't have a work permit on it. I want to stick as closely to the truth as possible, but I am afraid I won't be allowed in. After a very long pause, I finally say: "I am really just here to bring support to James from his family." She looks at me shrewdly and says:

"I think you work for the FBI."

Stunned, I laugh nervously: "No No, I don't work for the FBI," thinking: *Wouldn't someone from the FBI have a better cover story?*

"I'll give you one hour every week until you leave Thailand," she says.

I nod politely, inside screaming: *YES!*

I get a fantastic visit with James, both of us laughing about the FBI thing. On the way out of the prison, I see the Turkish man again – in despair, he begged Kuhn Fah to let him in to see his cousin but Kuhn Fah refused him entry. I take his cousin's name and promise I'll arrange some visits for him in the coming months.

Knowing how tenuous any agreement is in Thailand, I want to seal the deal with Kuhn Fah and I decide that a New Year's 'gift' will be perfect. That evening, as I sit at a local eatery, I ask the Thai owner, a friend of mine, what an appropriate and respectful gift would be for me to bring to a prison official. She recommends a basket of *Bird's Nest*. After a few confusing rounds of conversation, and a quick check online, I ascertain that 'Bird's Nest' is an edible delicacy, made apparently from a harvested bird's nest (?). As several foreigners and I try to decipher the incomprehensible Wikipedia description as to the exact nature of this stuff, the bar owner disappears and reappears a few moments later with a jar of white gelatinous mush she bought at 7/11. The box it comes in describes in English that the Bird's Nest is mixed with sugar and 'hygien- ically prepared' – a big red flag in Thailand, meaning that the product is extra nasty and assembled under distinctly unsanitary conditions. The only other clue as to what this snot-like substance might be comes from the phrase – 'saves you long hours of preparation.' *Preparation for what?* I wonder. I assume that the phrase Bird's Nest is a euphemism for something else, but I cannot figure out what. The waitress offers me a spoonful and I gingerly taste the sweet, white pus-like substance, while continuing to mine the box for clues as to what this stuff actu- ally is. Tellingly, the two ingredients added to the Bird's Nest are not translated into English. I ask my friend, and she translates for me that there is 88% Sugar, 10.4 % Bird's Nest, and 1.5 % Borax. *Borax?* "Are you sure?" I ask. Yup, apparently the same stuff you clean your toilet with. *Excellent*, I think, *that must be the 'hygienic' part*. I am feeling queasy now from the one mouthful I had. "Are you sure I should bring this stuff to the prison tomorrow?"

"Yes," she insists. Apparently, it's what all Thais give at New Year's for business 'gifts,' that is, bribes.

Next morning, dressed in my FBI best, I go to the local supermar- ket where I see aisles and aisles of gift baskets of Bird's Nest for every budget. The most expensive brand is the White Fungus brand. I pick out a medium gift basket costing 1000 baht, a not insignificant sum. My Western sensibilities make me also grab a tin of lemon cookies (*to wash the snot down with,* I think), and I stand in line surrounded by Thais buying dozens of baskets of Bird's Nest – they're flying off the shelves. I strap the basket to the back of my *motorbai*, ride to the prison, where I present Kuhn Fah with the gift, thank her for her help, and wish her a Happy New Year. "See you next week," she answers, and I skip out of the prison, stoked that I've apparently successfully greased the wheels. I am hopeful I'll see James next week, but I know not to count on it. This is Thailand, after all. Anything can happen.

LETTERS

Dear Samantha:

I appreciate your thoughts on how to engage with prisoners. Most first-time pen-pals and/or visitors have similar questions about what to say to an inmate.

Many people are worried that they should not talk too much about their interesting lives, as it will 'depress' or 'overwhelm' the inmate. I can assure you, the opposite is the case. These men are leading exceedingly boring lives with no variation and little to engage them. (Remember these are NOT Western prisons, with activities, libraries, gyms, etc.). After years of seeing the same faces, the same men, having exhausted all possible conversation with the same people they live with, they they crave new sights and sounds.

If he gets a visit from the outside world, an inmate WANTS to hear all about the interesting things you do: where you're from, where you've travelled, what your life is like, or what you did today. This provides them with mental images: colours, sights, sounds, energy that they feed off of for days, months, years. This is the case for all inmates I have worked with, regardless of their country of origin and the length of their incarceration. If you do decide to become a pen-pal, the inmate will want to hear about your life. Tell him of your travels, your hobbies, your joyous events. This allows them to transcend the place they exist in and to dream. Many report that they feel 'alive' from visits, suddenly able to be seen as human, to engage as human, and to live vicariously through hearing about another's life, whereas before they merely 'existed.' As one inmate said to me: 'my biggest activity is remembering and imagining, hoping and dreaming.'

Every first-time visitor enters with a lot of fear and concern about what to say to what they expect will be an exceedingly depressed inmate. The visitor invariably walks out of the prison totally shocked that they had such a joyous conversation. The inmate is thrilled to see another person, has a vested interest in making the experience positive, and gets to engage as a person, rather than how he normally feels.

Our topics of conversation are varied: current events, families, emotions, and much, much more. Each relationship I develop is different and yet over the years I have observed many commonalities in how inmates react to, cope with and process their incarceration, even as they are just as widely diverse as all of us on the outside are. In general I allow the inmate to lead if he is needing to vent, or to share his feelings or thoughts. Often, though, an inmate has little to report and wants instead to hear anything and everything from the outside. I agree with your comment that the topic of conversation is less important than just connecting as two people.

In the case of some of the men that I visit regularly, we forge more intimate relationships and we share fears, worries, terror, and suffering, as well as joys, hopes, and triumphs. As I alluded to in the letter I wrote before, I see a pronounced psychological and physical withdrawing occurring at or around the tenth year of incarceration. The inmates themselves talk about how they seem to change around year eight, dramatically, for the worse. From where I sit, I see men who have become unable to converse normally. This becomes quite pronounced, where I see uncertainty in conversation, repetition, obsessive thinking and dwelling on the most minute details of their day, as well as odd speech patterns. They may tell a story and immediately restart it, repeating it several times in succession. This may be an unfortunate reflection of the large number of hours to fill and the very limited stimulation to them. While totally aware of how tiny their physical and social world is, most inmates don't see the concomitant shrinking of their inner world as well. I do limit, as you suggested, their highly repetitive discourse to a small amount of time in our conversation.

I have researched and witnessed it, but that does not prevent me from feeling deep grief at what we humans are capable of doing to others in the name of 'justice' or 'retribution.' This is what I was venting about in my previous email. I would not be human or good at what I do here if I were unaffected by the horrific stuff I see, thus sometimes my letters are experienced as quite shocking or distressing to people who do not engage with what I do.

It can be hard for people to understand the world these inmates exist in. Time slows down to a crawl and the minutes pass like hours. There is absolutely no change in their routine, their monotony. Thus novelty, no matter how tiny, can elicit elation for an inmate.

Last year, a guy told me in our visit that he had had 'a fantastic week.' He explained that he had heard, from inside the prison, the single honk of a car horn coming from outside the concrete walls. This was the first time he had heard such a sound in five years. He reported that single sound sent his mind spinning into thoughts of cars, of driving, and he spent the whole week on a cloud of 'joy,' just imagining the sensations of going on road trips and of being in a car.

For longer term inmates, novelty can also provoke panic or fear. When one is deprived of autonomy over every single aspect of one's existence – one's movement, one's environment, one's activities, severely controlled and restricted for a very long time, it can be terrifying to encounter novelty.

Many men at this point express a fear that they will no longer know, if they do get out, how to walk down a street with other human beings or how to order food in a restaurant, or how to open a door, or how to apply for a job, or how to hug a person. Although I can reassure them that they will adjust and learn again and that there will be support for them in doing so, I think it reflects a more existential fear – that they really are no longer human.

Thanks for listening to my rambles, I appreciate your comments because it helps me to reflect more deeply on some of this work.

XO Heather.

JANUARY 18, 2556

Dear James:

It is only hours after I last saw you and I really want to try to connect. I would prefer to write with pen on paper, but I have laptop and motivation right now, so this is how it is.

I am still thinking about our visit, and I know that by the time this letter reaches you in a few days, things will have changed. What you brought to our visit, the beating that you witnessed this morning was very disturbing. I am sorry you witnessed that violence, and I can't imagine how awful that was for you and everyone present. I know by the time you read this there will be a new chapter in the story but I wanted you to know I heard what you said. I hope tensions have lessened, that the situation is less stressful and that there is movement towards peace and safety in your building, and more joy in your world.

When we visit, I try to take my cues from you as to whether you want a distraction from what you experience, or a witness, or both. I sometimes get mixed messages from you, and the emotional tone of what you present dissonant with the content of your stories. This confuses me as I try to learn how to read through what you tell me to see how I can best be of support to you. Same for the very disappointing news about a judge possibly making it only in March. You said that I might think that your news is 'no big deal' – that you have still more months to go. It IS a big deal, James. It is so disappointing, I can't imagine the agony of the seemingly endless waiting waiting waiting and how hard that is on you.

I wonder if you don't really let yourself be present in the painful feelings before you push them away to 'find the silver lining.' In dismissing the hard stuff always with a smile, I worry that you don't allow the feelings of what you are experiencing to be acknowledged and for your hurt to be seen. Not sure how to be present in what was going on today for you, I left with sadness and a strong desire to hug you.

I am constantly moving in my seat when you and I talk, shifting my position and posture and moving my head an inch to the left or a foot to the right in response to your movements. It's because of the weird glare on the glass between us – I can only see you clearly when the shadow of my head falls on yours – otherwise, you are invisible. It is a little like the dance I do in trying to understand the emotional affect that you often mask, but that nonetheless seeps out in other ways, despite your cheerful jokes. Sometimes I am unsure whether to shift to make clearer what you try to keep opaque.

I am learning as we get to know each other a little more, and hopefully I will get better at providing what you need in terms of support and witnessing. I will make mistakes as we go along and not say the right thing at the right moment or may misread what you need. I thank you for sharing with me what you do, and I will continue to listen and try to hear it.

I care about what you are experiencing, James, and I send you love and light, hoping some of that will penetrate the dark places.

XO Heather.

JOURNAL

I didn't know how to respond today during out visit, because the affect James presented was so different from the horror he described. He witnessed three men being beaten. In the five plus years in three different Thai prisons, he said he had never seen torture like this before. He described the sound of men's bones being hit with sticks, the sounds of hands, fingers, arms, bottoms of feet being beaten mercilessly with batons, the thwacking sounds of bones cracking. As all the other inmates watched, after the beatings, the men were forced into barrels and rolled back and forth for hours. He says he left this scene to come to our visit while the violence was continuing.

As the only foreigner who speaks Thai fluently, James was told by the guards he would have to tell the other foreigners in English that the rules had changed and tonight there would be no more food allowed in their rooms, in fact nothing brought in with them at lock-up. They are locked 16 hours per day from afternoon until the following morning in crowded rooms of up to 80 men. James, housed in the punishment building, luckily shares his room with maybe ten other men. With his typical grin, James laughed: "So here I am announcing in English: ok, foreigners, as of tonight, only our bodies and a pair of shorts are allowed into the rooms." We continued to joke and laugh about the absurdities of prison life and I shared my own crazy week where not a bloody thing was positive, in fact, very hard days at different prisons with many men. Yet James and I always manage to joke and to laugh.

He says the inmates have decided to protest tonight by refusing to go into their cells. As I listen, I am scared for them. Apparently, the inmates are planning to revolt tonight. I have no idea what that means, but I can't help but worry. All I can do is listen, knowing that I understand nothing of the context he inhabits.

Later, I call a friend and we have dinner together and I cry on his shoulder and we go to a shitty comedy club and laugh. I crave wine, wanting to numb the rest of the emotions that still linger from a horrible week at the prisons. But I am grateful for my sobriety.

Well. I did it. I slammed down the phone and said: "Boo-Fucking-Hoo!" to Ivan and walked out. Did not go back, even as I briefly considered it. I am really shocked by his total arrogance, his refusal to take any responsibility for his crime and for his self-righteous insistence that he is the victim in this whole affair. That anybody getting robbed at gunpoint in a bank should really know that they are just there to get robbed and that the armed robbers are not there to hurt anyone. That the guy who died really should not have started shooting at them, and that it was his fault for getting killed. I said incredulously to Ivan: "Surely you accept some moral responsibility: If you men had not gone into a bank with weapons, with an intention to rob and terrorize people, and to take whatever you could, that man would not have died."

"Yeah, but if that guy had woken up later or stopped for a cup of coffee, and arrived ten minutes later at the bank he would not have died, too," Ivan responded. Invoking fate or destiny, Ivan insisted he bore no responsibility for the man's death. I was stunned. A total lack of empathy or awareness of the victims' perspectives. In his griping about his plight, Ivan even used his mother's suffering over his incarceration to elicit sympathy, but not once did he take any responsibility for creating the situation which caused her suffering. He repeated bitterly: "It's not fair! This other guy in prison killed his wife and got eight years. I only robbed a bank and my mom is now suffering for over ten years..." At another point he yelled out that his grandfather died after his arrest, proof of another 'injustice' committed against Ivan. I can't listen to his self-pity today.

I was feeling mildly guilty about leaving, but now, hours later, I laugh, recalling the scene: "*BOO-FUCKING-HOO!*" I yelled at him and slammed down the phone.

WEDNESDAY

I took a mental health day yesterday to do some self-care: a little meditation, a little praying to try to temper my self-righteousness and to release my fears to the wind and the waves... A great massage, a great rest and workout at the gym in the afternoon helped.

Today I came, with positive intentions, with prayer to not be self-righteous and still managed to be angered, irritated, humbled, and shocked in moments about how much I had hurt Ivan. I know I broke trust between us, and for that I take responsibility – he says he feels like our friendship is a cup that was broken and maybe can be used for a while, but will never be as strong. He's angry, defensive, and pushes me away: "I don't need you," he says, putting up walls that took years to come down between us.

AND there was also all the self-justification and rationale of his self-pity and not taking responsibility for his actions. So I had to really ask myself: *What is more important?* And I realize that I have to release all expectations of him being other than he is. My support and love and friendship with him is not contingent on him taking moral responsibility for his crimes. I can calmly disagree, explain my position and move on. It is controlling of me to expect him to conform to an ideal of what an inmate 'should' do or feel. I have done harm here.

MONDAY, MARCH 4, 2556

Writing in the cab between Bangkwang and Klong Prem: saw Ivan today and I find him increasingly difficult – so angry, so bitter, and so much narrower in scope of what he can and will talk about. When I bring it up, he reacts angrily. I worry about his new strategy of retreating to a bare existence he calls his 'submarine world' – yet I have no right to judge his coping strategy.

GOING INSIDE

I can't believe that I might actually get to go inside the prison, having learned never to count on anything as fact until it happens, but as the day approaches (Feb. 28), it appears that all is falling into place. Ivan tells me that the volunteer art instructor has helped to make arrangements for me to consult with a group of inmates who are working on a prison mural. I am excited at the possibility of actually seeing Ivan and others without bars between us and during our visits, we are both cautious and excited, finalizing plans for the big day that we are both uncertain about and yet hoping for. I realize that I am now daring to believe that for the first time in the many years I have visited the liminal space between inside and outside, hearing countless stories of inmates' mundane, surreal, monotonous, daily existence that I may get to go inside into this world that, until now, exists for me only in my imagination. I will be allowed to bring in my laptop and a USB stick with a presentation for the inmate artists. This is so hard to believe, given that no one is ever allowed recording devices or cameras. It is surreal to make these arrangements only through visiting Ivan, with no independent information that this unprecedented event may actually occur.

Over the years, I have prepared various times with various inmates for an 'inside' visit, the usually once per year occasion when an inmate can meet with their visitor at a table with no barriers between them and share a few hours of conversation. I am envious of the people who have had these rare occasions, grilling them about the experience: they say one hug with the inmate is allowed. In previous years, I have tried to have an inside visit with Johann, Liam, James and Ivan but each time last minute rule changes or circumstances have thwarted these, and bitter disappointment has turned to resignation. To think that I might be allowed to visit for a whole day with a group of inmates seems inconceivable.

As the day approaches, I become increasingly nervous. Relying only on the information from Ivan that this 'inside' visit he and others have been working on tirelessly over months to orchestrate may come to fruition, I am required to put my trust in his word. The potential consequences of this going 'wrong' are immense. I remember fearing the first time I came to this prison nearly a decade ago that I would not be allowed to exit again. This old fear is resurfacing as I put my safety and trust into someone who, by objective definition, cannot be trusted. Fearful and mistrustful of people in general, I became a fiercely self-reliant person first by necessity, then by habit. I often joke that my best friends are behind bars and glass because it is safer for me to develop intimate friendships with people who cannot hurt me.

I have known Ivan for over five years, have expended incalculable efforts and energy for him, much more effort than for any of the other inmates. Although I love him as I do several of the men I have become close to, I am realistic about our vastly differing agendas and interests.

A few weeks before the intended big day, Ivan asks me to download some files from an ex-inmate who was repatriated to Britain last year after over 20 years inside Bangkwang – files that will help Ivan develop further his artwork techniques. Ivan assures me that he has received prior approval from the guards to receive these files from my USB, but I am skeptical. I do not want to participate in any activity that could be construed as illegal, fishy, or otherwise jeopardize my safety. He insists, so I agree to check it out cautiously, with misgivings. I make contact with the ex-inmate in Britain, JP, on the weekend and he sends me files by email. I start to peruse the many files, and suddenly, see one marked "Phillipino Ass-Fucking." Stunned, I delete all the files and email a short missive to JP, incensed that he would jeopardize my safety by sending me items that could get me incarcerated. I am furious. At both Ivan and JP. How could men who profess their undying gratitude and appreciation for the support I've given them over years throw me under the bus like this? And how could they think I am so stupid that I would walk into a maximum security prison with any items I had not vetted ahead of time?

Forty-eight hours before the big day, I visit Ivan and I cannot contain my fury. I arrive and sit down across from him, pick up the phone, and through gritted teeth I coldly ask: "How dare you jeopardize my safety, my LIFE, for porn?" After a few back and forths, Ivan states incredulously that he had no idea that JP included such material. "Bullshit," I say. Ivan looks furious – he cannot believe that I don't trust him and gets up and storms away. Our visit is over. Bemused at the melo-dramatic display, I don't believe a word of his denial. Shaken, I ride my motorbike to the next prison through chaotic traffic, but I can't focus. I have a decision to make. Wiping the grime and sweat off my face, I join my friend and colleague Henk for our weekly lunch at Klong Prem prison. We catch up and eat while we wait for our respective afternoon visiting times with inmates.

I fill Henk in on the week's events, including the files with porn, and Ivan's reaction to me confronting him. I rage at the callous self-ishness of these men and Henk is amused: "It's not like these guys are known to be saints." True, but I guess I foolishly expected more of Ivan. After all I've done for him, thousands of hours of my own time and work to support and promote his art, thousands of my own dollars to set up exhibits in Canada to promote his incredible artistic achievements and to sell his art in order to give him the funds. *After all we've been through together*, I think petulantly. I am incredulous that these men who live the hell it is to be in a Thai prison have no compunction to put me in jeopardy of the same fate.

Now, I am supposed to show up in two days at Bangkwang at 9 am, trusting Ivan's assurance that the delicate negotiation of an unprec-edented visit by a foreign woman is all 'fine,' as he presents it. The negotiations over months to make this arrangement involves officials I cannot access in a language I don't speak and involves exchanges and hidden deals I am not privy too. Nothing in Thailand, and especially in the closed world of Bangkwang is arranged unless there is a distinct benefit for each person involved. I cannot know what purpose my visit serves for all involved, nor the hidden costs. This feels very risky. I want to call it off: in part to punish Ivan, but mostly out of fear. I ask Henk what he would do: clearly, it is too risky to put my trust in an inmate who has already demonstrated that my safety is not of paramount importance. Yet another part of me is infinitely curious – the unprece-dented possibility of going inside to this forbidden, closed prison is too appealing. I tell Henk that I deleted all the files JP sent me and that after my angry email, JP 'unfriended' me on Facebook. We laugh.

Am I simply too naïve, too trusting by considering going inside, based on only information I get fed by Ivan? I am surprised by what comes next: Henk tells me I should go anyway, and to simply snub Ivan while inside: that it is a once in a lifetime opportunity I should take advantage of. After all, I am doing nothing illegal by entering the prison with official permission, thus what am I risking? *But what if I am not allowed out again*, I secretly worry. I am still unsure after our conversation, but as I continue on with my day, sharing laughs and buying food for other inmates, I decide to proceed on Friday. I don't sleep much the following two nights.

On the morning of February 28th, I arrive outside the gates. I arrive on my motorcycle, dressed as instructed in long dark jeans and a long-sleeve top and sneakers over a bandage wrapping a swollen ankle I sprained a few days earlier on broken concrete. It is five to nine and the morning sun is already unforgiving. Sweaty, uncomfortable and grimy from the 45 minute commute through diesel-belching traffic, I am jittery from nerves, excitement and from lack of sleep. A middle-aged Thai man greets me in rudimentary English. Kip, the art teacher then introduces me to a Thai journalist who will be taking pictures and recording the event for Thai media. We enter a side door. I am told I cannot bring in my laptop, but I am allowed the USB stick containing my lecture with images of prison murals from around the world. We go through the customary frisking, metal detector and removal of our shoes. An official walks us through the courtyard of the visiting area I have been in hundreds of times before. My heart is beating quickly – I can't believe I am approaching the inner gates I have seen men taken into countless times. Fear has given away to curiosity and excitement. I look around at the inscrutable faces of the guards, but adopt an outward expression that this is all normal. A buzzer sounds from the inside to admit us and the large gold-painted gates swing slowly open.

Inside, twenty or so inmates stand at attention to be counted and frisked. We stop in front of a small desk to sign in. We proceed to the right along a dusty path toward building 14, where I am to meet with the art students, passing one of many concrete buildings. Towering over us is building five, punishment building. "This is where the bad men are punished", says Kip in his halting English. Screams and shouts emerge from closed windows. I make a conscious effort not to imagine what is inside. As we walk past in silence, I am grateful I cannot understand the meaning of the shouts, yet these entreaties are unmistakable in any language. We enter an open archway along a portion of the concrete wall, and as we enter the Building 14 area, one of twelve such compounds in this 80 acre prison, I am struck by a seemingly idyllic scene. Building 14 is where dignitaries and guests are hosted and special ceremonies take place. The building houses several air-conditioned classrooms and meeting areas. Outside, brightly coloured flowering shrubs, trees and small fountains adorn the exterior. Scanning from the entrance of the building to the rest of this compound, my eyes take in a football-field sized grassy area surrounded by the concrete wall, metal fence and barbed wire. The iconic Bangkwang tower presides over a two-hundred foot segment of this twelve-foot high wall, where a dozen inmates are busy painting a mural under hot sun. Some are standing on ladders, others standing back, scrutinizing their work or talking. I see few guards in this open area and our small group gravitates towards the shade offered by a small stand of trees. Inmates turn and look at me curiously and several wander over to where we stand. Kip cautions me that I am to stay one meter away from inmates, to never touch them, and certainly not to accept anything from them. I nod in agreement. I am introduced to a few, and we smile politely, nervously and shyly at each other. I see Ivan standing in the field fifty feet away talking to another inmate in front of the mural when he catches sight of us and starts to walk over.

All is totally surreal, including Ivan walking towards me like a normal human. I stand rooted as he approaches tentatively, wariness in both of us palpable from our last encounter. For the first time in five years there are no bars and walls between us. He stops at a respectful distance several feet away. We greet each other politely, but my insides are doing cartwheels. I decide in that instant to let all that came before go and to just revel in this incredible moment that could never have happened without his indomitable spirit, concerted tireless efforts and perseverance over months of lobbying. After eleven years in this prison, Ivan has made possible a whole day of sharing his world with a friend from the outside. Resentment and anger evaporating, I tell him we will speak of the other stuff at another time, but that today is magical and I simply want to enjoy the day with him and his artist comrades. "Can you believe I'm really here?" We shake our heads, both grinning like little kids. As most of the other inmates don't speak English, they soon leave us and resume their work in progress. An inmate brings two plastic chairs and offers them to Ivan and I, who are standing awkwardly at an unnaturally large distance from each other. Ivan and I sit down and start to converse nervously. It is weird to be able to see Ivan's whole physical being, with no part of his body or face obscured by barriers. As Ivan relaxes, his speech accelerates and soon he is yammering rapid-fire, barely pausing for breath, as is his usual manner, outlining ideas for future art and life projects. My nervousness abates; listening to his grandiose plans and excitement, I am soon at ease; all feels normal between us. Every few minutes, I look around to take this all in and we grin: it is dream-like. Yet, the muffled anguished sounds from the adjacent punishment building are an audible backdrop to this scene.

The next six hours pass in a blur, even as I try to be present and absorb every second of this experience: I am inside Bangkwang prison talking openly with inmates about their art, their lives. The guards wander casually to and fro or approach to take pictures, to converse with me, Kip or an inmate. I walk slowly along the twelve-foot high concrete wall, admiring the roughly two hundred foot long mural, painted in a series of twenty-foot wide panels. I ask questions through two Thai inmates who speak some English, blown away by how freely I am allowed to wander and converse with them, and to hear their stories. I have been invited as an art consultant, due to the prisoner art exhibits I curated in Canada, and because of my long-time experience supporting Bangkwang's inmates, and I spend the next few hours taking the role seriously, admiring the work, asking questions, discussing techniques and perspectives, colours and styles, but mostly just listening and absorbing all the inmates share of their stories of this mural.

The mural is themed: *Always Remember*, and has been conceived and designed by the inmates themselves after securing special permission. Kip, their volunteer art teacher has been working with this group of very lucky 15 inmates, out of a population of over 6000, for four years. This mural spearheaded by Ivan and other inmate artists, who have been coming for the past nine months every Friday to this area. They designed the panels, which, together, tell a compelling story: moving from their criminal past to imprisonment, the panels depict the inmates' existence inside and their struggles to hold on to their humanity through meditation and art. Poignant expressions of regret, despair, struggle, dreams of freedom and hope for enlightenment adorn this massive concrete canvas.

One image I return to over and over, entitled: 'Visiting Area'. Handprints and footprints travel into and exit from two separate areas: on the left side dark colours with horizontal bars, and on the right side, brightly coloured origami peace cranes spill out. It is sobering to see from the inmates' perspective the very same stifling, awkward dirty visitor's space I have been accessing for years, this bridge between outside and inside. Over and over I return to this panel, very much moved. It conveys both the tumultuous mixed emotions, and a sense of exhilaration and freedom that I glean too from my time spent in the visitor's area. Although I cannot know what the experience is for an inmate, I identify with the flight of the paper birds, uplifted from the shared joy created in the gloom of the surroundings.

I am frantically scribbling notes as each inmate describes the meaning of the work he has put in to the mural. All speak about transformation, about the possibility of redemption and using art to somehow give back and contribute, even as people who face incarceration for the rest of their lives.

Dripping sweat in the burning sun, an inmate offers me a hat to protect my face and I frequently take breaks from standing by the wall to return under the shade of trees to rest or get a drink of water. Although I know the inmates are accustomed to this, it still seems crazy that I am offered coffee and water on a tray while the inmates simply endure the oppressive heat.

I am surprised to see one panel depicting a biblical scene: Jesus speaking to a group of people from a mount. An unusual image in this largely Buddhist country, I am reminded of the respect I see Thai people showing towards all religions. Speaking through a translator, I learn of this Thai Christian inmate's faith that gives him comfort in his incarceration. The mural also contains many images of Buddha and lotus flowers, representations of enlightenment sought by these men.

After a few hours, the inmates set a table under one of the trees and bring out dishes of food. Kip, the media woman and I are served a feast – a delicious array of Thai food purchased and prepared by the inmates themselves. I cannot guess how much it cost each inmate individually to prepare and pay for this event – I am humbled and also realize that each one is as nervous and excited by this day as I am. I am distinctly uncomfortable eating seated at a table while the inmates stand or crouch nearby – it offends every part of my sensibilities, but I know enough not to comment. I am already on high alert to not make Kip or the guards lose face by an inadvertent cultural blunder. I don't dare look at Ivan, not wanting to compound the humiliation I feel on his behalf. As we pick at the delicious meal, a guard brings a bowl of Massaman curry – Kip explains that as so many popular books critique the conditions of the prison, including the inmates' food, they want me to try the "actual food" served to inmates. I test the curry and pronounce it good, while several guards watch me, nodding, in this bizarre, orchestrated moment.

Exhausted from the afternoon heat and the meal, I find myself wanting to sleep, but it is time for my presentation. We move towards the building, relieved to get out of the sun and into an air-conditioned room where a table and chairs face a pull-down screen. A guard sits with a laptop connected to the projector. Through a translator, he asks for my media device so he can check it for content. As the students file in, I look over to the table under the tree on which I placed a pen, my notes and the USB stick hours earlier, and my heart stops. The USB stick is gone. A sinking in my gut, I say to Kip and Ivan in English that I don't know where the device is. A second part of my brain hears me saying this and knows how pathetic, irresponsible, and frankly, *criminal* my words sound. Immediately, the students get up as the word gets around that the foreign teacher has lost her media device. I look desperately at Ivan and his expression is inscrutable, as is everyone's. Several guards, Kip, and all the inmates file outside and start what can only be a futile search of the field, the building, and surrounding areas. I retrace my steps of this morning, including a search of the guest bathroom, in vain. Time slows down and my mind speeds up. I can't recall when I last had it in my possession. Calm on the outside, inside, I am shitting bricks. How could I do this? How could I walk into *this* prison with a data device and not take more precaution to safeguard it? I am terrified. Every possible scenario of my worst fears plays out in my mind – that I will be arrested and sent directly to the women's prison for having orchestrated an elaborate ploy to smuggle an illegal device into this prison. I wonder if the small device is being passed around right now somewhere in another part of the prison, and I wonder how much it is being sold for by the inmate who delights at his fortune for having scooped up such precious contraband. I wonder what horrors will face my daughter as she learns over the next days and weeks that her mother is incarcerated in Bangkok. I laugh ironically and bitterly at all the years I have spent counseling potential prison visitors on ethical boundaries and how to be cautious and respectful of Thai customs and prison policies. And now this. What a fucking idiot I am. Fifteen tense minutes pass during which I am hardly breathing, frozen in fear, wondering how I will get out of this, and if I will ever see freedom again. Finally, word comes that one of the inmates found the USB stick on the football field. He hands it over to the guard. No high fives, no smiles, no one comments, and soon everyone files back into the classroom. I start to breathe again. It takes a few minutes before my heart is beating normally.

A guard I haven't seen before enters the classroom and takes a seat in the front, closest to the screen, saying nothing and looking bored. I am under no illusion that he is there out of personal interest: no doubt he is one of the few who understands English and is there to ensure I say nothing controversial or illegal. I have tailored my presentation to ensure my safety and that of the students – we will simply be discussing examples of murals in prisons around the world and how prisoners use this artform as rehabilitation and to contribute to their communities.

I show them the first image, worried that this will be of no interest to them, but the students seem keen. The teacher in me takes over and I passionately describe mural projects from prisons in the US, Asia and Europe. One of the older inmates, a doctor with a gentle demeanour, translates between me and the others. There are murmurs at each new photo and the students start to ask questions. Although I was told to keep my presentation to five minutes, we discuss the context and images in each slide and the discussion runs a long time – the students are asking questions and we are all connected to a world-wide community of artist inmates. Ivan and I occasionally catch each other's eye and a million thoughts are transmitted in our expressions of delight and astonishment. It feels incredible to be sharing this conversation with these men about the creative process, about the possibilities of personal transformation, restitution and redemption.

After, the class presents me with two works of art: one by Ivan, a stunning piece made in ballpoint pen, and a second piece, made by a long-term Thai inmate, Nit. Nit's job inside Bangkwang for many years was to clean the execution room. I learn through haltingly translated words that he was deeply affected by the stories and spirits contained within the walls, soil, dust, and blood splatters of the execution chambers. Using the soil of the prison as the paint in tribute to the 325 people executed inside Bangkwang, he created this piece for me for this occasion and the whole art class signed the back. I am humbled and speechless.

The inmates thank me and start to leave the classroom. Too soon, it is time for them to return to be counted and locked up in their buildings until the following morning. First, they propose we take a few pictures at the wall. Standing next to Ivan in front of the mural, each holding one of the art pieces given to me, my whole body is buzzing. I can't believe I am standing next to him, and I can tell by the stunned, vacant expression on his face, that none of this has really sunk in for him, either. As we pose for the camera, I lean into him, letting my shoulder touch his. He glances at me nervously. I reach over and squeeze his leg and whisper: "See, I am real, this is real!" We both laugh nervously and then move apart. The Thai journalist has been taking pictures all day and a prison guard offers me copies of these to load onto my data stick, which I gratefully accept – another shock in this wholly surprising day.

It is time to leave and, exhausted from the emotions and events of the day, we guests file to the exit, watching the inmates stand at attention to be counted and return to their respective buildings.

In silence, we go through the gauntlet of checks and metal detectors, gather our belongings and exit to the busy street. I thank Kip for hosting me on this incredible day and he promises to be in touch. That night I am dancing on clouds, as I replay the whole day in my mind, not wanting to forget a single moment.

Three weeks later, it is arranged that I enter again, and I spend another magical day, this time accompanied by another of Ivan's friends, a Russian who carves marble and brings in samples to show the art students how to create his unique form of sculpture. While Ivan translates from Russian to English, an inmate then translates from English to Thai.

This second time around, I am far less nervous, and as soon as we enter the building 14 area, I run up and greet all the artist inmates as old friends. Although Kip gave me shit for hugging Ivan on the previous visit, he did so with a smile, and I didn't know if it was the face-saving Thai smile masking anger or whether he was gently ribbing me. Today, no one seems angry about it. After the success of three weeks ago, everyone is far less jittery this time. Ivan and I are allowed to hug hello. I pepper the inmates with questions and we speak more freely about personal matters, hearing about hopes and dreams as I spend much of the morning just hanging out with them. At one point I run out to the field to do cartwheels in part just to release the surge of energy I feel. The inmates look at me like I'm crazy. I feel so incredibly happy to be inside this prison, albeit with the knowledge that I can leave at the end of the day, but my giddiness is infectious and we are all laughing, joking, and speaking more easily, and I feel emboldened to approach and start conversations with the more withdrawn inmates who kept to themselves on my first visit. This time at lunch, Ivan and the doctor inmate are allowed to join the Russian visitor and I at the table under the canopy of the trees while the rest of the inmates eat ten feet away from us.

The inmates bring out from a storage area all canvases they have worked on over the past four years in their art class, propping them around the bushes. I spend time admiring each incredible art piece. Engaged in easy conversation with guards and this exceptionally privileged group of inmates in this garden-like setting, I could be lulled into a false impression. Knowing that I don't see the whole picture, it is still hard to reconcile this scene with my experience of bearing witness to the ravaged spirits of countless men. After years of experiencing the mind-fuck that is Bangkwang, albeit only in the visiting area, I am under no illusion that the seemingly placid exterior doesn't conceal an ineffable darkness that viciously erodes men's bodies, spirits and souls.

Mid-morning, I set out in search of a toilet I can use, as the 'guest' toilet I made use of last time is barricaded. I walk to the far end of building 14, passing windows where I see some startled faces glancing up at me. Behind the far end of the building, I discover some small garden plots with inmates working away in them, their heads, arms and shoulders covered by black cloth to guard against the sun. I am dripping with sweat, dying for some running water to cool myself off. The inmates look up at me then quickly look down again. I approach a guard lounging in the shade and ask politely in rudimentary Thai for directions to the nearest *hong nam*. After relieving myself and splashing water on my face from a dribbly dirty faucet, I walk back to rejoin our group, now lounging in the sun talking, others painting, still others resting in the shade of the trees, or putting away the dozens of canvasses they had brought out that morning to display proudly for me. Suddenly, a small man comes streaking out of the building and across the grass towards me – he runs straight at me and before I can put out my hand to warn him to keep his distance, he stops a meter away from me as if by an invisible barrier and blurts out: "What are you doing here?" It is Otun, a Chinese-Thai man I have known a few years. He is astonished at my presence. We laugh as I explain why I am inside, and he tells me that he is taking a class inside the building and thought he was hallucinating to see me walk by the window. We chat a few moments, catch up then wave goodbye, and he runs off to rejoin his class.

The only point at which I am nervous comes when the brand new director of Bangkwang prison enters the area flanked by a small group of guards. I am standing by the mural in progress and I immediately adopt what I hope is a scholarly and professional posture and demeanour meant to convey the air of a foreigner who needs and deserves to be consulting inmates in a notorious Thai prison about how to paint their mural (!).

When the director leaves, we spend a relaxed few hours posing for pictures: guards, inmates and me, and when I leave the prison, I am again astonished to get copies of all of these pictures – here, from inside a prison that no one is allowed to photograph the outside of. They tell me I have permission to use the photos however I want, as long as I blur the faces of any inmate besides Ivan!

That evening I am buzzing, filled with the sights and sounds of those days inside, a most incredible experience. I am excited, envisioning those two days as only the beginning of a bigger initiative. I see worlds of possibilities opening up, and hope I can be a part of bringing more classes and opportunities to these isolated people, hungry for learning and for an avenue to express themselves.

I don't know how to write about these days, worried that the small scene I portray conveys a falsely bright impression of the much larger unfathomable darkness. Perhaps that was the purpose I was serving.

YOUR JOB IS NOT TO JUDGE

Today I draw a heart in coloured pencils and copy out the following words inside it, pinning it to the wall beside my desk.

> Your job is not to judge. Your job is not to figure out if someone deserves something. Your job is to lift the fallen, to restore the broken, and to heal the hurting.
>
> ~ UNKNOWN

Yesterday Ivan proudly described saving a rat's life. Earlier that week, he encountered the rat as he was released from his cell in the morning. Hurrying to where the communal 'showers' are before they get crowded, he heard a noise in a bucket and discovered the struggling creature. The swimming rat apparently entered the half-full bucket of water sometime during the night and was unable to get out. She was almost depleted, clearly straining, most likely swimming for hours. Scanning my face for a reaction to his story, Ivan hesitantly explained how he reached in and lifted her out and placed her on the ground. The rat collapsed and lay still. He kicked her a few times to get her going. Eventually, she crawled away. Clearly identifying with the determined creature, he added that the rat was worthy of saving because rats are smart, industrious, strong, resourceful and they get a bad rap. Chest puffed and face beaming, Ivan repeated proudly that he saved a rat's life. I pictured a filthy, hot corner of the prison compound, a space barren of nurturance, love or care, and this compassionate moment of grace. My thoughts turned to a few days earlier. I was at my friend and *de facto* colleague's Henk's house for a bbq.

A very kind advocate of inmates' families, Henk devotes considerable personal resources, time, effort, and energy to supporting female inmates from several African countries. He advocates and lobbies on their behalf and also supports some of the men at Bangkwang. We met a few years ago at the prisons and our friendship has developed from our shared, yet unique experiences of navigating an insane world impossible to describe to outsiders. So we bond over the complexities, the human tragedies, absurdities, injustices, harsh realities and incredibly mundane tasks of supporting these inmates. We meet at the Khlong Prem prison restaurant every Wednesday, "The Bar," Henk calls it. Each week, he takes a large Singha beer and orders a meal that includes "nothing that has a mother," while I order iced coffee and wing bean salad. We debrief in a ritual of catching each other up on our respective weeks: gossiping about the inmates, commiserating at the various troubles and triumphs at court; with Embassies, ever-shifting and worsening prison regulations, temperamental prison guards, as well as laughing at the cast of crazy characters who are the prison visitors. The latter round out the oddball scene at the prisons each day: missionaries shrieking a message of forgiveness across bars and glass, demanding inmates accept Jesus today!; a parade of white-robed nuns and saffron-clad monks receiving blessings and wise counsel from the incarcerated paedophile monk; various kindly, dedicated British Volunteer Ladies; weary family members; an occasional backpacker; and, a few deluded lunatics with marriage on their minds. Although neither of us places ourselves in any of the above categories, neither are we unaware of the uniquely dedicated type it takes to undertake this work, unpaid, day in and out, over years. Even as our personalities and politics are disparate, me 'too emotional' according to Henk, and him oddly dispassionate in my view, each of us offers a different type of invaluable support to inmates. Henk has my full respect and admiration and affection. Our weekly lunches save my ass when the insanity of the whole scene is overwhelming, and our friendship has evolved to include occasional bbqs at his home south of Bangkok.

On this day in July, he is describing some of the flora and fauna he has encountered in his lovely garden. Just as the inmates delight in the blind cats, rat families, lizards, toads, butterflies and cockroaches that often live along side them in their small world, Henk has been documenting the creatures he finds in his back yard. One morning recently, he discovered a two-foot long Monitor Lizard in his pool – also known as a Komodo dragon in Indonesia, the Thai variety is non-poisonous, but nonetheless bites. I ask how he removed it from the pool. Henk shakes his head, amused: "I drowned it." He matter-of-factly describes holding the struggling creature's head under water until it expired its breath and life, then calling the Thai building security personnel to help him lift the animal out. He learned from the scared man who refused to help him remove the dead animal from the pool that Monitor Lizards are a protected species in Thailand. He no longer bothers the security guards to dispose of the other Monitor Lizards he kills.

I think back a few months to my time inside the great walls of the prison in March: Sitting in the shade of a tree where inmates have set out our feast, Vladimir and I are being served lunch as honoured guests while fourteen inmates eat their own food standing or squatting near us. I have been invited inside the prison as a guest to lecture on prison art for the few inmates who have been allowed the opportunity to create a large mural for an upcoming visit by the Princess. On this day, long-term inmates Ivan and Dr. Piyawat are allowed to join Vladimir and I at our table. Sitting in the shade of a tree in 38 C heat, I look around in wonder that I am sitting inside this infamous prison with a group of inmates as we share food and talk of art under the beating hot sun. I have no idea how this has all been arranged, but I hear Dr. Piyawat had a major hand in facilitating this day. I know not to enquire about what that means in terms of 'connections' – just accept that's how things operate in Thailand. I ask Dr. Piyawat casually if he has any children. A pause, a gentle smile.

"Yes." He answers.

"I have a twenty year-old daughter," I say, making conversation, trying to find common ground to share with this older man.

Later, as I review the events of the entire surreal day in my mind, I kick myself as I recall that Dr. Piyawat killed his wife and dismembered her. I find myself irritated: Do his children even speak to him? Was I not supposed to ask about his family because he murdered his wife? What's the etiquette on that? No idea. Why am I supposed to feel uncomfortable – you are the guy who apparently flushed your wife down the sewer system of the university where you both worked and other parts of her in a hotel toilet. Her remains were only identified months later by forensic analysis of DNA, according to an article in the *Bangkok Post*.

Yet here, in the shade of this tree under merciless midday sun beating down on one of the hottest days of 2014, inside Building 14 compound of Bangkwang prison, we sit together on plastic chairs at a picnic table, food spread out before us and politely pick at a meal together, sharing rice and chicken and he offers me an extra coconut custard dessert that he organized to have specially made for my visit, insisting that I eat a second one.

What does it mean to forgive someone but still want for them to 'pay' for their crime? What does it mean for them to 'pay' with a decade of their life but then walk freely out of the prison behind me as I sit talking to Ivan? Here, now, in August, 2014, Dr. Piyawat is freed since the takeover by the new military junta, enjoying numerous reductions to his original sentence, and he walks out of the prison, past Ivan who remains behind. The *Bangkok Post* runs a few articles over the next few days about the wife-chopping gynaecologist set free after a decade, then the brouhaha disappears into more recent gossip of what the former Prime Minister was seen eating at the local shopping mall.

Ivan is bitter. This is the second wife-murdering cellmate he has seen set free in the past few years, as well as dozens of other foreigner men repatriated to their home countries, while his Embassy does nothing. He confesses his bitterness and rage-filled revenge fantasies to me. Twelve years he has sat, unsupported, watching so many others set free due to their political connections or the efforts of their governments, all while his own government refuses to write a simple letter of support that would release him, despite countless letters and years of tireless lobbying. I hear him and understand and encourage him to not let this rage and bitterness rob him of the rest of his life...that bitterness and revenge only gives more power to those who hurt him.

It is so much easier to see in the guys what lessons I want to carry for myself. How some men's thoughts and moods are full of bitterness and anger at their situation, at people and at the world. Other men with less or more harm done to them use their thoughts and actions and words in different ways... some choosing joy. This lesson, so easy for me to forget in my own life, I re-learn from these inmates. Because we are all doing time... and we all suffer and feel wronged by others, either real or imagined, as well as do wrong to others. We all must learn how to deal with that. Do we sit in our victimhood or guilt and how do free ourselves from it? How free am I? I still find many ways in which old patterns can trap me in fear. When I judge others rather than simply show up to offer my best, then I am trapped in fear too. These men help to remind that only I can free myself from the trap of bitterness or fear or regret.

Today, I resent Ivan and his 'victim' bitching. Five years of whining to me about how he is the victim of an unjust system, how everyone and everything have wronged him. Yes, there is deep injustice here. And, most other inmates, no matter their situation use our visits as an opportunity to create something different – some laughter, some joy, a connection, share a dream, sing a song, be silent in sorrow or contemplation. Ivan uses most of our visits to complain non-stop about how he has been wronged, who is at fault, how wrong everyone else is. It is challenging to want to engage with him when he has been unable to take any one else's perspective, including the dozens of people he held hostage in an armed bank robbery and murder he and his compatriots committed.

I remember a short documentary about American jails. An inmate with a life sentence who killed three people in one family is interviewed: he says that because he knows God forgives him, he lives with a clear conscience. Watching, I am angry that he gets to use religion to let himself off scott-free – no remorse, no torment, because 'God' has forgiven him. A fucking mythological construct conveniently used to let himself off the hook? WOW... Makes my blood boil.

Where does my anger really come from, I wonder? Isn't self-forgiveness an equivalent mental construct we employ to bring about peace for ourselves, to release us from a life of the torment of remorse, pain, suffering, also self-imposed by our lovely brains? Is that inmate not accountable to society, to the people in the world who have been hurt by his actions? Indeed he is: he is serving life in prison. He is responsible for his actions, and is paying socially-agreed upon penalties of them. Yet the residual mental torment, or lack thereof, in his case, is what I seemingly judge people on, even as I think I don't judge inmates. I apparently have an internal criterion of how much torment or remorse I think someone should show for their actions: that is, someone should have just enough torment to satisfy others, but not so much that they must remain in this state for too long. No, life-long torment is too much for my sensitivities to will upon someone, because even some degree of suffering on anyone's part impels me to come along and try to alleviate that pain.

I can't reconcile my hypocrisy: I encounter normal, understandable strategies of inmates surviving a violent dog-eat-dog system and yet I am nonetheless resentful when an inmate is manipulative and deceitful with me. I am resentful some days of the inmates' selfishness, conceit, narcissism and when they question my support. Some days I just want to walk away and tell them to go *Fuck Themselves*. Other days, I try to bring a spirit of curiosity to these situations, trying to unravel what is triggered in me and what I can do to bring a more gentle and loving reaction to an already very difficult space.

Today, Ivan tells me that I am not really helping him by visiting, that I should be doing something else. He tells me that he hopes he can 'count on me' to give him cash when he is released to help him get a start in life. I tell him that I'm not a cash machine for current or former inmates. He scoffs and tells me that there are many people who 'shake their head' coming back from a visit with me and don't feel I am being helpful. It is hard not to be stung by his obvious and childishly transparent attempt to wound me, to punish me for not giving him what he wants and for my recent revelation that I have a boyfriend. Anger, rejection and hurt have been at the forefront the past few visits, and now it is coming out in petty grousing. I smile gently to mask my growing anger. I will not rise to the bait, I tell myself, as he tries to tell me how I should be doing my job differently and living my life differently.

Ivan berates me again today for not having a 'business plan' for my non-profit society and he warns me to be cautious in my financial dealings. I want to laugh at him, but I nod and listen. Ivan insists that he will fix and sort out my life when he gets out, as well as a few other people's lives, who are obviously running things poorly, in his estimation. Former cell-mates describe him as a bully, a pain in the ass, as he is always berating them for their lack of industriousness and physical discipline. I have experienced him as many things, not least: determined, unrelenting, focused, self-disciplined, creative, superstitious, curious, exceptionally skilled artistically, self-absorbed, manipulative, and demanding. He requests Henk and I write and send countless letters to the Russian President, to the Ukrainian President, various Embassies, and the King of Thailand. Initially, these letters were reasonable pleas for Ivan to be repatriated to his home country. In recent years, though, the letters are more likely to be self-absorbed, hard to read or to take seriously, something the Ukrainian Consul pointed out to me not so delicately when I visited him last year to plead for Ivan's case. He produced the most recent letter from Ivan, translating it for me, and I had to agree with him. Although Ivan's persistence and determination in advocating for his freedom are commendable, his diplomacy and tact leave something to be desired. As the Consul put it, Ivan is a 'common criminal' in his Embassy's eyes, and the delusions of grandeur, sense of entitlement and narcissism evident in his correspondence win him few allies.

Over delicately grilled tofu and veggie sausages, Henk and I shake our heads over the latest missive Ivan has us post to the Ukrainian president, detailing Ivan's plan to solve the current Russian/Ukrainian conflict and to remedy the Ukraine's reliance on Russia for natural gas, while fixing the Ukrainian economy. Ivan has the solution for every problem in everyone's life, if only they would realize that he knows better and if only people would listen to him and act on his advice. Often on the receiving end of his patronizing life and business advice, I bite my tongue, sometimes not able to hide my irritation. Today, I smile and tune out as he rattles on at me about my failings and his remedy for them, and I imagine myself interrupting him to say: "And how's your life working out for you, Ivan?"

I wonder at the limits of my patience with this wounded population in an incredibly inhumane environment. And at what point I am still allowed to hold expectations of a certain degree of respect and reasonableness in their behaviour towards me. Like everything, my position changes on this day by day, as I have less or more ability to hold the encounter in a place of compassion and kindness. If I show annoyance at him, I beat myself up for a long time after. You may rob people, deal drugs, be a thug, kill someone, yet, believing in your inherent dignity as a human, I will offer emotional and humanitarian support, but if you are a bit of a jerk to me, then I want to withdraw that support?

Why do I expect the men I have been visiting for years to behave in certain ways – respectful or somewhat kind or remorseful? They are not in prison for being saints nor emotionally mature nor kind. I am human and allowed to draw the line at how I am personally treated, but how is this consistent with my principles that all people deserve to be treated with dignity, regardless of their actions?

Who gets to forgive whom? And for what?

The paradox of my vegan compassionate colleague drowning an endangered animal in his backyard pool with the manipulative criminal rescuing a common rat from a bucket in the prison invite simplistic analogies as to how we decide which acts and events we are to be judged for, or feel justified in condemning others for. For me, questions, uncertainties, paradoxical experiences with any given person in any given moment, are all I can draw attention to: The care and attention the kindly doctor showed me and other inmates in March in helping to facilitate an apparently selfless opportunity to give a group of long-term inmates a chance to have a day sharing their art project with a foreign visitor. No idea what his motivations were, I know only that Dr. Piyawat helped to facilitate with great difficulty an absolutely magical day in which I was granted access inside the prison and on that day we spent hours sharing about creativity, about personal transformation and art. We also shared food, and he translated my lecture on prison art for the other inmates. His mellow and serene countenance impressed me and stayed with me long after.

And, yes, he murdered his wife. He created incalculable suffering to his children and to many others in this heinous act. I have no idea how to hold that piece in my brain as well. It is not for me to forgive, yet also not for me to accept and ignore, either.

Maybe I just need to keep bringing myself back to each present moment, and living each with less attachment to the others.

Can I offer kindness and acceptance here, right now, rather than judgment? This simple question is the one I return to as truth for me. That is, there are moments of grace everywhere among all other moments and I can only live each moment one at a time and hope to recognize this grace and offer love.

In these simple human moments: in sharing food, a smile, in a hand lifting a struggling creature out of danger, there is a person in front of me who is living the consequences of his past actions. In the present, in the here and now, do I have the courage to be loving in my words and actions and authentic in how I expect to be treated in return?

EPILOGUE

JOURNAL: FIRST DAYS BACK IN BANGKOK

Six am. traffic noises, street vendors shouting, cats yowling, and creeping heat in my tiny stuffy room wake me just a few hours after I collapsed onto the bed, after arriving from the airport. So excited to be back in Bangkok, I take a cold shower, get a coffee and jump on the riverboat to Bangkwang prison.

Motorcycle taxi alongside Nonthaburi Road, running along the concrete perimeter wall of the prison, the iconic tower staring out over the wall. The guards greet me warmly, big smiles and waves, and some *wais*: this is fantastic to get this greeting on the one hand, and surreal in such a place to have all the uniformed people treating me like an old friend.

Ivan is jumping up and down waving frantically across dirty bars and glass, and the visit is rushed; we spill words on top of each other, half-finished sentences and broken fragments of thoughts, big smiles. Next week, we'll slow down to breathe and take our time, we promise. Daniel also jumps up and down and waves at me, and we briefly trade phones so his visitor can talk to Ivan, while I catch up with Daniel. He implores me to please write another letter to the president of his country to ask for his release. I say I will, even though I'm convinced all the letters go straight to the dustbin.

On my way out, I see Zaw, who has a visitor: I learn that since February, Zaw has been in the prison 'hospital' – not a medical treatment facility as would normally be conjured by the word, the 'hospital,' is a dreaded place where terminally ill inmates go to die. Zaw is battling HIV and TB. We are both emotional seeing each other – he is one of the first people I met and this will be the ninth year I visit him. His spirits are higher than in recent years: he says his goal is to die in his home country.

At another prison in the afternoon, after more hours spent waiting in the heat, I get to see Jason and he is distressed by the water rationing, and increasingly overcrowded conditions. There are now 77 men in his cell. I am fighting my jet-lagged brain as I try to absorb the ever-shifting situations of each of the men. His cell-mate Glen, an older quiet Canadian has spent much of his adult life behind bars in Canada and now in Thailand, and is getting very skinny. I buy them a bunch of fruit, meat and snacks at the prison shop before I leave.

Each one has a carefully elaborated plan that he wants me to participate in to help ease his time, to secure his freedom – many of their requests are futile, and I wonder each year how much of my time and energy I can devote to fulfilling requests that are pointless, in my mind. But it is so hard to refuse a request that re-kindles a spark of hope, something to latch on to for each inmate that maybe, perhaps, this time, something will change for the better. My purse is full of my scribbled jottings of inmates asking to just send this or please contact that person on their behalf...already overwhelmed by the tasks ahead, I make a mental note to follow up on all these next week, before new visits add more scribbled notes.

Walking back through my neighbourhood, looking around for a place to rent, Tip, the Thai massage parlour owner I've known for years runs out of her shop to greet me, but stops short and scrutinizes my body, stating that I should be able to soon lose the fat I've gained in Canada. Her sister, Anna, who runs the beauty parlour a few shops down also stares at my belly, shaking her head, disapprovingly. I am fat, but not too bad, I am told. I laugh at their words, but it is a sobering reminder of hyper youth and beauty obsession here, girls primped and primed to be only sexual objects for men: everywhere, botoxed and surgically-constructed children walk three steps behind the men who have purchased them for a day, a month, a year, until their novelty or utility wear out.

I go to an evening twelve-step meeting to re-connect with friends I haven't seen in seven months, but see few familiar faces. I learn that a friend overdosed last week, another reminder of the severity of this disease. A chair scrapes behind me, and I turn to see a wonderful friend I met last year. We embrace. His eyes are moist and red. He exclaims: "You've been sober this whole time, I can hear it in your voice. You've softened and changed so much. And now you're radiating."

Stopping at a sidewalk stall on Sukhumvit, hundreds of tourists heading in all directions, mostly out for a night of drinking or buying sex, it would seem, I am looking at pirated dvds for sale to pick up a movie to watch. A fat drop of warm rain lands on my nose. A chorus of "*fontok*

UNFORGOTTEN

fontok" ripples through the voices of the street vendors up and down the street. All whip into action, pulling large sheets of clear plastic out from under their stalls and hastily rig them up. Everyone is laughing as they race against time to cover their merchandise before the downpour hits. As the warm rain pours onto the street, bouncing high off the ground, I make my way across packed streets through honking vehicles, to the cover of a taxi. We wind our way through crowds of wet protestors chanting anti-government slogans to my guesthouse and I collapse on my bed.

Today, I am supposed to take a Burmese friend to the public hospital to treat a nasty abscess on his face. Win Oo lost his job a month ago, as his boss doesn't want customers seeing Win Oo's infected and swollen face. He is relying on his small community of migrant worker friends to survive, to eat, squeezing the angry-looking golf-ball-sized mass that has swollen his left eye shut. At a clinic I dragged him to yesterday, the doctor confirmed that this is very serious and must be treated in hospital. I cancel my plans to head to a prison south of Bangkok this morning where one of my guys was recently transferred, and arrange to meet Win Oo first thing to go to the public hospital, where treatment will be relatively cheaper. I am aware of my privilege of being able to buy medical treatment for him that he cannot afford, at just a cost of a few dollars.

Thousands of anti-government demonstrators and truckloads of military and police are swarming into Democracy Monument, a few blocks from my room, protesting against the government's proposed plan to grant a general amnesty.

Exhilarating moments: motorcycle taxis in the rain, winding through gridlocked Bangkok traffic, coughing up clouds of black diesel from the back of buses; re-connecting with friends who greet me with love; fresh fruit and warm skies.

I get up early, regretfully cancelling skype plans with my daughter, annoyed the internet in my room hasn't worked properly in 24 hours. The final push of my fundraising campaign that I recorded on my mini-cam at 1 am cannot be uploaded, so I simply accept that my paltry efforts at internet fundraising are over. As the hours roll by this morning with no word from my Burmese friend, my impatience grows into anger. I'm pissed that I've cancelled my plans today to reconnect with one of the inmates who has been desperately sending letters to Canada, begging me to not forget him, now that he has been moved to a prison outside of

Bangkok. He has no way of knowing whether his postcard detailing his new circumstance, sent eight months ago to an obsolete address in Canada, has even reached me. If I hadn't received it by chance months after it arrived, I would no longer have any idea where to find him. I wrote him back, saying I was coming this week to find him. I have no way to know if he received my letter. As inmates exist in an information vacuum, I cannot send word that I can't come today because I felt getting Win Oo's septic face to the hospital was more urgent. Despite trying to be 'culturally-sensitive," and knowing that what I see as a concrete plan of action at a certain time rolls completely differently in this part of the world, I still get angry when my time is wasted, as if my notion of how the day should go is the most important one. It's a hard habit to break, though, and right now, I'm having an angry conversation with Win Oo in my mind, justifying to myself that my desire to 'help' him by throwing my few dollars at his urgent medical problems should take precedence over whatever it is that he is doing, like sleeping and taking his sweet time. I know he'll simply show up whenever that suits him. I have learned that from all my Burmese friends. I must accept this, but I am seething and trying not to make this about ME and MY precious time...

Today I am questioning myself – feeling defeated and discouraged – about most things. In the topsy turvy adjustment to this completely different universe I have re-entered, I find it hard to convey the intense reality I see to those back in Canada. I see myself withdrawing already from people I wish I could share my days with, unable to bridge the two disparate worlds and exhausted from the effort. Today I unfairly resent friends in Canada for not understanding what goes on here, and for saying: "Oh, I haven't seen anything about that on the news." As if the Canadian news dominated by incessant coverage of a crack-smoking mayor or the latest fear-mongering mis-interpretation of scientific studies has ever interested itself in covering the global reality of people without access to basic human rights like clean water, medical attention and housing. So many are struggling everywhere, every day. "These people are not a 'cause' – they are human: they are you, me, us – why aren't we doing things differently? Why are we complacent?" I want to scream. But that is so unbelievably unfair, I know this. Tired and drained after just two days here, I remind myself to pace myself to meet the unrelenting demands and to take it slowly.

I am 'supposed' to be writing a cheery letter to people who have supported my fundraising campaign, to tell them how great the inmates appreciate their contributions – but today, I have no interest. Frankly, I am just angry at the pointless suffering I see, the despair and violence lived by so many in this one tiny corner of one prison in the world...the total waste of human lives, the devastating effects of violence, and the degradation that never fails to stun me.

In my room, I rant alone at the billions spent yearly on waging wars against the poor, against addicts, against the most marginalized of people. When do we stop funding Wars on Drugs that serve only to create so much more addiction, more marginalization and suffering? Where is the funding for humanity, healing and treatment? When will the world devote significant resources, energy, hearts and work towards justice for all?

I try yoga and to meditate, but I am too agitated. Too annoyed that nothing is working the way I want it to today. I must accept that I can do very little to change anything. I remind myself to carve out spaces of gratitude today. Every choice I make that moves me towards kindness and away from fear or judgment changes things. These words ring hollow in my head, but that's the best I can come up with right now. I will trudge my way to a café and try to get a working speck of internet, while I wait for Win Oo to show up.

A friend and I are meeting today after my six-month absence. I want to buy a plant and something to sit on for my room, so she feels welcome – and as the morning goes by and I give up on all the things I've been pressuring myself to do today before we meet – go to the gym, make my bare-bones room more hospitable, I feel my anxiety mounting, as I feel a 'real' friend would try to make her experience as warm and welcoming as possible. She texts me that she's having a hard time getting out of bed and facing the world. I decide to let myself off the hook, a little. Sure, my head has been running with the old stories of rejection, and fears that old friends will have moved on when I re-connect with them, as sometimes happens, painful as that is. And I've been so excited to see her again, I am afraid she won't love me anymore or our friendship won't be the same.

What would I say if I saw her pressuring herself to get things 'just right' before we meet? I'd tell her I love her no matter how empty or hollow her space is, and to let go of her secret fears that she is not good enough, with nothing to offer. That just being together is all that matters. So I slow down, make a cup of tea, give myself permission to be a little out of shape, my room a little cold and empty, and maybe even smoke cigarettes all day today, to not be perfect. To just BE with her, together, sharing friendship, seeing each other warts and all. I remind myself to celebrate feeling this vulnerable: it is a gift of living.

How Free Do You Want to Be?

Staring at these words in my journal, I wonder why I can't start writing – How free do I want to be? Do I feel I deserve to be free? The cage I am often trapped in, of fear, is a shape-shifter and although I have tackled it in various ways over my life, it often takes a long time for me to realize that in some of my choices, I have traded one cage of fear for another.

I was contacted yesterday by my alcoholic ex-partner who made repeated credible death threats against me and who was in Bangkok, asking to meet with me. It jarred me – fear to a real threat as well as stirring up lots of feelings about this sick individual: compassion, grief, painful memories, pain, rage, heartbreak, and disgust.

I used to rage against the world when I was fearful. Wanting to run directly towards a perceived threat, in order to better 'manage' or 'control' it, today I instead choose not to use this well-worn response to fear. Cultivating and nurturing peace, and listening for quiet stillness is a response too. Frequently agitated at kindness directed towards me, and angry at my own perceived 'weakness' or vulnerability, I had to remind myself that responding to a threat to my safety from a peaceful place is not the same as being passive, or a victim. Long ago, I saw myself as a victim, then a survivor, and I have spent many years now a warrior. I am unlearning this fighting response to life's challenges – I don't want to fight anything or anyone, including myself anymore. Today, I pause and listen for the heart-centred choices. I want to become a gardener. I am responsible for planting and nurturing seeds of peace in me and for listening to the softer places grow.

First weeks back at Bangkok prisons. Lots of emotions of both sides of the bars, turbulence, and getting adjusted again, as much as I can ever get fully adjusted to this craziness. I have seen over a dozen inmates in the two short weeks here, from: Iran, Burma, US, Canada, Russia, Ukraine, Kazakhstan, China, Britain, and Sweden. I am as elated as they are.

Today, I celebrate with Ivan his joy at calculating that he may be on the final stretch of his prison sentence – possibly only three or four more years to go. Liam looks terrible, moves slowly, speaks little, all life drained from his face. On our second visit in as many weeks, he perks up a little, and I am secretly thrilled that I make him cry – it is beautiful to see tears of laughter streaming down his face.

I almost pissed my pants at lunch with Henk on our first day back to our Wednesday weekly routine of gossiping about the insanity of the prison world. He's been lobbying the [--] Embassy to have a modicum of consideration for a foreign woman he's been visiting at the women's prison for years. She was very ill, and her Embassy neglected her and let her suffer, unattended, until she recently died a horrible, painful, lonely death in there. No one was allowed access to her, no access to family or a single person from her Embassy to even comfort her in a shitty filthy prison with no medical attention. Henk was disgusted and fought them every step of the way to get to visit her as she lay suffering for months. The officials simply ignored repeated pleas for consideration.

Now that this woman is dead, the Ambassador agrees to meet Henk and postures all manner of care and concern. No one knows what has happened to the woman's body – it got lost in the black void that is the prison system here, and the woman's family is too poor to pay for her body to be flown back to them in her home country. After months of no consideration for the loneliness and pain suffered by this dying woman, and repeatedly denying Henk's attempts to be able to comfort the woman, her country's Ambassador now says to Henk: "If you can locate the body and get her cremated, we'll use our official diplomatic envelope to mail the ashes back to the family free of charge!" *

I absorb this information for a few seconds, then burst out laughing. Tears streaming, Henk and I picture a generic official Embassy condolence letter in a clear plastic baggie, covered in grey ashes and soot arriving from across the globe to her family, free of charge, courtesy of the generous Ambassador. Couldn't be bothered to let others provide comfort nor to alleviate her suffering while she was alive, but you will fly her ashes in a baggie home for free. Wow...thanks for the consideration. Fuck, people are callous.

---

* I omit the woman's country of origin to respect her family's privacy, and not to spare the callous Embassy officials the shame they should feel for their reckless indifference.

On the weekend, I got a phone call from London, England from a woman who found me from my website. She is desperate to locate her brother from Burma whom she heard was executed last week in Bangkwang. I am highly doubtful, as there have been no official executions here in a few years, but regardless, I will try to locate her brother for her to at least reassure her that he is alive, if not well. Locating an inmate is not an easy task in the black void that are the prisons here, especially for the people from the poorest countries. She has emailed me twice this week and I agree to look into the situation, but now she is calling me on my cell, highly agitated. Although it's understandable, given her situation, I have to set boundaries, as I am regularly inundated with agitated family members searching for loved ones. I tell her I will do my best and will email her as soon as I have any news.

One of my American guys has been in a funk, but seeing his spirits and energy rise, the smile on his face and light in his eyes today feels really good. The heartfelt "Thank Yous" and the visible changes in the inmates' demeanour really affect me, charging my reserves for the many days when this feels only draining and thankless.

On days that I don't feel I can show up in a place that has so much suffering and so little hope, these smiles makes the biggest difference. The inmates tell me countless stories of hope and joy spreading outward from our visits, in ripple effects. That keeps me going back.

Tomorrow, I will get on a stinky, sweaty bus and head south of Bangkok to another town and another prison, where I hope to locate of my guys who was transferred there last year.

I make no progress on locating the Burmese man whose sister is frantic – but I did get some disturbing information from another inmate that a few guys were taken from their cells and executed last week, unofficially, low-key, to avoid alerting the Thai media in the midst of the political unrest here. A little shocked, I am hoping this information is baseless prison rumour.

Over years, I have learned that I must focus not on what I cannot do, whom I cannot reach, but on all the small victories: that reaching one person with kindness, a smile, and some food isn't futile.

A new day: I receive an email from a friend back in Canada who comments that the female inmate's death I wrote to him about is horrendous. I worry a little that he thinks I am indifferent to her suffering because I could laugh over lunch about her Embassy's response.

The conditions of this woman's death, the months leading up to it are detestable. I will encounter dozens more incomprehensibly horrible stories like this this week. From my narrow window into their lives, I will bear witness to horrors that are mundane, routine and unremarkable in these prisons, as well as the lived cumulative effects. I carry these people with me, and sometimes I buckle at a soul-less system that warehouses countless people under the guise of justice, and carelessly crushes them, a juggernaut of reckless indifference. Regular people doing regular jobs are complicit in these heinous acts, not necessarily due to any particularly malicious intent on their part. Simple, mundane disregard for humanity – 'the banality of evil.' I couldn't continue this work, these efforts of the past decade, if I couldn't find away to laugh at this stuff to release the chokehold that these human tragedies have on my heart.

"Make no mistake that my heart is not breaking," I email back my friend. Often, after a day at the prisons, I want to vomit, scream, cry, or punch walls. I used to abuse alcohol to numb this pain. Although I don't self-destruct in response anymore, I still need to release. For me, among other things, writing and sharing these stories is critical. Laughing in the face of anguish, pain, fear, horror and injustice has been my saving grace, loosening the stranglehold of what used to destroy me.

Each of the men I visited inspired me in different ways and taught me about choosing our reality. James was determined to be the happiest prisoner ever. One day, he told me that he had just seen guards beating three inmates who were caught with cell-phones. Describing the vivid sounds of the beating, he had a smile on his face. I learned during other interactions with him that his big grin indicated neither sadism, lunacy nor a hardening to others' pain. Instead, he lived his mantra, 'attitude is everything,' by smiling at me as he shared his horrible story. He chose positivity wherever he could, no matter the circumstance. This was very different from the North American insipid and shallow pre-occupation with 'being happy.' I saw in his smile that day a rallying cry for his own life, for freedom, for the survival of his spirit and soul.

He supported and inspired me in many ways. Through our interactions, somehow this untrusting, wary and guarded woman whose only close relationships were across metal bars and glass trusted enough in his friendship and love to allow him to guide me gently towards facing the truth about my drinking, and towards recovery from alcoholism, for which I will always be grateful. The depth of our connection and mutual support was immeasurable; through it he helped breathe life back into a woman who was dying on the inside. James also reminded me every day when I would show up at the prison overwhelmed by the weight of despair, inhumanity and broken lives I saw that happiness is a choice, no matter what darkness surrounds me. Sourcing laughter in darkness does not disrespect the dignity of those who have suffered or continue to suffer; instead, it holds space that affirms the preciousness of life.

When I do not succeed at choosing joy or laughter, I will rant and scream. Succumb to despair. Maybe I will curl up in a ball and weep, or say hurtful words to those I love because I am really scared and angry at the world – angry at its perceived lack of caring. This rage and grief at injustice is real and valid and needs to find expression. But I find myself less and less willing to waste a precious minute more of my life focusing on what doesn't work. I try to source laughter and to focus instead on what does work – reaching out to all those in pain with care, re-connecting us to each other. This includes gratitude for the community of people, activists, many of them strangers to me, who have contacted me to offer words of support and love that sustain me, the inmates and each other in our hopeful embrace. I hope that in sharing small parts my journey, I inspire others to use our words and actions towards love, justice, hope, humanity and connectedness. We are all responsible to create the world we want.

Not only is another world possible, she is on her way. On a quiet day, I can hear her breathing.

~ ARUNDHATI ROY

Untitled sculpture I constructed in 2010 using scavenged scrap material and exhibited at *Through The Glass*, an art exhibit of Bangkwang prisoners' art I curated on Salt Spring Island. The sale of this piece covered the costs for me to get to Bangkok to support inmates that year.

In order to protect inmate privacy, I do not include close-up pictures of any inmates, except for 'Ivan,' who specifically requested that he be shown. More photos of Thai prisons, the Bangkwang mural, my fishing trip, and more can be found at: luna-roseprisonersupport.org and on Facebook under *Luna-Rose Prisoner Support*.

Pencil drawing Ivan dedicated to me, calling it: *Living the Spaces Between Wall and Freedom.*

Ivan created this sketch for me, using found copper bits etched onto paper, the hands indicating the 11 years and 5 months he had served at the time.

Posing with inmates and guards inside Building 14 area, in front of the *Always Remember* mural in February, 2014. I'm in the middle of the back row, 'Ivan' is in the back row, far left. Below, the lucky select small group of inmates working on the prison mural.

The Visiting Area, as depicted by the inmates on the Bangkwang prison mural.

Ivan and I in front of the Bangkwang prison mural, holding the two pieces of art they presented to me. The first time we have seen each other without bars and glass in-between, I am reaching over to touch Ivan's leg and whispering: "See, I am real!"

Giving a presentation to inmates in a classroom in Bangkwang prison, building 14, in February, 2014. Several guards and a dozen other inmates are present, not visible in picture.

Posing with frozen Tuna.

On deck in Victoria, BC, during a stop to unload fish and change crew, August, 2012. Next page: Fishing, open ocean, September 2012.

My daughter Morgan
and I
in Thailand,
February 2014.

AUTHOR'S NOTE

As we go to print in Sept 2015, Liam is in his thirteenth year in Bangkwang, still hoping for a transfer to an Australian prison, where he will serve the remainder of his sentence. Zaw was re-leased on a King's amnesty to Burma in April 2015, after serving 18 years, one month. He lives with his sister. Johann lives free, at least in body, in the Netherlands while his wife remains in prison in Thailand. Daniel was repatriated to Kazakhstan after a decade, married within a year of gaining his freedom, and his wife has just given birth to a baby girl. Ivan has had his sentence reduced through King's amnesties and hopes to be freed in 2016 and reunited with his mother in the Ukraine. James is on parole in the US, recently became engaged and bought a house. Joe, the American whom I paid to cry on his shoulder one night in a bar was arrested and I have visited him as he awaits trial in Bangkok Remand. Many more men whom I did not share about in these pages remain in prison. I hope to visit each of the men who have been released to document on video their stories. Or at least to hug them as free men.

One night in December, 2013, In Bangkok, a few weeks before I celebrated my first year of sobriety, I got an eery and strong premonition that I needed to 'go find' David, my alcoholic ex-, whom I had not seen in over a year, since before I left on the Tuna fishing trip. Not even knowing what country he was in, I left my room and walked down a street with a strong sense that I was supposed to see him. Not five minutes later, I heard his voice: "Hi Heath." He was sitting on the street, almost unrecognizable, body bloated and yellowy, unable to walk, in the final stages of liver failure. I sat with him and told him about my newfound sobriety. He was very proud of me and agreed to come to a recovery meeting. A passerby and I lifted David and his whiskey bottle to a cab. After the meeting, we held hands and said the serenity prayer, the first time in the nine years we had known each other, both alcoholic, that we attended a recovery meeting together. We cried, then we hugged and he left. My understanding is he passed away shortly thereafter.

Luna-Rose Prisoner Support responds to requests regularly from people hoping I can visit their loved ones in Bangkok prisons and I do my best to fulfill these requests. Please support my work by making a contribution at luna-roseprisonersupport.org

Peace to All.
– HLR